A HY
COMPANION

A HYMN COMPANION

INSIGHT INTO THREE HUNDRED CHRISTIAN HYMNS

FRANK COLQUHOUN

HODDER AND STOUGHTON
LONDON SYDNEY AUCKLAND TORONTO

British Library Cataloguing in Publication Data

A Hymn companion : insight into three hundred
    Christian hymns.—(Coronet books)
    1. Hymns—History and criticism
    I. Colquhoun, Frank
    264'.2   BV310

ISBN 0-340-34657-4

CONTENTS

THE HYMNS

PREFACE

Hymn-singing is one of the features common to all the churches and as such is one of the factors which helps to unite them. While they differ from one another on points of doctrine and in modes of worship, they all sing very much the same hymns. This in itself is a significant and encouraging sign. There is no doubt that hymn-singing has a wide appeal and that its appeal is by no means limited to those within the churches. The popularity of such BBC programmes as *Songs of Praise* and *Sunday Half-Hour* are evidence of this. Clearly all sorts and conditions of people enjoy singing hymns and listening to them.

Yet while this is true, the fact remains that for the most part people do not know much about the hymns they sing or hear sung: who wrote them, how or why they came to be written, and what they are all about. And it is to help in this direction that I have written the present book.

Purpose
My purpose has been to provide a popular work of reference giving information about a representative selection of hymns now in general use. It is written not for the experts, who already have their own books on the subject, but for hymn-lovers in general; for churchgoers and non-churchgoers alike; for clergy, ministers, teachers, choristers and others whose work involves the use of hymns.

In addition to supplying purely factual details of the hymns selected (e.g. authorship, sources, dates, and so on) I have sought to fill in their background, to offer simple comments on their contents, to interpret their teaching and message, and to note any points of special human interest. My hope is that this may enable those who sing hymns to appreciate them better and to sing them with more understanding.

Selection

I have made a selection of 300 hymns for study and comment.
It has not been easy to keep within those limits, as the material
available is so abundant. But the line had to be drawn some-
where to avoid producing an unwieldy book; and in any case
whatever further additions had been made, it would not have
been possible to include everyone's favourites. My endeavour
has been to make the selection as wide and representative as
possible.

As already indicated, there is a large body of hymns common to all the churches and which virtually select themselves.
These are the great classical hymns of the past, including
translations of ancient Latin and Greek hymns as well as the
works of such acknowledged masters of English hymnody as
Isaac Watts and Charles Wesley (thirty-one of whose hymns
have been given a place). In addition, there are certain hymns
which are well known to Anglicans but largely unfamiliar to
members of the Free Churches. And the reverse is equally
true.

Again, apart from the established hymns of the more distant
past, a considerable number have also been written during the
present century. Many of these are now well known and firm
favourites; while at the same time some excellent hymns by
contemporary writers have gained recognition and are coming
into ever wider use. With these facts in mind, upwards of fifty
20th century hymns are included. And in addition to hymns
proper, a handful of popular 'gospel songs' (most of them
originating from the Moody and Sankey missions of the last
century) have been given a place as representing another aspect
of hymnody.

Arrangement

The hymns have been grouped in five main sections, according to subject. The first comprises hymns of praise and
thanksgiving; the second follows the seasons and festivals of
the Christian year; the third relates to the Church of God, its
fellowship, worship, mission and future glory; the fourth is
concerned with the life of Christian discipleship in its various

aspects; while the fifth gathers up the fragments that remain in reference to times, seasons and occasions.

The grouping may appear somewhat arbitrary in places. Some hymns could certainly be allocated to more than one section. However, any particular hymn can readily be traced by reference to the alphabetical index of first lines. There is also an index of authors and translators. The hymns are numbered for convenience of cross-reference.

Tunes

The book is concerned mainly with the *words* of the hymns, with only passing reference to their tunes. No attempt has been made to give technical details of the latter, something outside the scope of the present work. It is true, of course, that hymns cannot be separated from their tunes and that the tunes are important. Sometimes in fact the tunes have occasioned the writing of the hymns and often have contributed much to their popularity. In such cases attention has been drawn to this fact; but in general a line or two has simply been appended to the notes indicating the tune or tunes – and their composers or sources – most commonly associated with the hymns in question.

Biographical Notes

Short biographical notes have been added at the end of the book providing basic information about the chief hymn-writers represented. To indicate when this applies, an asterisk has been attached to the names of the authors or translators printed at the head of the notes. In the case of other writers, brief details about them are included in the notes themselves.

Acknowledgments

No one can write about hymns without being indebted to the works of others in this field. In a short bibliography I have listed the books chiefly consulted. For historical information I have turned constantly to Julian's massive *Dictionary of Hymnology* and to the handbooks of the standard hymnals. For the comments on the hymns and their teaching, I myself must accept a large measure of responsibility; but here the

writings of the late Dr Erik Routley have been of particular
value.

Finally, I wish to express my thanks to those whom I have
consulted about this enterprise: the Reverend Alan Luff, Pre-
centor of Westminster Abbey, and the musician Mr John
Wilson (respectively honorary secretary and treasurer of the
Hymn Society of Great Britain); the Right Reverend Timothy
Dudley-Smith, Bishop of Thetford; and the Reverend Eric
P. Sharpe, formerly minister of St Mary's Baptist Church,
Norwich. For their helpful advice and encouragement I am
most grateful.

FRANK COLQUHOUN

SELECT BIBLIOGRAPHY

J. Julian, *Dictionary of Hymnology*, 1907.

M. Frost (ed.), *Historical Companion to Hymns Ancient and Modern*, 1962.

J. Moffatt (ed.), *Handbook to the Church Hymnary*, 1927.

P. Dearmer (ed.), *Songs of Praise Discussed*, 1933.

J. Telford, *The New Methodist Hymn Book Illustrated*, 1934.

K. L. Parry (ed.), *Companion to Congregational Praise*, 1953.

H. Martin (ed.), *Baptist Church Hymn Book Companion*, 1962.

W. Milgate, *Songs of the People of God*, 1982.

A. E. Bailey, *The Gospel in Hymns*, 1950.

E. Routley, *I'll Praise my Maker*, 1951.

E. Routley, *Hymns and Human Life*, 1952.

E. Routley, *Hymns and the Faith*, 1955.

A. S. Gregory, *Praises with Understanding*, 1949.

H. A. L. Jefferson, *Hymns in Christian Worship*, 1950.

ABBREVIATIONS

AV	Authorised (King James) Version of Bible, 1611
RSV	Revised Standard Version of Bible, 1946 and 1952
NEB	New English Bible, 1961 and 1970
JB	Jerusalem Bible, 1966
TEV	Today's English Version of Bible (NT), 1966
BCP	Book of Common Prayer, 1662
Julian	*Dictionary of Hymnology*
A&M	*Hymns Ancient and Modern* (edition as indicated)
EH	*The English Hymnal*, 1906
CH	*The Church Hymnary*, 3rd edition, 1973
SP	*Songs of Praise*, 1931
CP	*Congregational Praise*, 1951
WOV	*With One Voice*, 1979

SECTION ONE
PRAISE AND THANKSGIVING

1 All people that on earth do dwell
W. Kethe,
16th century

St Augustine defined a hymn as 'a song with praise of God', and commented, 'If you praise God and sing not, you utter no hymn. If you sing and praise not God, you utter no hymn. A hymn then contains these three things: song, and praise, and that of God.'

The definition is too narrow, for hymnody like psalmody gives voice to other elements than praise. But praise is – or ought to be – the dominant note; and few hymns have provided a finer example of this than William Kethe's magnificent paraphrase of Psalm 100. First published in both Geneva and London in 1561, it is the earliest of the old metrical psalms to find a place in our hymn books.

Little is known of its author, not even the dates of his birth and death. He was a Scotsman who, like many Protestants of that time, sought refuge on the Continent during Queen Mary's reign. He took an active part in the compilation of the *Genevan Psalter* and contributed many items to it. The latter part of his life was spent in England as rector of Childe Okeford in Dorset.

The hymn as we now have it is much as Kethe wrote it. The third line of the first stanza begins, 'Him serve with fear'; but the psalm says 'Serve the Lord with gladness', so the Scottish Psalter later changed 'fear' to 'mirth', as in several modern hymnals. In the next stanza the words 'We are his folk' occur, meaning (as the psalm says) 'We are his people.' But the word 'folk' was originally spelt in its old English form of 'folck', and

later this was thought to be a misprint for 'flock' – a mistake
which persisted for three centuries. 'For why?' at the beginning of the fourth stanza means 'Because' and gives the reason
for praising God.

TUNE: *Old Hundredth* (Louis Bourgeois, born Paris
c.1510), from the *Genevan Psalter*, 1551.

2 Come, let us join our cheerful songs   *I. Watts**,
1674–1748

Could there be a better opening to a church service than this
exhilarating hymn by Isaac Watts? That it invites us to
worship is clear from its first word – *Come*; and as the model
of our worship it points us to the adoration of the whole
company of heaven. Hence the caption which Watts gave the
hymn: 'Christ Jesus, the Lamb of God, worshipped by all the
Creation. Rev.5:11–13.' In that passage the living creatures,
elders, and myriads of angels gathered round the throne of
God, are heard praising Christ and crying, 'Worthy is the
Lamb who was slain to receive power and wealth and wisdom
and might and honour and glory and blessing!' That song of
heaven we echo here on earth:

> 'Worthy the Lamb,' our lips reply,
> 'For he was slain for us.'

Like so many of Watts's hymns, this one not only sounds
the note of joy but also has a cosmic outlook. Christ is Lord of
the universe and 'the whole creation' is called upon to pay
honour to his name. This idea is further expressed in the stanza
omitted by many hymnals:

> Let all that dwell above the sky,
> And air and earth and seas,
> Conspire to lift thy glories high,
> And speak thine endless praise.

TUNE: *Nativity* (H. Lahee, 1826–1912).

3 Let all the world in every corner sing

George Herbert★,
1593–1632

From Herbert's collected poems *The Temple*, published in 1633, a year after his death. He entitled the poem 'Antiphon', a term denoting a musical work to be sung in alternate parts by two bodies of singers. In the present instance there is a chorus, repeated four times, in which the larger number of people (e.g. the congregation) join:

> Let all the world in every corner sing,
>> My God and King.

The verses between the chorus in each stanza constitute the hymn proper, to be sung by a small group or a soloist.

The keynote of the work is found in the chorus, which is a call to universal praise. The note of praise sounds out equally in the two verses, but in different ways. In the first, the world of *nature* is bidden to sing God's praise – the heavens above and the earth beneath. In the second verse the praise is that of *people*: both the corporate worship of the Church at large and the personal devotion of the heart which 'must bear the longest part'. The poet indicates here that while the Church's official acts of worship take place only at certain times, the praise of the heart is unceasing: it is prolonged through every hour and every day.

TUNE: *Luckington* (Basil Harwood, 1859–1925).

4 Ye holy angels bright

R. Baxter★, 1615–91,
and J. H. Gurney, 1802–62

Despite its opening words, this is not a hymn about angels. From beginning to end it is a call to praise God, a call addressed in turn to the angels who stand before his throne, to the 'blessed souls at rest', to the Church on earth ('Ye saints who toil below'), and last of all to the singer of the hymn:

> My soul, bear thou thy part,
>> Triumph in God above,

And with a well-tuned heart
Sing thou the songs of love!

Richard Baxter must be given chief credit for this fine
hymn, though in the form we have it today it is by no means
wholly his work. The first, second and fourth stanzas are
based on some verses of a hymn he appended to his *Poor Man's
Family Book*, 1672. A little over a century and a half later John
Hampden Gurney, who for twenty years served as curate of
Wycliffe's old parish of Lutterworth, selected three of Baxter's
stanzas, revised them, added one of his own (v. 3) and included
the finished work in his *Collection of Hymns for Public Worship*,
1838. Thus in a somewhat strange way the hymn assumed its
present shape, the combined effort of a famous Puritan
preacher and a humble Anglican curate. Gurney also wrote
'Fair waved the golden corn' and 'Lord, as to thy dear cross we
flee'.

TUNE: *Darwell's 148th* (John Darwell, 1731–89).

5 How shall I sing that majesty   *J. Mason, 1645–94*

This fine 17th century hymn of praise remained virtually
unnoticed and unsung for many years until it appeared in the
English Hymnal, 1906. It fully deserves a place in our hymn
books and happily it is now coming into wider use.

The hymn extols God in his heavenly glory and contrasts his
greatness with our own littleness here on earth. While countless angels on high ceaselessly adore his majesty, we in our
lowly state can but catch the echo of their song and add our
alleluias to their praise.

John Mason, the son of a Dissenting minister, graduated at
Cambridge and took orders in the Church of England. He was
one of the very earliest Anglican hymn-writers. It was when
he became rector of Water-Stratford in 1683 that he published
his *Spiritual Songs* in which this hymn was included. The book
went through twenty editions and was highly praised by Isaac
Watts in the next century. But Watts's own hymns and those
of Wesley gradually overshadowed and eventually supplanted

Mason's works. His name is certainly worthy of honour. Richard Baxter, who was a close friend, called him 'the glory of the Church of England'.

TUNES: *Old 137th (Anglo-Genevan Psalter,* 1556); or *Soll's Sein* (melody from Corner's *Geistliche Nachtigal,* 1649).

6 O worship the King all glorious above
R. Grant,
1779–1838

Sir Robert Grant was of Scottish birth, the son of Charles Grant, sometime MP for Inverness. After graduating at Oxford he entered the legal profession and was called to the Bar in 1807. Later, following in his father's footsteps, he embarked on a parliamentary career and in 1832 was made Judge Advocate General. He was knighted two years later on being appointed Governor of Bombay.

His hymn is a free paraphrase of part of Psalm 104, which celebrates in rich poetical language God's work in creation. Beginning with the words 'O God, thou art very great, thou art clothed with honour and majesty', it goes on to speak of him as one who covers himself with light as with a garment, who stretches out the heavens like a curtain, who makes the clouds his chariot and walks on the wings of the wind, who laid the foundations of the earth and covered it with the deep as with a garment (vv. 2–6).

Here clearly is the material on which the opening stanzas are based. The last two are of a more personal character and remind us that he who is 'measureless Might' is also 'ineffable Love', so that we may sing,

Thy mercy, how tender, how firm to the end,
Our Maker, Defender, Redeemer and Friend!

The hymn was published in Sir Robert's *Christian Psalmody,* 1833. His only other hymn to have survived, though now little known, is 'Saviour, when in dust to thee'.

TUNE: *Hanover* (usually attributed to William Croft, 1678–1727). An alternative is the *Old 104th* (from Ravenscroft's *Psalter,* 1621).

7 The God of Abraham praise   *T. Olivers*, 1725–99

Thomas Olivers, who as a profligate youth was converted
through the preaching of George Whitefield in Bristol, became one of John Wesley's most active itinerant preachers. In
1770 when he was staying with his friend John Bakewell in
Westminster, he visited the Great Synagogue at Duke's Place,
London. There he heard the *Yigdal* – a paraphrase of the
thirteen articles of the Jewish faith – sung antiphonally by the
congregation and a chorister, Signor Leoni (Meyer Lyon).
The tune haunted him; and soon afterwards he set about
writing a Christian hymn to fit the melody.

   'Look at this,' he said to a friend, 'I have rendered it from the
Hebrew, giving it as far as I could a Christian character.' It was
published in twelve verses as a leaflet entitled *A Hymn to the
God of Abraham*. The tune's origin is uncertain but was probably a traditional Jewish melody. Olivers, having arranged
and adapted it, named it 'Leoni' after the synagogue chorister.

   The hymn soon sung its way into Methodist circles, and it
has maintained its popularity to the present day. A selection of
stanzas is to be found in all the standard hymnals. It is a
magnificent piece of writing, combining Hebrew imagery and
idiom with distinctive Christian truth. From beginning to end
it is an outpouring of praise to God in his holiness, glory and
power. In this praise all must unite – and each individual as
well. So the hymn concludes, somewhat surprisingly, on a
personal note:

> Hail! Abraham's God and mine!
>   (I join the heavenly lays),
> All might and majesty are thine,
>   And endless praise.

TUNE: *Leoni* (see above).

8 Praise the Lord, ye heavens   *Foundling Hospital*
adore him   *Collection*, 1796

The author of this hymn is unknown, but we do know where
and when it originated. The Foundling Hospital in High

Holborn, London, was a well known orphanage for the care and education of deserted children. It had its own chapel, the organ being the gift of Handel who took a keen interest in the institution. Members of London's fashionable society often attended the Sunday morning services, at which hymn-singing by the children was a feature.

The words of this hymn were first printed in a four-page leaflet which formed a brief supplement to the hospital's large collection of psalms, hymns and anthems, published in 1796. The hymn would therefore be of later date, possibly 1801. No indication is given of its authorship, but the lines are headed 'Hymn from Psalm cxlviii, Haydn'. This tells us something about the words and music. The hymn is based on Psalm 148, which calls upon the whole creation – the angelic host, the heavenly bodies, the family of mankind and finally the chosen people – to unite in praise of God. The word 'Haydn' is a reference to the celebrated composer's tune *Austria*, with which the hymn is still closely associated.

TUNE: *Austria* (F. J. Haydn, 1732–1809). Some hymnals print the hymn in four stanzas of four lines and set it to *Laus Deo* (R. Redhead, 1820–1901).

9 Songs of praise the angels sang

J. Montgomery*,
1771–1854

This hymn first appeared in Cotterill's *Selection of Psalms and Hymns*, 1819. Montgomery gave it the title 'Glory to God in the highest'. Its theme is epitomised by the phrase 'songs of praise' which runs all through the hymn. It occurs at least once in every stanza, ten times in all, and its repetition gives strength and unity to the hymn.

The six stanzas follow a clear and orderly pattern. The first three link the songs of praise to the great crises of biblical history: creation, redemption, and judgment. The last three apply the principle of praise to the life and worship of the Church, both on earth and in heaven.

When the hymn was included in *A&M*, 1861, the final verse was omitted and replaced by a trinitarian doxology, probably the work of Sir Henry Baker. This has been adopted by some other hymnals, but Montgomery's original ending is to be preferred:

> Borne upon their latest breath,
> Songs of praise shall conquer death;
> Then, amidst eternal joy,
> Songs of praise their powers employ.

TUNES: *Northampton* (composed for the hymn by C. J. King when he was organist of St Matthew's, Northampton). Alternatives are the ancient *Culbach* (Breslau, 1657) or the modern *Lauds* (John Wilson, *b.*1905).

10 Bright the vision that delighted   *R. Mant*, 1776–1848

Who was this 'Judah's seer' to whom the opening stanza refers: the prophet who was once delighted with a dazzling vision and entranced by the music of 'countless tongues'? Probably the majority of people who sing the hymn would find it difficult to answer the question. However, the footnote appended to the hymn in *A&M* comes to their aid: 'This hymn is based on the account of Isaiah's vision in Isa.6.' Here is the clue to these stanzas, which are a free paraphrase of verses 1–3:

> In the year that king Uzziah died I saw also the Lord sitting upon a throne, high and lifted up, and his train filled the temple. Above it stood the seraphim: each one had six wings; with twain he covered his face, and with twain he covered his feet, and with twain he did fly. And one cried unto another, and said, 'Holy, holy, holy, is the Lord of hosts: the whole earth is full of his glory.'

On account of its repeated *Ter sanctus* ('Holy, holy, holy') the hymn is commonly associated with Trinity Sunday; but it is too fine an act of worship to be limited to any particular occasion. It was published in 1837 when Richard Mant was Bishop of Connor and Down. The only other hymn for which he is now remembered is 'For all thy saints, O Lord'.

TUNE: *Laus Deo* (R. Redhead, 1820–1901), or *Sanctus* (J. Richards, 1843–1908).

11 Praise, my soul, the King of heaven   *H. F. Lyte*★, 1793–1847

In the past Henry Francis Lyte's name was chiefly associated with 'Abide with me'. Now he is probably better known as the author of this hymn, which has become one of the most popular in the English language. It was published in 1834 in Lyte's *The Spirit of the Psalms*. The hymns in this book were not simply paraphrases, like the old metrical psalms. They were rather poetical interpretations of the psalms in words which made them suitable for use in Christian worship. Among them was 'God of mercy, God of grace' (Ps. 67), 'Pleasant are thy courts above' (Ps. 84), and the present hymn, which is a masterly treatment of Psalm 103. It consisted of five stanzas, not just the four to be found in most hymnals; and the refrain in each was 'Praise him! Praise him!', not the twofold 'Alleluia!' in *A&M* and other books.

Obviously the best way to appreciate Lyte's work is to compare the hymn with the original psalm. This shows the skilful way in which he caught the 'spirit' of the latter. It also illustrates his very real gift as a poet. When a student at Trinity College, Dublin, he won the prize for an English poem three years running. There are some memorable lines in the hymn e.g. 'Ransomed, healed, restored, forgiven' (v. 1); 'Slow to chide, and swift to bless' (v. 2); and 'Father-like he tends and spares us' (v. 3).

The stanza often omitted from hymnals covers verses 15–17 of the psalm ('The days of man are but as grass . . .') and is worth quoting:

> Frail as summer's flower we flourish,
>   Blows the wind, and it is gone;
> But while mortals rise and perish,
>   God endures unchanging on:
>   Praise him! Praise him!
>   Praise the high Eternal One.

TUNE: *Praise my soul* (J. Goss, 1800–80) has taken over as favourite from *Regent Square* (H. Smart, 1813–79).

12 Praise to the Lord, the Almighty, the King of creation

J. Neander, 1650–80
Tr. C. Winkworth*, 1829–78

Julian describes this as 'a magnificent hymn of praise to God and of the first rank of its class'. So indeed it is. Based freely on Psalm 103, verses 1–6, and Psalm 150, the hymn was published in 1680 and consisted of five stanzas. Catherine Winkworth translated four of these in her *Chorale Book for England*, 1863, to form our hymn.

The whole work is an unbroken outpouring of praise to Almighty God as the Creator and Sovereign of his people. He shelters and sustains them, defends and befriends them, and is worthy of their highest adoration. 'All that hath life and breath come now with praises before him!' (cf. Ps.150:6).

Joachim Neander's short life was by no means an uneventful one. After squandering his student days in riotous living he was converted and became a Christian pastor. Later he was appointed headmaster of the Latin School, Dusseldorf; but his evangelistic activities and pietistic views met with opposition from the authorities and he was obliged to resign. His last days were spent in Bremen, his birthplace, where he died of consumption at the age of thirty. He was a highly gifted young man and wrote about sixty hymns, many of which are still sung in Germany. See also 'All my hope on God is founded' (198).

TUNE: *Lobe den Herren* (a chorale melody which Neander himself chose and adapted for his hymn from *Stransund Gesangbuch*, 1665).

13 Sing praise to God who reigns above

J. J. Schutz, 1640–90
Tr. F. E. Cox, 1812–97

Another hymn of German origin and another hymn of praise. Its author, Johann Jakob Schutz, was a distinguished Frankfurt lawyer who had strong sympathies with the pietistic (Evangelical) movement in the Lutheran Church. In later life he left the Church and became a separatist. He published five hymns in 1675 of which this is the best known.

It was headed 'Hymn of Thanksgiving' and the text attached to it was Deuteronomy 32:3: 'I will proclaim the name of the Lord. Ascribe greatness to our God!' The hymn fulfils this purpose and celebrates the greatness of the Lord: his grace and power, his love and faithfulness, his justice and mercy. He is the God of creation and all living things praise him. So do the angel-hosts above. What then of us on earth? To those who confess Christ he is the God of salvation and all such have a tribute of praise to offer:

> O ye who name Christ's holy name,
>   Give God all praise and glory;
> All ye who own his power, proclaim
>   Aloud the wondrous story!
> Cast each false idol from his throne,
> The Lord is God, and he alone:
>   To God be praise and glory!

The hymnals print a selection of between three and five stanzas from the English translation. We owe this to Frances Elizabeth Cox, who like Catherine Winkworth specialised in the translation of German hymns. See also 'Jesus lives!' (99).

TUNE: *Luther's Hymn* (from *Geistliche Lieder*, 1535).

14 Immortal, invisible, God only wise   W. Chalmers Smith, 1824–1908

This very popular hymn is of Scottish origin, the work of an Aberdonian. It is based on 1 Timothy 1.17: 'Now unto the King eternal, immortal, invisible, the only wise God, be honour and glory for ever and ever.' It is essentially a hymn of praise to God as creator of the universe: the invisible God whose works in nature proclaim his glory and majesty, his goodness and love. He is the giver of *life* to all creation, 'the true life of all'. But the special emphasis of the hymn is on *light*.

God is said to dwell 'in light inaccessible' – an echo of Psalm
104:2 *AV*, 'Who coverest thyself with light as with a garment.'
He works 'silent as light'; and in the final stanza he is the 'pure
Father of light', light before which the angels veil their faces.
So our failure to see him is not due to the lack of light but rather
to the excess of it: ''Tis only the splendour of light hideth
thee.'

Dr Chalmers Smith was a well known Presbyterian divine
who held charges in London, Glasgow and Edinburgh. He
was honoured by being elected Moderator of the Free Church
of Scotland in its jubilee year, 1893. Among his many published works was *Hymns of Christ and the Christian Life*, 1876,
from which the present hymn is taken.

TUNE: *St Denio*, a Welsh folk melody, known in Wales as
'Joanna'.

15 All creatures of our God and King

W. H. Draper, 1855–1933
Based on St Francis of Assisi,
1182–1226

St Francis' famous 'Canticle of the Sun' was written at the end
of his life when he was in an extremely weak state of health,
with failing eyesight and increasing pain. For many days he lay
in a rough rat-infested hut in total darkness, for he could not
bear the light of the sun. Yet, as Bishop Moorman states, 'In all
that pain and discomfort his joy rose triumphant, and at last he
burst forth into one of the greatest of all Christian hymns.'

Sometimes called the 'Song about Creatures', it gives praise
to God for Brother Sun and Sister Moon, for wind and air,
water and fire, and for 'our Mother the earth, who sustains us
with her fruits and brings forth flowers of many colours.' This
song Francis taught his friars to sing. When later on he knew
he was dying he added a final stanza, beginning (in Dr H. C.
Robbins' translation, 1939):

> For death, our sister, praisèd be,
> From whom no man alive can flee.

The splendid version of the song by William Henry Draper
is not so much a translation as a free paraphrase and makes an

excellent hymn. He wrote it when he was rector of Adel, Yorkshire, for a schoolchildren's Whitsun festival in the city of Leeds.

TUNE: *Easter Song* (from *Geistliche Kirchengesang*, Cologne, 1623).

16 All hail the power of Jesus' name
E. Perronet,
1726–92

Edward Perronet, a member of a French Huguenot family, began life as an Anglican. His father was for fifty years vicar of Shoreham, Kent, and was an intimate friend of the Wesley brothers. Edward thus came under their spiritual influence and for a while his evangelical zeal found an outlet in their service. But he was a somewhat hot-headed character and eventually he parted company with the Methodists, turned Dissenter, and ended his days as minister of a small Independent chapel in Canterbury.

His fine 'Coronation Hymn' as it has been called was published in the *Gospel Magazine* in 1780 under the title 'On the Resurrection, the Lord is King'. It consisted of eight stanzas. A number of changes were made by Dr John Rippon, a Baptist minister, when he included the hymn in his *Selection of Hymns* seven years later. Some of Perronet's verses were omitted, others rewritten, while Rippon added two of his own. But this does not affect the hymn's grand design, which is to affirm the kingship of Christ and to call upon all and sundry to 'crown him Lord of all'.

In his version of the hymn Dr Rippon attached a suitable title to each of the stanzas. In the table below we follow this pattern in regard to the stanzas most commonly in use.

Title	Stanza
Angels	'All hail the power of Jesus' name'
The Created Order	'Crown him, ye morning stars of light'
Martyrs	'Crown him ye martyrs of your God'
Converted Jews	'Ye seed of Israel's chosen race'
The Church, the New Israel	'Hail him, ye heirs of David's line'
Redeemed Sinners	'Sinners, whose love can ne'er forget'
All Mankind	'Let every tribe and every tongue'
Ourselves	'O that with yonder sacred throng'

TUNES: *Miles Lane*, which Elgar pronounced the finest tune in English hymnody, was written for the words by William Shrubsole (1760–1806). A popular alternative is *Diadem* (James Ellor, 1819–99); also the more recent *Ladywell* (W. H. Ferguson, 1874–1950).

17 Join all the glorious names   I. Watts*, 1674–1748

Watts headed this hymn 'The Offices of Christ, from several Scriptures' when it was published in his *Hymns and Spiritual Songs*, 1707. It consisted of no less than twelve stanzas, setting forth in orderly procession the various 'offices' ascribed to Jesus in the Bible. *Congregational Praise* and *With One Voice* include eleven of these; but most hymnals make a selection of no more than four or five to provide a hymn of suitable length for congregational worship. The three most favoured verses are those beginning:

> Great *Prophet* of my God . . .
>
> Jesus, my great *High Priest* . . .
>
> My dear Almighty *Lord* . . .

Among the other 'glorious names' which Watts dwells on are Redeemer, Counsellor, Shepherd, Advocate and King.

Here undoubtedly is one of Watts's finest hymns; but like so many of his works it is little known in Anglican circles. For the benefit of those who are unfamiliar with it, here as a sample is the penultimate verse:

> Now let my soul arise
> And tread the tempter down;
> My *Captain* leads me forth
> To conquest and a crown.
> A feeble saint shall win the day,
> Though death and hell obstruct the way.

TUNES: *Croft's* 136th (W. Croft, 1678–1727); or *Warsaw* from Chetham's *Psalmody*, 1832 (attributed to T. Clark, 1775–1859).

18 O for a thousand tongues to sing *C. Wesley**, 1707–88

'If I had a thousand tongues,' said the Moravian Peter Böhler to Charles Wesley, 'I would praise Christ with them all.' The words set the heart of the poet aglow. He was approaching the first anniversary of his evangelical conversion in May 1738 and to celebrate the joyful event he wrote this hymn. For over 200 years it has been the opening hymn in every edition of the *Methodist Hymn Book*. When published in 1740 under the heading 'For the Anniversary Day of One's Conversion' it consisted of eighteen stanzas. John Wesley made a selection of these for his *Collection* of hymns, 1780, beginning with the original seventh stanza, 'O for a thousand tongues'.

In another hymn, Wesley wrote shortly afterwards:

> My heart is full of Christ, and longs
> Its glorious matter to declare.

In the same strain he now celebrates what God has done for him. His hymn, like his heart, is full of Christ. As he sings his great Redeemer's praise, he glories in the triumphs of his grace. The name of Jesus makes music in his ears, the music of salvation – 'life, and health, and peace'. For:

> He breaks the power of cancelled sin,
>   He sets the prisoner free;
> His blood can make the foulest clean,
>   His blood availed for me.

This is the heart of the matter. Here Wesley is writing out of his own experience, for he had found in Christ an all-sufficient Saviour who not only cancels the *guilt* of sin but breaks its *power*.

TUNES: The Methodist people love *Lydia* (T. Phillips, 1735–1807). Other more conventional tunes are readily available such as *Richmond* and *University*.

19 Let us with a gladsome mind   *John Milton*, 1608–74

Milton was only fifteen years of age when he wrote this hymn. At the time he was a scholar at St Paul's, the famous school founded a century earlier by John Colet to provide boys with a liberal education more in line with the New Learning. A year later Milton entered Christ's College, Cambridge, where he distinguished himself in Latin and English. Despite being disabled by total blindness in 1652, he lived to become the nation's greatest Christian poet.

His hymn is a paraphrase of Psalm 136. There are twenty-four stanzas in the original version, corresponding roughly to the Psalm's twenty-four verses, each of which ends with the words 'for his mercy endureth for ever' (*AV*). This becomes the hymn's refrain:

> For his mercies ay endure,
> Ever faithful, ever sure.

The psalm includes verses praising God for the exodus of the Israelites from Egypt, and corresponding stanzas are contained in Milton's paraphrase; but these of course are omitted from our hymn books. A shortened version of some seven to nine stanzas is now provided, concentrating on God's works in the natural order. This makes it particularly suitable for harvest thanksgiving, but its use is by no means limited to such occasions.

TUNE: *Monkland* (J. Wilkes, 1785–1869).

20 O praise ye the Lord   *H. W. Baker**, 1821–77

Written by Sir Henry Baker for the 1875 edition of *Hymns Ancient and Modern* and based on parts of Psalms 148 and 150. Both psalms begin and end with the words 'Praise the Lord!' and the hymn admirably catches their spirit. The words 'Praise him in the height' in the first stanza and 'Praise him upon earth' in the second are derived from Psalm 148, verses 1 and 7. In the third stanza 'all things that give sound' refers to the musical instruments enumerated in Psalm 150:3–6: trumpet and cymbals, lute and harp, strings and pipe. The last verse of this psalm calls upon everything that has breath to praise the Lord, and this finds an echo in the hymn's final stanza.

The hymn is ideally suited for a musical festival as well as being a general hymn of praise.

TUNES: *Laudate Dominum* (H. J. Gauntlett, 1805–76) was originally composed for this hymn in the 1875 edition of *A&M*. The splendid tune of the same name by Sir C. H. H. Parry (1848–1918) has since replaced it.

21 For the beauty of the earth   *F. S. Pierpoint*, 1835–1917

What sort of hymn is this? Is it to be regarded, in accordance with its original intention, as a eucharistic hymn? Or should it be treated, as is often done, as an ordinary hymn of praise?

The answer depends on which version is used. In its complete form of eight stanzas (as in *EH*) it takes its place among the communion hymns, and the refrain is:

> Christ our God, to thee we raise
> This our sacrifice of praise

– the 'sacrifice' being the eucharistic thanksgiving. In most hymnals, however, the hymn is reduced to five or six stanzas and the refrain is altered to something like:

> Lord of all, to thee we raise
> This our grateful hymn of praise.

In this form the hymn becomes a 'general thanksgiving' for our material blessings: for the loveliness of creation, earth and sky, day and night, sun, moon and stars; for our physical faculties of hearing and sight; for human love, family and friends; and for every good gift so freely bestowed on us and our race. This version of the hymn is particularly suitable for harvest and flower festivals and for family services.

It is the three final stanzas which give the hymn its distinctive character, beginning with:

> For thy Bride, that evermore
> Lifteth holy hands above,
> Offering up on every shore
> This pure sacrifice of love.

Some hymn books include this verse, changing 'Bride' to 'Church'. The two remaining stanzas offer praise to God for the martyrs, prophets, confessors, and virgins, and finally for Jesus himself, 'Victim undefiled', whose death and passion we celebrate in the eucharist.

Folliett Sandford Pierpoint was a West Countryman. A classical scholar and devout Tractarian, he wrote a good deal of poetry in his long life.

TUNES: *England's Lane* (traditional English melody); *Dix* (adapted from C. Kocher, 1786–1872); *Lucerna Laudoniae* (David Evans, 1874–1948).

22 All things bright and beautiful   *C. F. Alexander★*, 1818–95

Mrs Alexander published her *Hymns for Little Children* in 1848, a year or two before her marriage to the Revd William Alexander. The hymns were written to explain the Church Catechism (*BCP*) and make it more interesting to children by the use of poetry and pictorial language. The best known of the hymns are those connected with the Apostles' Creed, and three of these are to be found in every hymn book (see also 57 and 85).

The present hymn, headed 'Maker of heaven and earth', illustrates the doctrine of Creation. It employs concrete imagery, not abstract ideas. God is the *maker*: that is the point. The flowers and fruits, trees and meadows, mountains and rivers, summer and winter – 'The Lord God *made* them all.' The verb is the key to the hymn. It occurs seven times in the original seven stanzas (the first verse was not repeated as a refrain). One stanza is now invariably omitted:

> The rich man in his castle,
> The poor man at his gate,

> God made them, high or lowly,
> And ordered their estate.

The words have been much criticised but also much mis-
understood. The imagery certainly is outdated but not the
intended teaching. Mrs Alexander here is not expressing class
distinctions but affirming an important truth, that men of all
estates are equal in God's sight, the poor no less than the
rich – for he *made* them all.

TUNE: *Royal Oak*, adapted from an English traditional
melody by Martin Shaw (1875–1958), or *All things bright and
beautiful* (W. H. Monk, 1823–89).

23 Through all the changing scenes of life

*N. Tate★ (1652–1715)
and N. Brady (1659–1726),
New Version*

The names of Tate and Brady are associated with the *New
Version* of the metrical psalms published by royal authority in
1696 and dedicated to William III. It was intended to replace
the older version of 1562 edited by Sternhold and Hopkins,
'men whose piety was better than their poetry,' as it was said.
Their versifications were admittedly poor, crude sort of stuff.
Nevertheless Tate and Brady's new psalter met at first with
strong opposition and only gradually did it gain general
acceptance. Whatever its shortcomings, it was poetically a
distinct improvement on the old.

The present hymn represents the work at its best. It is a
paraphrase of part of Psalm 34 which begins, 'I will bless the
Lord at all times: his praise shall continually be in my mouth.'
The whole psalm occupied twenty-two stanzas. The five
which make up the hymn cover verses one, three, seven, eight
and nine. A comparison shows the measure of freedom which
the paraphrasers allowed themselves. For example, the
psalmist's words, 'O taste and see that the Lord is good:
blessed is the man that trusteth in him,' become:

> O make but trial of his love,
> Experience will decide

How blest they are, and only they,
Who in his truth confide.

The only other psalm from the *New Version* to survive is 'As pants the hart for cooling streams', part of Psalm 42.
TUNE: *Wiltshire* (Sir George Smart, 1776–1867).

24 Holy, Holy, Holy! Lord God Almighty!   *R. Heber*★, 1783–1826

It is strange to reflect that 'From Greenland's icy mountains' was once Reginald Heber's most renowned hymn. It is now so dated as to have practically dropped out of use. The same fate is not likely to overtake his Trinity Sunday hymn, for it deals with eternal, unchanging truth – the truth of God himself, the Three in One. It is undoubtedly the finest as well as the most famous of his hymns and well illustrates the high standard he set himself.

The hymn is a paraphrase of the passage (Revelation 4) which forms the Epistle for Trinity Sunday in *BCP*. The seer catches a vision of God enthroned in heavenly glory, surrounded by the twenty-four elders with their golden crowns and the four living creatures chanting endlessly, 'Holy, holy, holy is the Lord God Almighty, who was and is and is to come!' It is this imagery that Heber weaves into his hymn, which echoes much of its apocalyptic language.

The language of the passage accounts for the distinctive vocabulary of the hymn. The solemn and sonorous 'Holy, Holy, Holy' with which each stanza begins sets the keynote of the work, which from start to finish is pure adoration of God in his holiness or 'wholly-otherness'. Admittedly we mortals cannot apprehend the mystery of the Holy Trinity; but there are things about God we *can* understand, as the hymn affirms. That he is 'merciful and mighty' we can certainly grasp. He is also 'perfect in power, in love, and purity'; and since we sing 'All thy works shall praise thy name,' we ourselves can share in that praise, for we too are his workmanship (Eph. 2:10).
TUNE: *Nicaea* (J. B. Dykes, 1823–76).

25 My God, how wonderful thou art
F. W. Faber★,
1814–63

It was a saying of one of the old Puritan divines, 'Think magnificently of God!' Faber helps us to do this in his hymn. It takes a big view of God. It is an excellent hymn for an age in which, as is often said, man has lost his sense of wonder. Today's world is so full of wonders that they have become a commonplace. What is there left to wonder at?

The answer is – God himself. He is the supreme wonder. So in this hymn we are invited to capture or recapture our sense of wonder by contemplating him in his eternal glory and majesty:

> How wonderful, how beautiful,
>   The sight of thee must be,
> Thine endless wisdom, boundless power,
>   And aweful purity!

Such a vision of God must create within us a spirit of holy fear, deep penitence, adoring worship. And that is right and proper. It cuts us down to size. It compels us to recognise our own littleness and unworthiness before the Almighty. But that is not all. Another wonder remains, for our relationship with God in Christ is not only one of fear and reverence:

> Yet I may love thee too, O Lord,
>   Almighty as thou art,
> For thou hast stooped to ask of me
>   The love of my poor heart.

TUNE: *Westminster* (J. Turle, 1802–82).

26 Jesus! the name high over all
C. Wesley★, 1707–88

First published in Wesley's *Hymns and Sacred Poems*, 1749, in 22 verses, the hymn is headed 'After preaching (in a church)'. It is believed that this refers to the occasion in August 1744 when Wesley preached in Laneast church, Cornwall, and was interrupted by a blasphemer; whereupon he asked, 'Who is he that pleads for the devil?' 'I am he that pleads for the devil,' was the answer. Wesley continued his sermon, and recorded afterwards, 'Much good I saw immediately brought out of Satan's evil. I set myself against his avowed advocate, and drove him out of the Christian assembly.' This hymn may well have been the outcome:

> Jesus! the name high over all
> In hell, or earth, or sky;
> Angels and men before it fall,
> And devils fear and fly.

Many years later (1781) Wesley wrote, 'I have nothing to fear, I have nothing to hope for here: only to finish my course with joy.' And then he quoted the hymn's final stanza:

> Happy, if with my latest breath
> I might but gasp his name,
> Preach him to all, and cry in death,
> Behold, behold the Lamb!

TUNE: *Lydia* (melody by T. Phillips, 1735–1807).

27 To the name of our salvation

15th century, Anonymous
Tr. J. M. Neale*, 1818–66

The origin of this Latin hymn, *Gloriosi Salvator*, goes back more than 500 years, but no one knows who wrote it. It is found in some of the medieval Breviaries (the books containing the daily offices), the earliest being dated 1446. Dr Neale described it as 'a German hymn on the Festival of the Holy Name of Jesus'. His translation appeared in 1851; but when ten years later it was included in the first edition of *A&M* numerous alterations were made. Most hymnals follow this revised text. Neale's own version is given in *EH*.

The anonymous author of the hymn looks at the name of Jesus from various angles, like a man holding up a diamond to the light and examining its many facets. He sees in it a name

which proclaims God's salvation, a name of utmost sweetness
and ineffable joy, a name to be prized and treasured, venerated
and adored; a name which is music in the ears of him who
preaches – and of him who prays; a strong victorious name,
exalted over every foe; a name to be engraven on the hearts of
God's people for evermore.

TUNE: *Oriel*, composed or written by Caspar Ett (1788–
1847), in his *Cantica Sacra*, Munich, 1840.

28 Crown him with many crowns *M. Bridges*, 1800–94
G. Thring, 1823–1903

What a magnificent opening line for a hymn! It is hardly
surprising that two men were drawn to it and had a hand in
producing the hymn as it is found in many hymnals today.
Chief credit must go to Matthew Bridges, a former Anglican
who followed Newman into the Roman Catholic Church in
1848. His hymn appeared in his *Hymns of the Heart*, 1851, in
six stanzas under the text 'On his head were many crowns'
(Rev. 19:12). Not till many years later did Godfrey Thring, a
prebendary of Wells Cathedral, make his contribution. His
initial effort, in 1874, had been to write a hymn modelled on
Bridges' but quite distinct from it. However, it seems that he
was not satisfied with this, for in his collection of hymns
published in 1880 he substituted (with acknowledgment)
Bridges' first stanza for his own. This opened the way for
other versions to be produced, incorporating stanzas by both
men. Their individual authorship can be identified by their
opening lines. Bridges' are those beginning:

Crown him with many crowns . . .
Crown him the Virgin's Son . . .
Crown him the Lord of love . . .
Crown him the Lord of peace . . .
Crown him the Lord of years . . .

Thring's stanzas begin:

Crown him the Son of God . . .
Crown him the Lord of life . . .

The theme of the hymn makes it specially suitable for Ascensiontide.

TUNE: *Diademata* by Sir George Elvey (1816–93), composed for the hymn in the 1868 *A&M*.

29 Come, we that love the Lord   *I. Watts*★, 1674–1748

> Come, we that love the Lord,
> And let our joys be known;
> Join in a song with sweet accord,
> And thus surround the throne.

This opening stanza strikes the keynote of the hymn. It expresses Isaac Watts's conviction that Christianity is a thoroughly joyful affair. 'Religion never was designed,' as he says in a later stanza, 'to make our pleasures less.' Of all people, Christians have no occasion to be gloomy. On the other hand:

> Let those refuse to sing
> Who never knew our God;
> But servants of the heavenly King
> May speak their joys abroad.

The hymn continues in the same exultant strain and states the grounds on which the Christians' joy rests. They have a mighty God who is sovereign over all things and rules the world in love. Moreover, set before them is the hope of glory when they shall see his face and partake of his endless pleasures. But those pleasures do not all belong to the future. When he published the hymn in 1707 Watts gave it the title 'Heavenly Joy on Earth'; hence the stanza:

> The men of grace have found
> Glory begun below;
> Celestial fruits on earthly ground
> From faith and hope may grow.

TUNE: *St Michael* (from the *Genevan Psalter*, 1551); *Mount*

Ephraim (B. Milgrove, 1731–1810); or *Marching to Zion* (Robert Lowry, 1826–99).

30 Now thank we all our God

M. Rinkart, 1586–1649
Tr. C. Winkworth*, 1829–78

It is often pointed out that this great hymn of thanksgiving was written during the grim days of the Thirty Years War when appalling conditions of famine and pestilence prevailed in the Saxony town of Eilenberg of which Martin Rinkart was the pastor. But in all probability these circumstances had no direct connection with the hymn. Rinkart said he wrote the first two stanzas not for use in church worship but as a grace to be sung at meals in his own household. The third stanza was not added till later, to make it a complete hymn with a Trinitarian doxology.

Some further points should be noted about the first two verses. Rinkart based them on the passage in Ecclesiasticus 50:22–24 beginning, 'Now bless the God of all, who in every way does great things.' The whole passage should be read in order to appreciate the way Rinkart treats the words and turns them into verse. Again, these verses form a complementary pair. The first is an act of *praise* and looks back to the past in grateful recognition of the 'wondrous things' God has done for us from our very earliest years. The second is an act of *prayer* and looks to the future, asking that 'through all our life' God may be near us and grant us his joy and peace, his grace and guidance.

The doxology, ascribing glory to the Father, Son and Holy Spirit, brings the hymn to a majestic conclusion in an outburst of adoring worship. For the English translation we are once again indebted to Catherine Winkworth.

TUNE: *Nun danket*, written by Rinkart's contemporary J. Crüger (1598–1662).

31 Ye servants of God, your Master proclaim

C. Wesley*,
1707–88

This hymn appeared in Wesley's collection of *Hymns for Times of Trouble and Persecution*, 1744. It is the first of a series of

hymns 'to be sung in a time of tumult'. This may seem
somewhat odd, for in the hymn as we now have it there is no
mention of tumult or trouble. This is because two of the
original stanzas are missing. What was originally a battle-song
becomes simply a magnificent hymn of praise, extolling God's
sovereignty and magnifying the glories of Christ.

The omitted stanzas reveal Wesley's original purpose:

> The waves of the sea have lift up their voice,
> Sore troubled that we in Jesus rejoice;
> The floods they are roaring, but Jesus is here,
> While we are adoring he always is near.
>
> Men, devils engage, the billows arise,
> And horribly rage, and threaten the skies;
> Their fury shall never our steadfastness shock,
> The weakest believer is built on a rock.

At the time the hymn was written the Wesleys were subject
to a lot of violent persecution. Repeatedly they were opposed
not only by unruly, drunken mobs but also by hostile clergy.
More than once they narrowly escaped death. But real as these
things were, even more real was their sense of God's presence
and the assurance of his over-ruling power. We can readily
picture the small but heroic Methodist bands facing the fury of
their enemies with a triumphant song like this upon their lips.

TUNES: *Laudate Dominum* (C. H. H. Parry, 1848–1918);
Paderborn (from the *Paderborn Gesangbuch*, 1765); *Houghton*
(H. J. Gauntlett, 1805–76).

32 Ye watchers and ye holy ones   *J. A. L. Riley,*
1858–1945

John Athelstan Riley, a scholarly layman and ardent Tractarian, was a member of the committee that produced *EH*, 1906.
He himself contributed seven translations to the book, and
also three hymns, this one among them. It was written for the
tune *Lasst uns erfreuen*, a melody from *Geistliche Kirchengesang*
(Colne, 1623), arranged and harmonised by Vaughan
Williams.

The hymn is an invitation to praise and rings with alleluias. The first stanza names the nine orders of angelic beings codified by Dionysius the Pseudo-Areopagite (c. 500). In the second the Blessed Virgin Mary, the 'bearer of the eternal Word', is summoned to magnify the Lord. The third stanza calls upon the 'souls in endless rest' to add their praises: the patriarchs and prophets of the old covenant, and the apostles, martyrs and saints of the new. Finally, we ourselves gladly blend our voices with the others to sing 'supernal anthems' to God the Holy Trinity.

TUNE: See above.

33 When morning gilds the skies
Anonymous, 19th century
Tr. E. Caswall*, 1814–78

There is no doubt about what type of hymn this is. The constantly repeated refrain sets the keynote: *May Jesus Christ be praised!* It is essentially a hymn of praise, not a morning hymn as is sometimes supposed from its opening line. Its use is not restricted to any particular time of day. It is a fine song of praise for all times, all circumstances, and is as suitable for evening as for morning. 'Alike at work and prayer' we sing the praises of Christ. The following stanza sums it up:

> Be this, while life is mine,
> My canticle divine,
>   May Jesus Christ be praised.
> Be this the eternal song
> Through all the ages long,
>   May Jesus Christ be praised.

The hymn comes from Germany, but its authorship is unknown. It was published anonymously in *Katholisches Gesangbuch*, 1828, where it is in fourteen stanzas. From the English translation by Edward Caswall the standard hymnals make different selections of verses, so that no two versions are exactly alike.

TUNES: *Laudes Domini* (J. Barnby, 1838–96), or *O Seigneur (Genevan Psalter, 1551).*

34 King of glory, King of peace   G. *Herbert**, 1593–1632

George Herbert's poem was published in his posthumous
work *The Temple*, 1633, entitled 'Praise'. Its first appearance as
a hymn was in the *Wellington College Hymn Book*, 1902, and
soon after in the *English Hymnal*. Set to the Welsh tune
Gwalchmai by Joseph D. Jones (1827–70) it makes a hymn of a
high devotional character.

It begins by reminding us that our praise is the expression of
our love for God:

> King of glory, King of peace,
>   I will love thee;
> And that love may never cease
>   I will move thee . . .

meaning that unceasing love is kindled by unceasing praise.
But our praise is not silent. God has given us voices with
which to praise him and there is no higher use to which we can
put them than that:

> Wherefore with my utmost art
>   I will sing thee,
> And the cream of all my heart
>   I will bring thee.

Note the metaphor, 'the cream of all my heart'. Cream is
the richest part of the milk; so we must bring to God the
choicest praise we can offer, with the aid of music's 'utmost
art'.

Again, our praise is not simply a Sunday occupation:

> Seven whole days, not one in seven,
>   I will praise thee;

for in our hearts we can prolong the note of praise throughout
the week and throughout every day. And even eternity itself
will not exhaust it.

TUNE: See above.

35 O Lord of heaven and earth and sea   C. Wordsworth*, 1807–85

Bishop Christopher Wordsworth wrote this as an offertory hymn and included it in his *Holy Year*, 1863. It consisted of nine verses. Most hymnals omit two of them, the two which gave the hymn its distinctive character:

> We lose what on ourselves we spend,
> We have as treasure without end
> Whatever, Lord, to thee we lend,
>   Who givest all.

> Whatever, Lord, we lend to thee
> Repaid a thousandfold will be;
> Then gladly will we give to thee,
>   Giver of all.

These stanzas have a somewhat sermonic tone and are in keeping with the bishop's declared aim in writing hymns. The first duty of a hymn-writer, as he saw it, was 'to teach sound doctrine and thus to save souls'.

There is certainly sound doctrine as well as poetic beauty in this hymn which, without the two stanzas quoted, becomes an excellent act of thanksgiving for 'all the blessings of this life', and above all for 'the redemption of the world by our Lord Jesus Christ, for the means of grace, and for the hope of glory' (General Thanksgiving, *BCP*). The hymn's second stanza makes it particularly suitable for use at harvest-tide.

TUNE: *Almsgiving* (J. B. Dykes, 1823–76).

36 When all thy mercies, O my God   J. Addison, 1672–1719

In the *Spectator* for August 9, 1712, there appeared an article by Joseph Addison on the subject of gratitude, in which he wrote:

> If gratitude is due from man to man, how much more from man to his Maker! Every blessing we enjoy, by what means soever it may be derived upon us, is the gift of him who is the great Author of good and Father of mercies.

The essay concluded with a poem beginning with the opening stanza of this hymn. The poem consisted of thirteen verses. Of these, no more than six or seven are selected to make up the hymn we sing today. This of course is inevitable; but the cutting out of so many verses unfortunately spoils the pattern of the poem as Addison devised it. In its entirety it expresses thanks to God for his mercies through the whole course of life, from conception, birth and childhood to old age, death and beyond. One stanza (the original 11th) sums up the theme:

> Through every period of my life
> Thy goodness I'll pursue,
> And after death in distant worlds
> The glorious theme renew.

TUNES: *Belgrave* (W. Horsley, 1774–1858); *Contemplation* (F. A. G. Ouseley, 1825–89); or *London New* (Playford's *Psalms*, 1671).

37 O love of God, how strong and true!   H. Bonar*, 1809–89

> O love of God, how strong and true!
> Eternal and yet ever new;
> Uncomprehended and unbought,
> Beyond all knowledge and all thought.

This fine hymn by the prince of Scottish hymn-writers is apparently little known in his native land, for it finds no place in the Church of Scotland's *Hymnary*. It is also unfamiliar to Anglicans, but is widely used in the English Free Churches. Bonar included it in the second series of his *Hymns of Faith and Hope*, 1861, in ten stanzas headed 'The Love of God'.

We cannot have too many hymns on that theme, for the love of God lies at the very heart of the Christian gospel. But it is redemptive love, not love in the abstract, that constitutes the good news. As William Temple pointed out, the essence of Christianity is not 'God is love' but *'God so loved that he gave'*, his love in action for man's salvation.

It is of that love that Bonar sings in his hymn. Although, as
one of the stanzas says, we read God in the wonderful works of
nature, that is but an imperfect revelation:

> We read thee best in him who came
> To bear for us the cross of shame,
> Sent by the Father from on high,
> Our life to live, our death to die.

TUNE: *Eisenach* (J. H. Schein, 1586–1630).

38 The Lord is King! lift up thy voice

J. Conder,
1789–1855

The strong, vigorous lines of this hymn affirm the great
biblical truth of the sovereignty of God. It is a truth that rings
out again and again in the Psalms – 'The Lord reigns!' Josiah
Conder, however, found his inspiration not in the Psalms
but in the book of Revelation: 'Alleluia! for the Lord God
omnipotent reigneth' (19:6). The hymn, as first published in
Conder's *Star of the East*, 1824, comprised eight stanzas. Modern hymnals usually include no more than five or six.

The hymn not only proclaims the sovereignty of God. It
also asserts the difference this truth should make to our daily
lives. For to believe that God reigns silences our doubts,
strengthens our trust, lightens our cares, and confirms our
hope in the final victory of God's kingdom:

> Through earth and heaven one song shall ring,
> The Lord omnipotent is King!

Josiah Conder was one of the leading Congregational laymen of his time. He possessed considerable literary gifts and
was the author of numerous works in prose and verse. Bernard
Manning called him 'a true poet'. In 1836 he edited the first
official hymn book of the Congregational Church which
included nearly sixty of his own compositions. His communion hymn, 'Bread of heaven, on thee we feed', is still
widely used.

TUNE: *Church Militant* (J. W. Elliott, 1833–1915), or *Niagra* (R. Jackson, 1842–1914).

39 Tell out, my soul, the greatness of the Lord
T. Dudley-Smith*, b. 1926

Few modern hymns have gained such rapid and widespread recognition as this rendering of the *Magnificat* (Luke 1:46–55) by Bishop Timothy Dudley-Smith. Since it was first published in the *Anglican Hymn Book*, 1965, it has found a place in numerous hymnals in all parts of the world. Sir John Betjeman spoke of it in a broadcast in 1976 as 'one of the very few new hymns really to have established themselves in recent years.'

The author says that it was among the earliest of his hymns, written in May 1961 when he was living at Blackheath. On reading the version of the canticle in the New English Bible (then just published) he was struck by the opening words, which suggested themselves as the first line of a hymn. The result was this metrical paraphrase of the song of the Virgin Mary. Much of the phraseology of the *NEB* text is woven into the hymn. It admirably catches the spirit of the canticle, with its exultant praise of God for his mercy and faithfulness to Israel, and its triumphant celebration of Christ's coming kingdom in the world.

The perfect matching of the text to the tune *Woodlands* by Walter Greatorex (1877–1949), sometime music master at Gresham's School, Holt, has doubtless contributed to the hymn's popularity. Other tunes are also available.

TUNE: See above.

40 God of love and truth and beauty
T. Rees, 1874–1939

Timothy Rees builds his hymn around the phrase in the Lord's Prayer *Hallowed be thy name.* The Jerusalem Bible renders this 'May your name be held holy', which gives the true sense of the word 'hallowed'. The prayer is in essence an act of adoration in which we reverence God as the All-holy.

The hymn follows a simple pattern. In the first stanza we acknowledge that God's name is to be hallowed by us on earth as truly as it is by the angelic hosts in heaven. The second is a prayer that we may have a clearer view of God's nature, so that we may hallow him:

> By our heart's deep-felt contrition,
> By our mind's enlightened vision,
> By our will's complete submission. ·

In the final stanza we ask that God's name may be honoured in every department of life: in our work as well as in our worship, in the affairs of the nation as well as in those of the Church.

Timothy Rees was ordained in 1897 and spent the early years of his ministry in Wales. In 1906 he became a member of the Community of the Resurrection, Mirfield. After the First World War, in which he served as a chaplain, he returned to Mirfield as principal of the College. He remained there till 1931, when he was appointed Bishop of Llandaff.

TUNE: *Carolyn* (Herbert Murrill, 1909–52).

41 God is Love: let heaven adore him
T. Rees, 1874–1939

A hymn with the motif 'God is Love' would seem to be obvious enough, but no other writer appears to have made use of it in this way. It was found among Bishop Rees's papers after his death and was sung at his funeral. Its inclusion in the *BBC Hymn Book*, 1951, helped to make it known and it has gradually come into general use.

The first stanza affirms that the God whose name (i.e. nature) is Love is none other than the maker of heaven and earth:

> He who breathes through all creation,
> He is Love, eternal Love.

Hence, as the next verse goes on to say, this eternal Love enfolds 'all the world in one embrace'. No one is outside his 'unfailing grasp'; and therefore those whose hearts are breaking with sorrow may know that at such times they do not suffer alone:

Then they find that selfsame aching
Deep within the heart of God.

The final stanza rings with the assurance that as God's eternal, unchanging love continues to hold and guide the life of mankind, so at the last, triumphant over 'sin and death and hell', it will rule the universe.

TUNES: *Alleluia* (S. S. Wesley, 1810–76); *Hyfrydol* (R. H. Prichard, 1811–87); *Rustington* (C. H. H. Parry, 1848–1918).

42 Lord of the boundless curves of space   *A. Bayly**, 1901–84

Albert Bayly is a hymn-writer who looks at life on a cosmic scale. Like the great Dr Watts, he writes with a constant awareness of the vastness, the wonder, and the mystery of the universe as God's handiwork. But again like Watts, he is not content to stop there. From the natural order he directs his thoughts to the higher realm of the spirit and to God's ultimate purpose for the world in Christ.

This hymn affords a good illustration of his approach and technique. It views God as both Creator and Redeemer. He is indeed, as another of Bayly's hymns states, the 'Lord of every shining constellation', the source of all nature's energy:

Your mind conceived the galaxy,
Each atom's secret planned,
And every age of history
Your purpose, Lord, has spanned.

But the universe is not God's crowning achievement. His greatest work is seen in the making and remaking of man:

Yours is the image stamped on man,
Though marred by man's own sin;
And yours the liberating plan
Again his soul to win.

This liberating plan is accomplished through Christ, the incarnate Word, in whom the sons of earth see the perfect revelation of God's love and respond in adoration and obediencc.

TUNE: *London New (Scottish Psalter*, 1635) and others.

43 New songs of celebration render *E. Routley*, 1917–82

The inclusion of this hymn enables us to pay a brief tribute to the leading hymnologist of the latter half of the 20th century. Erik Routley's encyclopaedic knowledge of hymnody in all its varied aspects – historical, musical, liturgical, theological – made him the acknowledged authority on the subject throughout the world. He wrote some thirty books and had a hand in editing numerous hymnals. During the last seven years of his life he lived in the USA and was Professor of Church Music at the Westminster Choir College, Princeton.

He will be remembered as a composer of hymn tunes rather than as a writer of hymns. Among the latter this is probably the most widely known. It is a paraphrase of Psalm 98 ('Sing to the Lord a new song') based on the 1970 revision of the *French Psalter* and was published in *Cantate Domino*, 1975. To appreciate its high qualities no knowledge of the French original is necessary. A glance at any English rendering of the psalm will show how skilfully the writer has not only paraphrased its language but also caught its exuberant spirit of praise. Take for example the second stanza:

> Joyfully, heartily resounding,
>> Let every instrument and voice
> Peal out the praise of grace abounding,
>> Calling the whole world to rejoice.
> Trumpets and organs, set in motion,
>> Such sounds as make the heavens ring;
> All things that live in earth and ocean,
>> Make music for your mighty king.

The whole hymn, like the psalm, is a joyous celebration of God as creator, sovereign and judge of all the world.

TUNE: *Rendez à Dieu*. Melody by L. Bourgeois, 1510–61, for Psalm 98 in the *Genevan Psalter*, 1542.

44 To God be the glory! great things he hath done   F. J. van Alstyne, 1820–1915

Mrs Frances Jane van Alstyne is better known by her maiden name of Fanny J. Crosby. Blind almost from birth, she was educated at a New York school for the blind, where later she was a teacher. In 1858 she married Alexander van Alstyne, a blind musician. Her output of hymns and gospel songs was enormous, estimated as nearly 8,000 in all. Among those still in use, in addition to the present hymn, are 'Blessed assurance' (218), 'Safe in the arms of Jesus' and 'Rescue the perishing'.

'To God be the glory' – which has taken on a new lease of life through the Billy Graham crusades – owes its popularity in part to its tune by W. H. Doane (1832–1916). It is a hymn which has something positive to say, and something about God: *Great things he hath done!* That is the keynote. Fanny Crosby was no theologian, but she would have agreed with Dr John Mackay's assertion that the primary element in the Christian religion is not a great imperative, something that man should do, but a great indicative, something that God has done, his redemptive act in Christ.

The hymn is about God's great indicative. He so loved the world that he gave his Son, who made atonement for the sin of mankind and opened the gate of life to all who truly believe in him. So – to God be the glory! Great is our rejoicing here and now; but how much greater will be our rapture 'when Jesus we *see*'; and to Fanny Crosby in her blindness that last word had a special meaning.

TUNE: See above.

45 I danced in the morning   S. Carter, b. 1915

Sydney Carter's popular song, which he wrote about 1961 and included in his *Carols and Ballads*, has been likened to the Christmas carol 'Tomorrow shall be my dancing day'. It clearly owes much to that carol, in which the Son of God is represented as saying that he came into the world 'to call my true love (viz. mankind) to my dance' – that is, to share in the joy and triumph of his salvation.

Sydney Carter's song takes the idea of the carol a stage further, 'and presents the whole of God's plan of creation and redemption (Eph. 1:3–10) as a dance led by one who is the creative Word and also the redeeming and ever-present friend' (*Songs of the People of God*). Hence it begins 'in the morning when the world was begun' and ends with the cross and the resurrection.

The *Shaker Tune* to which the song is set is one of the many rhythmic melodies found in the American Shaker hymn books. It has been arranged by John Birch (*b.* 1929). The Shakers were members of a movement which seceded from the Society of Friends (Quakers) in 1747 and taught the imminence of the Second Coming and the Millennium. They expressed their joyful assurance of salvation in dancing and singing.

TUNE: See above.

SECTION TWO
THE CHRISTIAN YEAR

ADVENT

46 Lo! he comes with clouds descending

C. Wesley★,
1707–88

In 1752 John Cennick, a friend of the Wesleys and the author of
'Children of the heavenly King' (230), published a somewhat
crude Advent hymn beginning:

> Lo! he cometh, endless trumpets
>   Blow before his bloody sign!
> Midst ten thousand saints and angels
>   See the Crucifièd shine.
>   Alleluia!
>   Welcome, welcome, bleeding Lamb!

The verses came to the notice of Charles Wesley, who six years
later put out his *Hymns of Intercession for All Mankind*. Included
in this collection was what had once been Cennick's hymn –
now not only entirely rewritten but improved almost beyond
recognition. This can be seen by comparing the grandeur and
power of Wesley's familiar opening stanza with Cennick's. As
Canon Ellerton remarked, 'Cennick's hymn is poor stuff
compared to that into which Wesley recast it, putting into it at
once fire and tunefulness.' So radically did Wesley 'recast' the
hymn that scarcely a trace of Cennick remains.

Like all Wesley's writings, the hymn is rich in biblical
phraseology. Most of it is borrowed from the book of Revelation, the work as a whole being based on the passage (1.7
AV):

Behold, he cometh with clouds, and every eye shall see him, and they also which pierced him: and all kindreds of the earth shall wail because of him. Even so, Amen.

The language here is 'apocalyptic' – that is, symbolical, not literal. It must be interpreted accordingly; so must the language of Wesley's hymn.

TUNE: *Helmsley* (an air adapted by T. Olivers, 1725–99).

47 O come, O come, Emmanuel	*Latin, approx. 13th century* *Tr. J. M. Neale*, 1818–66*

This somewhat obscure hymn has its origin in the seven great Advent antiphons sung in the medieval Church at Vespers before and after the *Magnificat*, during the week or so before Christmas. Each began with a long drawn-out 'O' expressive of deep yearning for the coming of Christ, who in each was addressed by a different Old Testament title. Some time around the 13th century an unknown poet selected five of the antiphons and turned them into a Latin hymn, adding a refrain ('Rejoice! Rejoice!') to be sung after each verse. The titles, with their meaning and biblical source, were as follows:

O Emmanuel – O Emmanuel ('God with us')	Isaiah 7:14
O Radix Jesse – O Root of Jesse	Isaiah 11:10
O Oriens – O Dayspring	Malachi 4:2
O Clavis Davidica – O Key of David	Isaiah 22:22
O Adonai – O Lord (Jehovah)	Exodus 3:15

The Latin original was translated by Dr Neale for his *Medieval Hymns*, 1851, and this forms the basis of the hymn as it appears in *A&M* and most other books. Another version was made by Canon T. A. Lacey for *EH*.

The key to the hymn lies partly in the meaning of the titles addressed to Christ and partly in the refrain, the second line of which in the Latin is *nascetur pro te, Israel*. The meaning of this is not 'shall come to thee' (as it is rendered to fit the tune) but 'shall *be born* for thee'. Clearly the reference is not to Christ's second coming but to his birth. As G. R. Balleine observed, 'The writer was thinking not of Doomsday but of Christmas. The original purpose of Advent was to prepare for Christmas, as Lent prepares for Easter.'

TUNE: *Veni Emmanuel*, adapted from a French missal by Thomas Helmore, 1811–90.

48 Hark the glad sound! the Saviour comes

P. Doddridge*,
1702–51

Most of Doddridge's hymns were designed to be sung in his chapel at Northampton after he had preached on the text prefixed to them. This one is dated 28 December 1735 and headed 'Christ's Message, from Luke 4:18,19' – evidently the preacher's text that day. The passage refers to the words of Isaiah 61:1,2 which Jesus read in the synagogue at Nazareth as being fulfilled in himself:

> The Spirit of the Lord is upon me, because he hath anointed me to preach the gospel to the poor; he hath sent me to heal the broken-hearted, to proclaim deliverance to the captives, and recovering of sight to the blind, to set at liberty them that are bruised, to preach the acceptable year of the Lord.

Out of these prophetic words Doddridge fashioned his hymn, announcing the good news of Christ's advent and illustrating his mission in the world. The hymn originally comprised seven verses. Most hymn books now print only four of them, those dealing with the Lord's work in liberating the captives, healing the broken-hearted and enriching the poor. But the prophecy also refers to the 'recovering of sight to the blind', and Doddridge took note of this in one of the missing stanzas:

> He comes, from thickest films of vice
> To clear the mental ray,
> And on the eyeballs of the blind
> To pour celestial day.

TUNE: *Bristol*, from Ravencroft's *Psalter*, 1621, is first choice among others.

49 On Jordan's bank the   *C. Coffin, 1676–1749*
    Baptist's cry   *Tr. by J. Chandler, 1806–76*

When he translated this hymn John Chandler was seemingly under the impression that it was of medieval or even earlier origin, for he included it in his *Hymns of the Primitive Church*, 1837. But though written in Latin the hymn is not ancient. It is the work of Charles Coffin, a distinguished French scholar, who wrote a hundred or so Latin hymns. The bulk of these appeared in the *Paris Breviary*, 1736, the present hymn (*Jordanis oras praevia*) among them.

In general terms it may be regarded as a commentary on John the Baptist's announcement of Christ's advent and his call to the people of Israel to repent and prepare for his coming. That call is now applied to us as we make ready for Christmas and prepare to welcome Christ into our hearts. Chandler's translation has been revised and adapted to a certain extent. In particular his fourth stanza did insufficient justice to the Latin text, which made reference to the Lord's power to heal the sick, raise the fallen and restore the earth to its pristine beauty. This was righted by the editors of *A&M* with their rendering:

> To heal the sick stretch out thine hand,
> And bid the fallen sinner stand;
> Shine forth, and let thy light restore
> Earth's own true loveliness once more.

TUNE: *Winchester New*, from *Musikalisch Handbuch* (Hamburg, 1690).

50 Wake, awake, for   *P. Nicolai, 1556–1608*
    night is flying   *Tr. C. Winkworth*, 1827–78*

Here is a German hymn in the authentic Lutheran tradition. Philip Nicolai wrote it during a terrible pestilence which raged in his parish of Unna, Westphalia, in the winter of 1597–8, when over 1,300 of his parishioners perished. From the tragic scenes of death and grief around him Nicolai directed his thoughts to Augustine's *City of God* and the life everlasting. In due course he turned his meditations into verse and published them, so as to leave behind him, if he were taken, a testimony to his own serene faith and to comfort other sufferers. He also composed the magnificent tune *Wachet Auf* to which the hymn is sung.

The verses were entitled 'Of the Voice at midnight and the wise Virgins who meet their heavenly Bridegroom: Matthew 25.' This provides the clue to the hymn's message. The parable of the Virgins is the main theme of the opening stanza:

> Come forth, you virgins, night is past:
> The Bridegroom comes, awake,
> Your lamps with gladness take,
> And for his marriage feast prepare,
> For you must go to meet him there.

The references to the shouts of the watchmen (vv. 1,2) are derived from Isaiah 52:8; and in the final stanza there are allusions to the imagery of Revelation.

In addition to Catherine Winkworth's English translation two others are still in use: those by Frances Cox ('Sleepers wake! the watch-cry pealeth', as amended in *A&M*) and Francis Burkitt ('Wake, O wake! with tidings thrilling', made for *EH*).

TUNE: *Wachet Auf* (see above).

51 Come, thou long-expected Jesus   C. Wesley*, 1707–88

From Wesley's *Hymns for the Nativity of our Lord*, 1744; so this is intended to be a hymn for Christmas rather than Advent. It has indeed a good deal to say about the birth of Jesus, who came to be not only the long-expected Messiah of Israel but the 'hope of all the earth' (v.2). However, the hymn's ultimate emphasis is on the kingship of Jesus, and therefore upon his kingdom (v.3).

It is this fact that gives the hymn its Advent character. Jesus was born a King. But his kingship is not of this world; it is exercised in human hearts and lives. So the hymn fittingly ends with the prayer:

> By thine own eternal Spirit
>> Rule in all our hearts alone;
> By thy all-sufficient merit
>> Raise us to thy glorious throne.

TUNES: Various, including *Stuttgart* (from a melody in *Psalmodia Sacra*, Gotha, 1715); *Cross of Jesus* (Sir J. Stainer, 1840–1901); and *Holton Holgate* (W. Boyce, 1710–79).

52 Mine eyes have seen the glory of the coming of the Lord

J. W. Howe,
1819–1910

This is very much an American hymn, written by an American author, closely linked with American history and sung (usually) to a rousing American tune. Mrs Julia Ward Howe wrote it in December 1861, six months after the outbreak of the American Civil War. At the time she was in Washington, attending a review of Union troops, and she heard them singing 'John Brown's body'. Someone remarked to her that such a fine tune deserved better and more permanent words. She took it as a challenge, and that night the words came to her. Before daybreak the hymn was complete. It was published in the *Atlantic Monthly*, February 1862, under the title 'The Battle Hymn of the Republic'.

The political background of the hymn is the struggle for the abolition of slavery, and echoes of this are evident throughout. But it strikes a strongly spiritual note. In the popular song that inspired the hymn it was John Brown's soul that was said to go marching on. Mrs Howe lifted this idea to a higher level. *Our God is marching on!* And he is marching on to judgment. Note the references to the grapes of God's wrath, his terrible swift sword, his sifting out the hearts of men. Note above all the allusion to Christ's sacrifice:

As he died to make men holy, let us live to make men free.

What Mrs Howe actually wrote was '. . . let us *die* to make men free.' In doing so she was indicating the costly character of the struggle in which the abolitionists were engaged.

TUNE: As noted, the hymn was written for the famous marching song, 'John Brown's body', now known as *Battle Hymn*. An excellent alternative is the tune *Vision*, which Sir Walford Davies (1869–1941) wrote for it in 1915.

53 Long ago, prophets knew   *F. Pratt Green**, *b*.1903

Fred Pratt Green wrote this hymn in 1970 in response to a request from John Wilson (of the Hymn Society) for an Advent hymn to the carol tune *Personent hodie*: Gustav Holst's arrangement of the melody from *Piae Cantiones*, 1582. Dr Pratt Green's 'Advent Song' admirably fits the tune and draws out the message of the season, beginning with the promise of Christ's coming:

> Long ago, prophets knew
> Christ would come, born a Jew,
> Come to make all things new,
>   Bear his people's burden,
>   Freely love and pardon.

The chorus which follows each stanza, 'Ring, bells, ring, ring, ring,' sounds a welcome to the one whose coming is anticipated and celebrated in the hymn. The second stanza is a reflection on God and Time and echoes the words of Galatians 4:4: 'When the appointed time came, God sent his Son, born of a woman'; and this is fittingly followed by a stanza on the Annunciation:

> Mary, hail! Though afraid,
> She believed, she obeyed.
> In her womb God is laid,
>   Till the time expected,
>   Nurtured and protected.

In the final stanza Bethlehem is glimpsed shining in the distance . . .

TUNE: *Personent hodie* (see above).

CHRISTMAS

54 O come, all ye faithful   J. F. Wade, c.1711–86
Tr. F. Oakley, 1802–80

The authorship of the *Adeste fideles* was long in doubt. Scholars were agreed that despite its Latin origin the hymn was not earlier than the 18th century. New light was thrown on the problem when in 1946 Dr Maurice Frost, vicar of Deddington, Oxfordshire, discovered a Latin manuscript of the hymn. As a result of his researches he concluded that both words and music were the work of a young Englishman, John Francis Wade, who worked in Douai, the famous Roman Catholic centre in France where there was an English college. The most likely date of the hymn is 1743.

In its original form it consisted of the four familiar stanzas. The first is an invitation to Bethlehem to adore the new-born babe; the second an affirmation of faith in the Incarnation; the third an exhortation to the angels to sing their Christmas anthem; and the fourth is our own greeting to the Holy Child on his birthday. The English version is based on the translation made in 1841 by Canon Frederick Oakley when he was incumbent of what is now All Saints', Margaret Street, London. He later entered the RC Church.

The hymn has two unusual features. One is its irregular metre: all four stanzas have a different metrical form. The other feature is the lack of rhyme, which is very unusual in a popular hymn; yet strangely we are not conscious of it when we sing the hymn at Christmas.

The three additional stanzas found in many hymnals were added later.

TUNE: *Adeste fideles* (see above).

55 Hark! the herald-angels sing   *C. Wesley*★, 1707–88

This, the most popular of Wesley's many Christmas hymns, is
arguably the best known of all his hymns. It has been translated into numerous languages and is sung all over the world.
Since it was first published in 1739 as ten four-line verses it has
undergone a good many alterations. As Wesley wrote it the
opening was:

> Hark! how all the welkin rings,
> 'Glory to the King of kings,
> Peace on earth and mercy mild,
> God and sinners reconciled.'

The last four verses have completely dropped out of use and
the remaining six have been paired off to make the now familiar
three stanzas of eight lines each.

The opening lines, altered by George Whitefield in 1753 to
their present form, became the refrain of the hymn when in the
mid-19th century it was set to a fine chorus from Mendelssohn's *Festegsang* (Op.68), a work composed for the Leipzig
festival of 1840 to celebrate the invention of printing. The
adaption was made by William H. Cummings (1831–1915)
when organist of Waltham Abbey. It met with Mendelssohn's
strong disapproval: he considered the tune to be too gay and
cheerful for sacred words. Nevertheless the tune has not only
stuck but has doubtless contributed largely to the hymn's
immense popularity.

TUNE: *Mendelssohn* (see above).

56 Christians awake, salute the happy morn   *J. Byrom*, 1692–1763

A pleasant story, and happily a true one, lies behind this hymn.
John Byrom wrote it for his little daughter Dolly who had
asked her father for a poem as a Christmas present. Sure
enough, when she came down to breakfast in her Manchester
home on Christmas morning 1749 the lines were lying on the
table in her place, entitled 'Christmas Day, for Dolly'. The

original manuscript is preserved in the Chetham Library, Manchester. Not long afterwards the poem found its way into a local newspaper and so was made public; and in his diary Byrom recalls that the following Christmas (1750) 'the singing men and boys with Mr Wainwright came here and sang "Christians awake".' The choir was that of Stockport parish church, and the organist John Wainwright (1723–68) had written the tune (now known as *Yorkshire*) for the hymn.

The fact that it was written for a child doubtless accounts for its simple and straightforward character. The first part is in narrative form and tells the story of the nativity as given in Luke 2:8–20. The latter part is a homily or reflection on the meaning of the story, beginning with the lines:

> Like Mary, let us ponder in our minds
> God's wondrous love in saving lost mankind.

Dr Byrom was a scholar of some distinction, a Cambridge graduate, well versed in theology, medicine and science, and a Fellow of the Royal Society.

TUNE: *Yorkshire* (see above).

57 Once in royal David's city   *C. F. Alexander*★, 1818–95

From Mrs Alexander's *Hymns for Little Children*, 1848 (see 22), to illustrate the words of the Apostles' Creed, 'Who was conceived by the Holy Ghost, born of the Virgin Mary'. Inevitably we now regard this as a Christmas hymn, but it was not written as such. The author's object was to teach children the meaning of what we celebrate at Christmas, so as to make clear not only *what* happened but *why* it happened, and to explain some of its implications.

The six stanzas fall quite naturally into three pairs. The first pair is concerned with the significance of the Lord's nativity; the second with the pattern of his childhood; and the third with his heavenly glory, in contrast to his lowly birth. The hymn is thus a skilful mingling of Bible story and Christian theology, combined with a bit of godly moralising – the sort of thing that was expected in children's hymns in Victorian times.

TUNE: *Irby*, composed by Dr H. J. Gauntlett (1805–76) for this hymn in his *Christmas Carols*, 1849, and later included in the first edition of *A&M*, 1861.

58 Of the Father's love begotten

A. C. Prudentius, 348–413
Tr. J. M. Neale*, 1818–66

This is quite certainly the oldest of our Christmas hymns. Aurelius Clemens Prudentius was, according to *Julian*, 'the most prominent and most prolific author of sacred Latin poetry in its earliest days.' After training and practising as a lawyer, he received promotion to a judgeship; but later in life he retired to a monastery, where he devoted his poetical gifts to the service of the Church.

Verses from his poems were selected to be sung as hymns in the monastic offices of the medieval church and so have come down to us today in English versions (see also 69). Dr Neale's translation of the present one (*Corde natus ex parentis*) in *A&M* underwent a good deal of revision by Sir Henry Baker and others. Its length (in full) makes it an ideal hymn for use as a processional at Christmastide.

It is, clearly enough, a hymn of the Incarnation. But it is more than that. It is also a battle-hymn contending for the Catholic Faith in face of the Arian heresy (the denial of the Godhead of Christ) which was so vital an issue in the 4th century. So the hymn views Jesus as the only begotten Son of the Father, the Alpha and Omega, the Creator of all things, who came as promised in the ancient scriptures, took our mortal frame and was born of the Blessed Virgin to redeem mankind. The whole work leads up to the final triumphant doxology in which the whole creation joins in praise to Christ.

TUNE: *Divinum mysterium*, from the medieval melody *Piae Cantiones*, 1582.

59 In the bleak midwinter

C. Rossetti, 1830–94

Christina Rossetti must be regarded as a poet rather than a hymn-writer. A member of an exceptionally brilliant family, she grew up in a circle of literary people and artists. She had a

deeply religious temperament and wrote a number of devotional works in prose as well as several volumes of poems.

Walter de la Mare spoke of there being 'a kind of magic in
her best writing, and a touch of what was once the fashion to
call the "numinous".' This quality can be seen in the present
poem, which is a deeply sensitive and vividly imaginative
expression of the Incarnation. Written about 1870, it was first
used as a hymn in the *English Hymnal*, 1906, set to the tune
Cranham which Gustav Holst (1874–1934) composed for it. As
Percy Dearmer observed, 'The music is simple and unpreten-
tious, and thus in accordance with the spirit and the expression
of the poem.'

Two other of Miss Rossetti's Christmas poems have
found their way into our hymn books: 'Love came down at
Christmas' and the children's carol 'The shepherds had an
angel'.

TUNE: *Cranham* (see above).

60 O little town of Bethlehem   *Phillips Brooks,*
1835–93

In 1866 Phillips Brooks, then rector of Trinity Church, Philadelphia, was on a pilgrimage in the Holy Land. Christmas
Eve found him in Bethlehem, where after visiting the Field of
the Shepherds he attended the midnight service in the Church of
the Nativity. For the young clergyman it was a moving and
memorable experience; and on his return to America he
decided to record his impressions in the form of a hymn. He
wrote it for the children of his Sunday school. The church
organist set it to music and it soon came into use in the
American churches. In Britain, however, it was little known
till its appearance in the *English Hymnal*, 1906. It was there set
to *Forest Green*, an arrangement by Vaughan Williams of a
traditional English melody. Walford Davies' *Christmas Carol*,
published a year earlier, also added to its popularity.

Against the background of the sleeping town of Bethlehem
the hymn gives poetical expression to the story of the first
Christmas night and the wonder of God's entry into human
life in the child born to Mary. It also has something to say

about what this should mean to us; for as it begins with Christ born in Bethlehem, it ends with Christ born in the heart.

Phillips Brooks, who late in life was elected Bishop of Massachusetts, gained renown as one of America's finest preachers. He continues to preach through this hymn.

TUNE: *Forest Green* or *Christmas Carol* (see above); or in USA *St Louis* (L. H. Redner, 1830–1908).

61 Away in a manger, no crib for a bed   *Anonymous*

This charming children's hymn is such a favourite with everyone at Christmas that it deserves a place in this companion. No one knows who wrote it. The only thing that can be said with confidence is that it is not by Martin Luther, to whom it used to be ascribed. The earliest date to which it can be traced is 1885, when it was included in the American Lutheran's *Little Children's Book* and stated to be anonymous. It consisted then of only the first two verses; the third was added later.

There seems no doubt that the hymn is of American origin, as is the attractive *Cradle Song* to which it is wedded. This was composed by William J. Kirkpatrick (1838–1921), who wrote tunes for many of the popular gospel songs of the last century, including 'Will your anchor hold' (222) and 'We have heard a joyful sound'.

TUNE: *Cradle Song* (see above).

62 Child of the stable's secret birth   *T. Dudley-Smith★*,
*b.*1926

Written in February 1969, the five stanzas of this hymn were not originally intended to be sung. They were written as a poem and published at the end of that year in the Christmas issue of *Crusade* magazine, of which Timothy Dudley-Smith was then editor. Six years later they were included in *English Praise*, set to the tune *Morwenstow* by Christopher Dearnley (*b.*1930).

Of the author's many Christmas hymns – most of them written in the first place as verses for the family Christmas card – this is probably the finest. As we contemplate the baby 'cradled soft in the manger bed', so small, so weak, so helpless, we are reminded of the cruel destiny that awaits him at the hands of sinful men – and also of the great redemption he is to accomplish through his suffering in fulfilment of the divine purpose. The final stanza epitomises the theme:

> Child of the stable's secret birth,
> The Father's gift to a wayward earth,
> To drain the cup in a few short years
> Of all our sorrows, our sins and tears –
>   Ours the prize for the road he trod:
>   Risen with Christ; at peace with God.

TUNE: *Morwenstow* (see above).

63 While shepherds watched their flocks by night
N. Tate*, 1652–1715

It was Nahum Tate, the Poet Laureate of his day, who collaborated with Nicholas Brady in the production of the *New Version* of the metrical psalms, 1696 (see 23). Four years later a supplement was added to the psalter containing various other paraphrases and also six hymns. Among the latter was a hymn for Christmas – the ever-popular 'While shepherds watched'. This is known to be the work of Tate alone.

The hymn is of course a straightforward paraphrase of the nativity story in Luke 2:8–14. No doubt its popularity lies partly in the story itself, which makes an irresistible appeal to the imagination. But Tate must be given credit for the skilful way in which he turned Luke's prose into poetry. It is an example of biblical paraphrasing at its best. While adhering closely to the text of scripture and taking no undue liberties, he produced lines which are easy to understand and easy to sing. Unfortunately not all the paraphrases of that age were of the same standard. The hymn remains as Tate's abiding memorial wherever English hymns are sung.

TUNE: *Winchester Old* (from Este's *Book of Psalms*, 1592).

64 Angels from the realms of glory   *J. Montgomery*★,   1771–1854

Montgomery was editor of a Sheffield newspaper called the *Iris* and this hymn first appeared in its columns on Christmas Eve, 1816. Like all his hymns, it follows a clear and orderly pattern as it summons in turn the angels, the shepherds, the magi and the expectant in Israel to come and worship the new-born King. In its original form the hymn had a strangely unsuitable fifth stanza, addressed to 'Sinners wrung with true repentance' which has quite rightly disappeared from our hymn books. The 1950 edition of *A&M* replaced it with a stanza from another of Montgomery's Christmas hymns:

> Though an infant now we view him,
> He shall fill his Father's throne,
> Gather all the nations to him;
> Every knee shall then bow down.

TUNES: *Lewes* (J. Randall, 1715–99); or *Regent Square* (H. Smart, 1813–79); or perhaps best of all the French carol melody *Iris*.

65 Still the night, holy   *J. Mohr*, 1792–1848   the night   *Tr. Stopford Brooke*, 1832–1916

Of the familiar Christmas hymns and carols that have come to us from the Continent, one of the most popular is Joseph Mohr's *Stille Nacht*. It was written in 1818 and first sung on Christmas Eve of that year in the village church of St Nicholas, Oberdorf, Upper Austria, where Mohr was assistant priest. Earlier that day he had asked his friend Franz Gruber (1787–1863), the acting organist of the church, to set the words to music. The haunting tune was apparently composed at once and so came to be used that same evening. As the church organ happened to be out of action Mohr sang the tenor part, accompanying himself on a guitar, while Gruber sang the bass, with a choir of village girls joining in the melody.

Of the dozen or so English translations which have been made only two are now in common use. The version beginning 'Silent night, holy night', popular in America, is ascribed to Bishop John F. Young (1820–85). In Britain the version based on Stopford Brooke's translation in his *Christian Hymns*, 1881, is generally used; but it has been so much altered in order to bring it into closer line with the original that his name is attached to it only as a matter of courtesy.

TUNE: *Stille Nacht* (see above).

EPIPHANY

66 As with gladness men of old   *W. Chatterton Dix★*, 1837–98

Without question this is the best known of Epiphany hymns. It was written by a layman, in fact a businessman – a point worth noting, since the vast majority of hymn-writers have been clergymen of one kind or another. William Chatterton Dix was a devout Anglican in the High Church tradition. He possessed genuine poetical gifts and among his other hymns are 'Alleluia! sing to Jesus' (145) and the harvest hymn, 'To thee, O Lord, our hearts we raise'.

Dix has left it on record that he wrote the hymn in 1860 while slowly recovering from a serious illness. One evening, when feeling somewhat stronger, the lines gradually formed themselves in his mind, and asking for writing materials he committed them to paper. The hymn was published a year later in the first edition of *A&M*.

Taking the Epiphany story in Matthew 2:1–11 as his theme, Dix draws out its spiritual lessons, likening the quest of the magi to our own Christian pilgrimage. The first three verses thus follow the pattern 'As they . . . so may we.' The last two stanzas abandon the story and are a prayer that we may obediently follow the path that leads at last to the heavenly country, of which Christ himself is the uncreated Light (*cf.* Rev.21:23).

TUNE: *Dix*, from a chorale by Conrad Kocher (1786–1872).

67 Brightest and best of the sons of the morning

R. *Heber*★, 1783–1826

This is the earliest of Reginald Heber's hymns. It was published in a weekly paper called the *Christian Observer* in November 1811. Despite its flights of poetical fancy the hymn appears to be innocuous enough and perfectly orthodox; but when it first appeared it was highly suspect in certain church circles on the ground that it involved the worshipping of a star! For this reason it was excluded from *A&M* for over fifty years.

The hymn is far from having any connection with nature worship. While using natural imagery as a background to its teaching, its real concern is to make clear the kind of worship that is acceptable to God. With a good deal of licence Heber portrays the nativity scene, with the hovering angels offering their silent adoration and the wise men paying homage with their costly gifts. Then he asks in effect, What worship shall *we* offer to the Christ? Does God demand our most lavish gifts, as represented by the gold, incense and myrrh of the magi? No, says the poet, something more is needed:

> Vainly we offer each ample oblation,
>   Vainly with gifts would his favour secure:
> Richer by far is the heart's adoration,
>   Dearer to God are the prayers of the poor.

In a sense the hymn is a commentary on the words of Psalm 51:17: 'The sacrifices of God are a broken spirit: a broken and a contrite heart, O God, thou wilt not despise.'

TUNES: *Epiphany Hymn* (J. F. Thrupp, 1827–67); *Liebster Immanuel*, from *Himmels-Lust*, Jena, 1679, arr. by J. S. Bach; or *Bede*, adapted from Handel's *Athalia* by Sir John Goss.

68 O worship the Lord in the beauty   *J. S. B. Monsell★*,
      of holiness   1811–75

Like Heber's 'Brightest and best' this is an Epiphany hymn
dealing with the subject of worship, and in much the same
spirit. It not only invites us to worship; it tells us *how* we
should do so:

> O worship the Lord in the beauty of holiness!
>   Bow down before him, his glory proclaim;
> With gold of obedience, and incense of lowliness,
>   Kneel and adore him, the Lord is his name!

The call to worship God in 'the beauty of holiness' rests on
Psalm 96:9 (*AV*). Obedience is likened to *gold* because it is so
precious an element in worship, while true humility, like
incense, imparts a fragrance to the praise we offer. The 'burden
of carefulness' in the next verse means the burden of our care
or anxiety, as in Philippians 4:6 (*AV*). The third stanza, with
its reference to the slenderness of the wealth we offer in God's
courts, recalls the story of the widow's mite; and in the fourth
the words 'mornings of joy' and 'evenings of tearfulness' are a
poetical paraphrase of Psalm 30:5, 'Weeping may endure for a
night, but joy cometh in the morning.'
  Of Monsell's nearly 300 hymns the best known is 'Fight the
good fight' (199).
  TUNE: *Was lebet*, from the Rheinhardt MS, Üttingen,
1754.

69 Earth has many a noble city   *A. C. Prudentius*, 348–413
                                  Tr. E. Caswall★, 1814–78

Although the Epiphany is an ancient feast, dating back to the
third century, comparatively few Epiphany hymns have come
to us from early Greek or Latin sources. Best known of these is
this one by Aurelius Clemens Prudentius, author of the
Christmas hymn 'Of the Father's love begotten' (58). The
English translation by Edward Caswall was included in his
Lyra Catholica, 1849, in which it began:

> Bethlehem, of noblest cities
> None can once with thee compare . . .

But most hymnals now adopt the revised version made by the
editors of *A&M*, 'Earth has many a noble city'.

The hymn acclaims Bethlehem as the noblest of cities
because it was the birthplace of 'the Lord from heaven'. It goes
on to tell of the star that announced his birth and led the magi
on their journey to the presence of the infant King, there to
offer him their gifts:

> Solemn things of mystic meaning:
> Incense doth the God disclose,
> Gold a royal child proclaimeth,
> Myrrh a future tomb foreshows.

This interpretation of the gifts as pointing to Christ's divinity,
royalty and mortality represents the teaching of the early
church fathers, however dubious it may appear to the modern
mind.

TUNE: *Stuttgart* (C. F. Witt, 1660–1716).

70 Songs of thankfulness and praise   *C. Wordsworth*★, 1807–85

The value of this hymn is its teaching about the meaning of the
Epiphany. This is exactly what Bishop Wordsworth intended.
He was first and foremost a scholar, not a poet, and he made it
clear that in his hymns he was concerned not so much with
writing fine poetry as with imparting sound teaching. And
this hymn is packed full of teaching in regard to the *epiphaneia*
(manifestation) of Christ in its varied aspects.

It begins with his manifestation as the incarnate Son in his
birth at Bethlehem. It goes on to his later epiphanies: at his
baptism in the river Jordan; at Cana's wedding feast when he
changed the water into wine; in his ministry of healing the sick
and afflicted; in his battle with the powers of evil. Finally there
is a reference, in the bishop's own words, to 'the future great
and glorious Epiphany at which Christ will appear again to
judge the world.'

When we have sung this hymn we have not only offered praise to God. We have also learned something more about the Epiphany – and something more about Christ himself.

TUNE: *St Edmund* (C. Steggall, 1826–1905).

71 Hail to the Lord's Anointed
James Montgomery*,
1771–1854

It is interesting to compare Montgomery's hymn with Isaac Watts's 'Jesus shall reign' (166). Both are free paraphrases of Psalm 72 which begins, 'Give the king thy judgements, O God.' The Jews believed that the *king* referred to was the promised Messiah and that the psalm was a prophecy of his glorious reign. The Church from the beginning adopted this interpretation and accordingly applied the psalm to Jesus – as Watts does quite specifically in his opening line. Montgomery is content to speak of Jesus as 'the Lord's Anointed, great David's greater Son'. In turning the psalm into poetry he keeps more closely to the biblical text than Watts. Indeed, the best way to appreciate the hymn is to open the Bible alongside it and note how the two match up.

The psalm speaks in glowing terms of the king's righteous rule, offering relief to the poor and oppressed, bringing peace and prosperity to the nation and extending its boundaries far and wide in the world. All these elements find expression in the hymn, especially in its complete form of seven stanzas (as in *CP* 326). It ends with a vision of the King's reign as not only universal but eternal: 'His name shall endure for ever,' wrote the psalmist; and this is echoed in the hymn: 'His name shall stand for ever.' But then the writer adds something of his own: 'That name to us is Love.' Many hymn books change this to 'His endless name of Love' – an unnecessary alteration.

The hymn, first published in 1821 and later revised, is probably Montgomery's finest work and is particularly suitable for the Epiphany season.

TUNE: *Crüger* (adapted by W. H. Monk, 1823–89, from a chorale by J. Crüger, 1598–1662).

LENT

72 Forty days and forty nights   G. M. Smyttan, 1822–70,
and others

In Anglican circles this is probably the best known of Lent
hymns proper. In its original form, as published by the Revd
George Smyttan in 1856, it consisted of nine stanzas. Francis
Pott, the author of 'Angel voices ever singing' (133), revised it
for *A&M*, and it is this version which is best known today.
Percy Dearmer also revised it for *SP*.

  Which ever version is adopted, we are compelled to admit
that this is not a great hymn. Its merit is that it does take as its
theme our Lord's temptation in the wilderness; but it is based
on Mark's short account (Mark 1:12,13), which is concerned
only with the outward circumstances, not with the Lord's
inner spiritual conflict described in the other synoptic Gospels.
The hymn therefore fails to deal with Jesus' temptations as
such but simply with the physical sufferings he endured in the
lonely desert. This is the picture provided in the two opening
verses. Those that follow seek to relate what Jesus endured to
our own Lenten discipline, as for example in the third verse as
Smyttan wrote it:

> Shall not we thy sorrow share,
>   Learn thy discipline of will,
> And, like thee, by fast and prayer
>   Wrestle with the powers of ill?

TUNE: *Heinlein*, probably by Martin Herbst (1654–81).

73 Christian, dost thou see them   J. M. Neale*, 1818–66

An element of mystery surrounds the origin of this hymn. It
was published in Dr Neale's *Hymns of the Eastern Church*, 1862,
as a translation of a hymn by St Andrew of Crete (660–732),
but no Greek text has been found from which this translation
could have been made. It seems that Neale composed the

Greek text himself in the spirit of St Andrew – who in his day put up a strong fight for the truth of the gospel – and then rendered it into English. Hence the theme of the hymn is the Christian's battle against the forces of evil.

Those forces attack the believer in different ways, as expressed in the opening lines of the first three stanzas (the italics are as in Neale's published version):

'Christian, dost thou *see* them . . . ?' There are powers of evil in our fallen world that are clearly visible, like 'the troops of Midian' which threatened Israel in Gideon's time.

'Christian, dost thou *feel* them . . . ?' Evil also takes a spiritual form. It is the evil we feel within us as we struggle againt pride, jealousy, greed and the lusts of the flesh.

'Christian, dost thou *hear* them . . . ?' A third type of evil disguises itself in false or beguiling speech, tempting us to listen to the voice of Reason rather than follow the path of self-discipline and prayer.

The fourth stanza, which brings the hymn to a triumphant conclusion, is different. Now another voice is heard speaking to us, the voice of the Lord himself, offering us sympathy and encouragement as we continue to fight and pray, and promising us a place near his throne at last.

TUNES: *St Andrew of Crete* (J. B. Dykes, 1823–76), or *Gute Bäume bringen*, from a melody by P. Sohren (died *c.*1692).

74 Take up thy cross, the Saviour said   *C. W. Everest,* 1814–77

The Christian path is not a bed of roses. Jesus spoke to his disciples about the necessity of taking up the cross and following him (Mark 8.34), and it is this teaching that finds expression in this hymn. Charles William Everest was an American youth of nineteen when he wrote it. He later graduated at Trinity College, Hartford, and in 1842 he was ordained to the ministry of the Episcopal Church. The text of his hymn

appears in a considerably revised form in most hymnals. A
version closer to the original is in *CP*, where for example the
third stanza follows Everest's wording:

> Take up thy cross, nor heed the shame,
>   And let thy foolish pride be still;
> Thy Lord refused not e'en to die
>   Upon a Cross, on Calvary's hill.

For a hymn written by a young man it paints a strangely
sombre picture of the fully committed Christian life: denying
self, renouncing the world, bearing the shame of the cross,
braving dangers and following Christ to the bitter end. Yet we
cannot deny that it comes uncomfortably close to what Jesus
himself said about the cost of discipleship.

TUNE: *Breslau*: melody in *As hymnodus sacer* (Leipzig,
1625).

75 O love, how deep, how broad, *Anonymous, 15th century*
how high!   *Tr. B. Webb*, 1819–85

This is part of a long Latin hymn on the Incarnation from
a Karlsruche manuscript of the 15th century. It has been
attributed to Thomas à Kempis on account of its affinity with
his known writings, but there is no direct evidence of
authorship.

The original hymn consisted of twenty-three stanzas. Our
English version is based on a translation by Benjamin Webb of
selected stanzas, beginning with the second: *O amor quam
exstaticus*. The hymn has two notable features. The first is the
breadth of its scope. It not only deals with the theme of the
Incarnation but covers the whole of our Lord's incarnate life,
culminating in his resurrection, ascension and sending of the
Holy Spirit.

The hymn's other feature is the emphatic way in which it
relates Christ's life and work to ourselves. *For us* is its key
phrase. It occurs some nine or twelve times, depending on the
stanzas selected. One which is often omitted is:

For us he prayed, for us he taught,
For us his daily works he wrought,
By words and signs and actions thus
Still seeking not himself but us.

A. S. Gregory said of this hymn that it 'contains almost all that Christians believe about Christ'. Hence what was originally a hymn of the Incarnation becomes a general hymn of praise to Christ for his redeeming grace.

TUNE: *Eisenach* (J. H. Schein, 1586–1630).

76 Lord Jesus, think on me *Synesius of Cyrene*, 375–430
Tr. A. W. Chatfield, 1808–96

The origin of this hymn goes back to the beginning of the 5th century. Synesius, a contemporary and friend of St Augustine, was in many ways a remarkable character. He was certainly a man of many parts: soldier, athlete, statesman, philosopher, poet – and last of all bishop. It was with some reluctance that he consented to be consecrated Bishop of Cyrene in 410 because his theological views, as propounded in his ten *Odes*, were somewhat unorthodox. He delighted to express the mystery of God's being in paradoxical and metaphysical terms. However, the final ode – on which the hymn is based – strikes a different note. Here the philosopher bows humbly in the presence of Christ and asks the Saviour to 'think on' him (or remember him), like the penitent thief on the cross.

The English version we sing is admittedly a free and expanded paraphrase rather than an exact translation of what Synesius wrote. It was published in 1876 by Dr Allen Chatfield, a classical scholar who specialised in translating the works of early Christian Greek poets.

TUNE: *St Paul's* (J. Stainer, 1840–1901), or *Southwell* (Damon's *Psalter*, 1579).

77 Father of heaven, whose love profound *E. Cooper,*
1770–1833

The name of Edward Cooper is practically unknown in the story of our hymns; yet he deserves to be remembered as being one of the pioneers of hymnody in the Church of England. Rector of Yaxall, 1809–33, he contributed this hymn among others to a collection published in Uttoxeter, Staffordshire, in 1805 – long before hymn-singing became a feature of Anglican worship or *A&M* appeared on the scene.

The hymn is based on the opening words of the Litany in the *BCP*, a penitential prayer beginning 'O God, the Father of heaven, have mercy upon us miserable sinners.' The hymn follows the same Trinitarian pattern and strikes the same penitential note. Thus the first three stanzas are addressed in turn to the three Persons of the Godhead – the Father of heaven, the incarnate Son, the eternal Spirit – and the fourth to the Holy Trinity:

> Thrice Holy! Father, Spirit, Son,
> Mysterious Godhead, Three in One,
> Before thy throne we sinners bend,
> Grace, pardon, life to us extend.

TUNES: *Rivaulx* (J. B. Dykes, 1823–76), or *Song 5* (Orlando Gibbons, 1583–1625).

PASSIONTIDE

78 All glory, laud,   *St Theodulph of Orleans*, 750–821
and honour   *Tr. J. M. Neale★*, 1818–66

No Palm Sunday service is complete without this hymn, written by the theologian and poet Theodulph in 820. Some twenty years earlier Charlemagne had brought him from Italy to France and appointed him Bishop of Orleans; but towards the end of his life he fell foul of the Emperor Louis, who accused him of conspiracy against the state and imprisoned him in a monastery at Angers. It was while thus confined that he wrote the hymn *Gloria, laus et honor*.

The original Latin version consisted of no less than thirty-

nine verses. Its length was due to the fact that the hymn was
intended to be sung in procession by choir and congregation
not only inside the church but outside as well. When Dr Neale
produced his English translation he considerably reduced its
length. It was published, with certain alterations, in the first
edition of *A&M*, 1861. It beautifully reflects the spirit and
imagery of the Lord's triumphal entry into Jerusalem. Neale
noted that, 'Another verse was usually sung till the seven-
teenth century, at the quaintness of which we can scarcely
avoid a smile.' That verse went:

> Be thou, O Lord, the rider,
> And we the little ass,
> That to God's holy city
> Together we may pass.

TUNE: *St Theodulph* by Melchior Tescher, published in
Leipzig, 1615.

79 Ride on! ride on in majesty! *H. H. Milman*, 1791–1868

Henry Hart Milman who in 1849 became Dean of St Paul's,
wrote this hymn about 1822 when he was Professor of Poetry
at Oxford. He sent a copy to his friend Reginald Heber, who
was seeking material from various poets for a projected collection of hymns to cover the Church's year. He was delighted
with the hymn. In acknowledging it he wrote to the author, 'A
few more such hymns and I shall neither need nor wait for the
aid of Scott and Southey!'

Each stanza begins with the arresting phrase 'Ride on! ride
on in majesty!' *Majesty* is the word we should keep in mind as
we sing the hymn. As he rides into Jerusalem Jesus is acclaimed
as King by the hosannas of the Jewish people. True, he is riding
there 'in lowly pomp to die'; but the death that awaits him is
not defeat or failure:

> O Christ, thy triumphs now begin
> O'er captive death and conquered sin.

Milman superbly invests the Passion of our Lord with royalty and interprets the cross in terms of victory. Moreover, with an imaginative touch he pictures the angels contemplating the scene with wonder and the Father waiting expectantly for his Son's hour of triumph. Throughout its five stanzas the hymn unites the elements of meekness and majesty, sacrifice and conquest, suffering and glory: a perfect expression of the Palm Sunday theme.

TUNES: *Winchester New* (from *Musikalisches Handbuch*, Hamburg, 1690, adapted by W. H. Havergal, 1793–1870), or *St Drostane* (J. B. Dykes, 1823–76).

80 My song is love unknown   *S. Crossman*, 1624–84

Samuel Crossman was one of the small group of 17th century writers whose sacred poetry has become part of our Christian hymnody. His name is closely associated with Bristol Cathedral of which, after serving as a prebendary for many years, he became dean a few weeks before his death. In 1664 he published a small book called *The Young Man's Meditation* which included nine of his poems. 'My song is love unknown' was among them. It was virtually lost to sight for 200 years until it was reprinted in the *Anglican Hymn Book*, 1868. It was there set to the tune *Lawes Psalm 47*, the work of Henry Lawes, 1596–1662 (as in *CP* and *WOV*).

In the present century the hymn has gained renewed popularity through the attractive tune *Love Unknown* which John Ireland composed for it at the request of Geoffrey Shaw. It is said that he wrote the tune on a scrap of paper in a quarter of an hour as soon as he received the request.

The words make an admirable passiontide hymn. Crossman's treatment of the theme is reverent and restrained, deeply devotional in tone and vividly pictorial in character. Beginning with the Incarnation (first two stanzas) it moves swiftly on to the events of Holy Week, dwelling in particular on the shame and tragedy of Jesus' rejection by his own people:

Sometimes they strew his way
And his sweet praises sing,

Resounding all the day
Hosannas to their King.
Then 'Crucify!'
Is all their breath,
And for his death
They thirst and cry.

The hymn is essentially a song of praise to Christ for his
unexampled love; and it ends, as it began, on this note.
TUNES: See above.

81 The royal banners   *Venantius Fortunatus, c.*530–609
    forward go   *Tr. J. M. Neale★,* 1818–66

Fortunatus was the leading Latin poet of his day. An Italian by
birth, he spent most of his life in France where he ended his
career by being elected Bishop of Poitiers in 599. It is with
Poitiers, though at an earlier date, that the writing of this
hymn (and the next one) is associated.

In his journeys Fortunatus became acquainted with Queen
Radegunda who, separated from her husband, had founded a
convent near Poitiers. She wished to secure some sacred relics
for its chapel and at length succeeded in obtaining these,
among them a supposed fragment of the true cross. To
provide processional hymns for the solemn ceremony at
which the relics were presented to the convent Fortunatus
wrote his two famous lyrics. It was therefore on that occasion,
19 November 569, that *Vexilla regis prodeunt* was first sung.
The English translation from Dr Neale's *Medieval Hymns,*
1851, is the basis of the version to be found in most hymnals.

The third stanza, as rendered by Neale, originally ran:

Fulfilled is all that David told
In true prophetic song of old;
Amidst the nations, God, saith he,
Hath reigned and triumphed from the tree.

No prophecy such as is here ascribed to David is to be found
in any version of the Psalms. The reference is to a faulty

rendering of Psalm 96:10 in some medieval psalters: 'Tell it out among the nations that the Lord is reigning from the tree [*a ligno*].' Fortunatus evidently followed this unauthentic text. Nevertheless, it remains true that the cross is the throne from which Christ rules his people and wins their allegiance.

TUNES: *Vexilla Regis* (Mode i), or *Gonfalon Royal* (P. C. Buck, 1871–1947).

82 Sing, my tongue,   *Venantius Fortunatus, c.530–609*
  the glorious battle   *Tr. J. M. Neale★, 1818–66*

For the background of this hymn, *Pange lingua*, see 'The royal banners forward go' (81). The original was in ten stanzas, which in the later medieval Breviaries were divided into two parts, as in *EH*. The opening words at once establish the theme:

> Sing, my tongue, the glorious battle,
>   Sing the ending of the fray;
> Now above the cross, the trophy,
>   Sound the loud triumphant lay;
> Tell how Christ, the world's Redeemer,
>   As a Victim won the day.

The Victim has become the Victor, for the battle is over and Christ has won redemption for mankind. The first part of the hymn traces the Christian story from the Fall to the Incarnation. The second part dwells entirely on the Passion, beginning:

> Faithful cross! above all other,
>   One and only noble tree!
> None in foliage, none in blossom,
>   None in fruit thy peer may be;
> Sweetest wood and sweetest iron!
>   Sweetest weight is hung on thee.

In singing these two hymns of Fortunatus we may forget that they were originally written in connection with a supposed relic of the cross. They make no allusion to the relic. 'Their whole theme,' as G. R. Balleine remarks, 'is the cross itself, the victorious cross, the cross that has spoiled and is spoiling the spoiler of his prey, the cross that has freed millions of souls from the bondage of sin.'

TUNES: *Pange lingua* (Plainsong melody, Sarum use); *St Thomas* (from S. Webbe's *Motets*, 1792); *Picardy* (French carol melody).

83 Praise to the Holiest in the height   *J. H. Newman**, 1801–90

Cardinal Newman published his poem *The Dream of Gerontius* in 1865. It traces the journey of a Christian soul (in this case the aged monk Gerontius) through the gate of death into the presence of Christ. The verses which make up the hymn are part of a longer poem, a chorus of praise sung by a choir of angels. It may seem strange that a hymn which is so occupied by the death of man should also be so full of praise. But the Christian believer is able to view death calmly and confidently in the light of Christ's redemptive work, and this is the hymn's majestic and triumphant theme.

It is not a popular type of hymn which readily yields up its meaning. It contains some difficult language which needs to be carefully interpreted. For example, in the second stanza reference is made to the *second Adam*. This is Jesus, 'The man from heaven' as Paul calls him, who came to do battle with sin and rescue us from its guilt and power (see Rom. 5:12 *f.* and 1Cor. 15:45–47).

Another unusual phrase comes at the beginning of the fourth stanza: *a higher gift than grace*, which refines flesh and blood. This is not a subtle allusion to the Roman doctrine of transubstantiation, as some Protestant critics have claimed. It is a reference to the Incarnation. In the perfect manhood of Jesus was embodied, enfleshed, not simply God's grace but 'God's presence and his very Self, and Essence all-divine'.

Again, the next stanza speak of *the double agony* which as the second Adam Jesus underwent for man. By the double agony is meant the Lord's physical and spiritual sufferings: all that he endured both in body and soul for our salvation.

TUNES: *Gerontius* (J. B. Dykes, 1823–76); or *Somervell* (Sir A. Somervell, 1863–1937). *Richmond* is a third alternative.

84 When I survey the wondrous cross   *I. Watts*★, 1674–1748

Matthew Arnold considered this to be the finest hymn in the English language. Certainly Watts himself wrote nothing greater. He included it among his hymns 'for the Holy Ordinance of the Lord's Supper' in his *Hymns and Spiritual Songs*, 1707, but clearly its use is not restricted to the sacrament.

It fixes our gaze wholly on the cross. In its original form it began:

> When I survey the wondrous cross,
>   Where the young Prince of glory died . . .

But Watts altered it to the present form when the hymn was republished in 1709. Many have since felt that the change was regrettable and unnecessary.

The second stanza echoes the text with which Watts headed the hymn: 'God forbid that I should glory save in the cross of our Lord Jesus Christ' (Gal.6:14). We glory not in ourselves:

> Forbid it, Lord, that I should boast
>   Save in the death of Christ my God.

We see in the cross the one thing we may boast about, the thing of supreme worth: God's saving act accomplished once and for all in the death of his Son Jesus Christ.

In the third stanza we look at the cross again and see in it an unveiling of the heart of God:

> See, from his head, his hands, his feet,
>   Sorrow and love flow mingled down.

The *sorrow* here is God's sorrow for our sin; the *love*, God's love for the sinner.

Watts's fourth stanza ('His dying crimson like a robe') is commonly omitted. The picture of Jesus bathed in his blood is startling, almost revolting. Watts probably intended it to be so. He wanted to disturb our complacency and make us feel something of the horror of the crucifixion. Thus we are prepared for the final verse, which confronts us with the demand of the cross:

> Love so amazing, so divine,
> Demands my soul, my life, my all.

TUNE: *Rockingham* (adapted by E. Miller, 1731–1807); or in USA *Hamburg* (arranged by Lowell Mason, 1792–1872).

85 There is a green hill far away   C. F. Alexander*, 1818–95

From Mrs Alexander's *Hymns for Little Children*, 1848, to illustrate the words of the creed, 'Suffered under Pontius Pilate, was crucified, dead, and buried'. She is said to have written the hymn while sitting by the bedside of a sick child. At the time she lived not far from Londonderry and was familiar with the sight of the massive city walls and the green hills beyond. This may have suggested the opening lines of the hymn. In any case it was an excellent idea of hers to begin it by painting a picture rather than by preaching a sermon. She knew her first task was to arrest the child's attention and capture his imagination.

She begins with a word of caution: 'We may not know, we cannot tell . . .' There are depths of meaning in the death of Jesus which are beyond our understanding. But that is not to say that the cross is a complete mystery. There are some things we *can* understand, and they are stated here at the end of the hymn. As the New Testament scholar, Professor A. H. Hunter, remarked, 'It was given to an Irish woman, in a hymn she wrote for children, to express better than many a learned tome the purpose, the necessity and the challenge of that sacrifice which has in principle redeemed our prodigal human race.' Look at the last three stanzas and you will find it all there: the purpose, the necessity and the challenge of the cross.

The author herself altered the 'Without' of the hymn's second line to *Outside*, to remove ambiguity; but most hymnals for some reason adhere to the original wording.

TUNE: *Horsley* (W. Horsley, 1774–1858).

86 O sacred head, sore wounded

P. Gerhardt, 1607–76
Tr. J. W. Alexander, 1804–59

This famous Passion hymn by the German hymn-writer Paul Gerhardt is based on part of a long medieval poem *Salve mundi Salutare*, commonly attributed to St Bernard of Clairvaux (1091–1153) but probably not earlier than the 14th century. In the work as a whole the unknown author addresses himself in turn to the various parts of the body of Jesus hanging on the cross. The last part is an invocation of the Saviour's head (*Salve caput cruentatum*) and it is this part of the poem that lies behind the hymn.

There are many English translations. Sir Henry Baker made his own version for *A&M*, 1861. The *EH* has a paraphrase by Dr Robert Bridges. The most widely used translation (much edited and revised) is by Dr James Waddell Alexander, an American scholar of Scottish descent, beginning:

> O sacred head, sore wounded,
>   With grief and shame bowed down!
> O kingly head, surrounded
>   With thorns, thine only crown!

The available versions in their different ways reflect the deeply devotional character of this hymn, which perhaps is more suitable for personal meditation than for singing in public worship. It is a hymn, as it has been said, which in passing from the Latin into the German and thence into the English 'proclaims in these tongues with equal effect the dying love of our Saviour, and our boundless indebtedness to him' (Philip Schaff).

TUNE: *Passion Chorale* (melody by H. L. Hassler, 1564–1612, arranged by J. S. Bach, 1685–1750).

87 Glory be to Jesus

Italian, anonymous
Tr. E. Caswall★, 1814–78

The author of this Italian hymn *Viva! Viva! Gesu* is not known. The earliest date to which it can be traced is 1843. The English version by Edward Caswall was first published in 1857. He gave it the title 'Hymn to the Precious Blood' and this is the key to its message:

> Glory be to Jesus,
>   Who, in bitter pains,
> Poured for me the life-blood
> From his sacred veins.

From beginning to end the hymn pursues this theme.

There are some Christians who find the *blood* of Jesus a difficult subject, even a repugnant one. As our hymns have so much to say about it we ought to be clear what it means. In the Bible the 'blood' is the *life* (Gen.9:4; Lev.17:11): not the life existent but the life forfeited, surrendered, laid down. Hence blood is symbolical of death, often violent death. This is the meaning of the NT phrase, 'the blood of Christ'. It signifies the pouring out of his earthly life in death, the total sacrifice he made on the cross for the salvation of mankind.

It is of this we sing in the present hymn, and this is why in the final stanza we lift our voices to God and 'louder still and louder praise the precious blood'.

TUNE: *Caswall* (F. Filitz, 1804–76).

88 In the Cross of Christ I glory

J. Bowring, 1792–1872

Sir John Bowring was an exceptional man in many ways. Among other things he was an outstanding linguist and claimed to know 200 languages and to speak 100. He was much involved in political life and occupied many important government posts, including that of Governor of Hong Kong. He was a Unitarian.

His *Hymns*, 1825, were among his early publications and included this one. It was based on the words of Galatians 6:14:

84 THE CHRISTIAN YEAR

'God forbid that I should glory, save in the cross of our Lord Jesus Christ.' The opening stanza views the cross in the light of history and sees it 'towering o'er the wrecks of time'. The reference is to the past civilisations and empires with which the story of mankind is littered. The cross has outshone and outlived them all.

The remaining stanzas take on a personal character. They speak of the consolation we derive from the cross amid life's trials and disappointments, and of the added lustre it imparts to our days of peace and bliss. The final verse sums up the message by bringing together these two contrasting aspects:

> Bain and blessing, pain and pleasure,
> By the cross are sanctified;
> Peace is there that knows no measure,
> Joys that through all time abide.

TUNE: *All for Jesus* (J. Stainer, 1840–1901), and others.

89 We sing the praise of him who died   T. Kelly*, 1769–1854

This passion hymn by the Irish hymn-writer Thomas Kelly has much in common with 'When I survey the wondrous cross' (84). Published in 1815, it was headed with the same text that inspired Watts's classical hymn (Gal.6:14). Likewise its opening words turn our eyes in the same direction, to 'him who died upon the cross'. It is the sight of the crucified Saviour that calls forth our praise, for:

> Inscribed upon the cross we see
> In shining letters 'God is Love'

– a strikingly imaginative touch. The Gospels tell us that over the cross was written, 'This is Jesus the King of the Jews,' the sentence of condemnation. To the eye of faith the inscription reads quite differently. It is transfigured into letters of gold and reads, 'God is Love' – the message of salvation. For 'God has shown us how much he loves us; it was while we were still sinners that Christ died for us' (Rom. 5:8 *TEV*).

The stanzas that follow relate the cross to our Christian life and experience. It releases us from the burden of guilt, supports us in time of weakness, consoles us in sorrow, nerves us for life's battles, and enables us to face death without fear. The final stanza sums it all up:

> The balm of life, the cure of woe,
>   The measure and the pledge of love,
> The sinner's refuge here below,
>   The angels' theme in heaven above.

Kelly was also the author of 'The head that once was crowned with thorns' (108).

TUNES: *Fulda* (from Gardiner's *Sacred Melodies*, 1812); *Bow Brickhill* (S. H. Nicholson, 1875–1947); *Wareham* (W. Knapp, 1698–1768).

90 My God, I love thee; not because
Anonymous Tr. E. Caswall*, 1814–78

There is no historical foundation for attributing this hymn to St Francis Xavier, the 16th century missionary, as was formerly done – and as some hymn books continue to do. It is a translation by Edward Caswall of a 17th century Latin hymn, based on an earlier Spanish sonnet which was doubtless known to Francis and quoted by him; but its authorship remains unknown.

Why do I love God? Or why should I love him? That is the question posed and answered by the hymn. It is an exploration of motives. I must not love God for selfish reasons: either in order to acquire merit and win heaven, or for fear of losing his favour and perishing eternally. I must love God purely and simply for his own sake and because of what he has done for me:

> Not with the hope of gaining aught,
>   Not seeking a reward,

> But as thyself hast lovèd me,
>   O ever-loving Lord.

'We love him, because he first loved us' sums up the message.
    TUNE: Choices include *Song 67* (O. Gibbons, 1583–1625);
St Francis Xavier (J. Stainer, 1840–1901); *Solomon* (G. F.
Handel, 1685–1759).

91 Nature with open volume stands   *I. Watts*★, 1674–1748

For a hymn dealing with 'The Wonders of the Cross' (its
original title) this has an unusual starting-point. It begins with
the world of nature, which is likened to an 'open volume', a
book in which we can read of God's mighty work in creation.
St Paul says the same in Romans 1:20: 'The invisible things of
him [God] from the creation of the world are clearly seen,
being understood by the things that are made.' The biblical
revelation, however, does not stop there, nor does Isaac Watts:

> But in the grace that rescued man,
>   His brightest form of glory shines;
> Here, on the cross, 'tis fairest drawn
>   In precious blood and crimson lines.

God's work in redeeming man shines more brightly than his
work in creating him. In the cross God's 'whole name appears
complete' – his power, his wisdom and his love.
    The fourth stanza presents a difficulty and is sometimes
omitted:

> Here I behold his inmost heart,
>   Where grace and vengeance strangely join,
> Piercing his Son with sharpest smart,
>   To make the purchased pleasure mine.

The difficulty is the use of the word *vengeance*. It was not a
happy choice on Watts's part. Doubtless he meant by it not
revenge but God's righteous condemnation of sin. The word

'judgment' would better serve the purpose and be more scriptural. We may rightly say, in the words of Dr J. S. Whale, that on the cross 'the sinless Son of God was saying Amen on behalf of humanity to the judgment of God upon sin.'

TUNE: *Eltham* (from *Harmonia Perfecta*, 1730), and others.

92 It is a thing most wonderful   *W. W. How**, 1823–97

Walsham How, as the greatly beloved bishop of what was virtually London's East End, earned for himself various titles such as 'the people's bishop' and 'the poor man's bishop'; but as he confessed later in life, the title he liked best was that of 'the children's bishop'. He had a true love and understanding of children and was always at home in their company – as they were in his. Not surprisingly he published a book of *Children's Hymns*, 1872, and it is from this that the present hymn comes.

The bishop headed it with the text 1 John 4:10: 'Herein is love, not that we loved God but that he loved us, and sent his Son to be the propitiation for our sins.' In the hymn he is endeavouring to look at the cross through the eyes of a child and to see in it a revelation of the love of God. It is a difficult theme to deal with realistically in a children's hymn, but this one succeeds. It has many sensitive and imaginative touches, yet it avoids being over-sentimental. And though it is a children's hymn, it is not childish. Adults can sing it without embarrassment. The death of God's Son on the cross is indeed a thing most wonderful, almost too wonderful to be.

TUNE: *Herongate* (English traditional melody, arranged by W. Vaughan Williams, 1872–1958).

93 See, Christ was wounded for our sake   *B. Foley,*
*b.*1919

> See, Christ was wounded for our sake,
>   And bruised and beaten for our sin,
> So by his suffering we are healed,
>   For God has laid our guilt on him.

The fifty-third chapter of Isaiah – Isaiah's Golden Passional as it has been called – would seem to offer ideal material for a Passiontide hymn. It has been left to a Roman Catholic priest of the 20th century to provide such a hymn. And what a fine hymn it is!

Its author Brian Foley, ordained in 1945, began writing hymns in the 1950s; fourteen of them are included in the *New Catholic Hymnal*, 1971. His Passion hymn is a paraphrase of selected verses from the Isaiah passage, interpreting it with reference to the suffering and sacrifice of Christ. The opening stanza quoted above serves as an illustration. As a further example we may take the second stanza, based on the words, 'Without beauty, without majesty [we saw him], no looks to attract our eyes; a thing despised and rejected by men, a man of sorrows . . .' (vv.2, 3 *JB*):

> Look on his face, come close to him –
>   See, you will find no beauty there;
> Despised, rejected, who can tell
>   The grief and sorrow he must bear?

TUNE: *Felinfoel*, written by Michael Dawney (*b*.1942) for the words, and named after the Welsh village where he composed it in 1969.

94 On a hill far away   *G. Bennard*, 1873–1958

> On a hill far away stood an old rugged cross,
>   The emblem of suffering and shame;
> And I love that old cross where the dearest and best
>   For a world of lost sinners was slain.

'The Old Rugged Cross' is immensely popular in the United States, the land of its birth. In Britain it does not find a place in the standard hymnals; but it is, of course, a gospel song rather than a hymn in the accepted sense.

Both its words and music were written by George Bennard, a Methodist minister. It had its origin in a revival mission he conducted in the town of Albion, Michigan, in 1913. The character of the song is accounted for by the fact that Bennard had been a Salvation Army officer and therefore knew the effectiveness of a good gospel song with a good chorus:

> So I'll cherish the old rugged cross,
>   Till my trophies at last I lay down;
> I will cling to the old rugged cross,
>   And exchange it some day for a crown.

As in the case of many gospel songs, the poetry is elementary and the work as a whole has no claim to literary merit. But without question its simple evangelical theology has a strong emotional appeal, aided by a haunting, memorable tune.

TUNE: See above.

EASTER

95 Jesus Christ is risen today   *Anonymous, 14th century*

It has been pointed out that the most popular of our Easter hymns are translations from other languages – Latin, Greek or German. The present hymn is an example of a Latin translation. It is probably the best known of all Easter hymns, yet its authorship is entirely unknown. Nor do we know who composed the magnificent tune *Easter Hymn* to which it is always sung. All that is certain is that the hymn is based on an Easter carol of the 14th century beginning *Surrexit Christus hodie*.

The English translation and the tune first appeared in *Lyra Davidica*, published in 1708. It was later revised; and in its present form it became widely known through its inclusion in the 1816 *Supplement* to Tate and Brady's *New Version* of the Psalms. No doubt it owes its popularity to its tune as much as to its words. Nevertheless the words, for all their simplicity, are not to be ignored. They unite the two great themes of

Easter, the Cross and the Resurrection, and do so in an interesting way.

Each of the three stanzas consist of two couplets; and in each case one couplet refers directly to the Lord's triumph over death and the other to his passion. In the first and second stanzas the couplets celebrating his triumph come first, followed by those which refer to his suffering. In the third stanza the order is reversed. It is a small point but worth noting; and it means that the hymn has the merit of presenting the whole of the Easter message – Christ crucified *and* risen.

TUNE: *Easter Hymn* (see above).

96 The day of resurrection! St John of Damascus, d.780
Tr. J. M. Neale*, 1818–66

Two points of interest may be noted about this hymn. First, it comes from the Greek or Eastern Church, which has always laid particular stress on the resurrection of Christ; and second, it is written by St John of Damascus who is acknowledged to be the greatest poet of the Greek Church. Little is known of his life, most of which was spent in the monastery of St Sabas, lying ten miles south-east of Jerusalem, not far from the Dead Sea. It is good to know that the joy of Easter invaded that remote and lonely place.

The hymn is the first ode of what is known as the Golden Canon of Easter. It is sung in the Greek churches at midnight before Easter. As the congregation light their candles the darkness gives place to a blaze of light and the silence is shattered by the sound of drums and trumpets. Then everyone joins in the cry, 'Christ is risen! He is risen indeed!'

The first stanza celebrates the Easter victory by employing the OT imagery of the Passover and the Exodus. The crossing of the Red Sea becomes an image of the resurrection and what it has achieved for us:

> From death to life eternal,
>   From earth unto the sky,
> Our God hath brought us over
>   With hymns of victory.

The second stanza moves from the Old Testament into the New. Now it is indeed the day of resurrcction, and like the first disciples we catch a glimpse of Christ in his risen, radiant glory and 'raise the victor strain'. This leads on to the final stanza, which calls on the whole of creation to swell the chorus of praise.

TUNE: *Ellacombe* (melody from *Mainz Gesangbuch*, 1833).

97 Come, ye faithful, raise   *St John of Damascus, d.*780
    the strain   *Tr. J. M. Neale**, 1818–66

Another Easter hymn by St John Damascene (see 96) which like the previous one appeared in Dr Neale's *Hymns of the Eastern Church*, 1862. It consists of the first ode for the canon of St Thomas's Sunday, the name given in the Greek calendar to the Sunday after Easter.

The first stanza is based on the Song of Moses (Exod. 15) and like the other hymn employs the Passover story as an image of the great redemption wrought by Christ's triumph over death. But the most striking feature of the hymn is its use of the Spring – 'the Queen of seasons' – as an allegory of the resurrection. Just as the sun comes back victoriously from its winter retreat and the days grow brighter and warmer, so Christ the Sun of Righteousness has returned from the grave to bring us life and light:

> 'Tis the Spring of souls today;
>   Christ hath burst his prison,
> And from three days' sleep in death
>   As a Sun hath risen;
> All the winter of our sins,
>   Long and dark, is flying
> From his light, to whom we give
>   Laud and praise undying.

This note of praise and joy is developed in the third and fourth stanzas.

TUNES: *Ave Virgo Virginium* (from Leisentritt's *Gesangbuch*, 1584), or *St John Damascene* (A. H. Brown, 1830–1926).

98 Christ the Lord is   M. Weiss, 1480–1534
risen again   Tr. C. Winkworth*, 1829–78

Michael Weiss began life as a Roman Catholic priest and was for many years a monk at Breslau. Influenced, however, by the writings of Martin Luther he left the monastery and became a member of the Bohemian Brethren (later the Moravians) at Landstrewn. Here, in addition to writing hymns and other works, he edited the Brethren's first hymnal. *Julian* remarks: 'Many of his hymns possess considerable merit. His style is flowing and musical, the religious tone is earnest and manly, but yet tender and truly devout.'

His Easter hymn *Christus ist erstanden* is based on an older German hymn dating from the 12th century. English translations appeared as early as 1750, but it was not until Catherine Winkworth included it in her *Lyra Germanica*, 1858, that it became popular, due chiefly to its finding a place in *A&M* 1861. Miss Winkworth entitled it 'The Song of Triumph'. This indicates the keynote of the hymn, which stresses not only the Lord's resurrection but also his exaltation to the throne of heaven as King of kings.

TUNES: *Wurtemberg*, adapted by W. H. Monk from *Hundert Arien* (Dresden, 1694), or *Orientis Partibus*, a medieval French melody harmonised by R. Vaughan Williams.

99 Jesus lives! thy   C. Gellert, 1715–69
terrors now   Tr. Frances E. Cox, 1812–97

Christian Gellert was a lecturer in poetry, and later Professor of Philosophy, at the University of Leipzig. A man of deep piety, he exercised an enormous influence over his students on account of the unselfish and saintly quality of his life.

His Easter hymn, *Jesus lebt, mit ihm auch ich*, reflects his strong and vigorous faith. In the form in which he wrote it each verse ended with the triumphant cry, 'This shall be my confidence!' In Miss Cox's translation, published in 1841, 'Alleluia!' becomes the equivalent of this.

Gellert based the hymn on the words of Jesus, 'Because I live, you shall live also' (John 14:19). Hence the ringing affirmation with which each stanza begins – *Jesus lives!* This is the heart of the Easter faith, and the five stanzas show how this faith affects our Christian lives. The living Lord robs death of its power, opens to us the gate of life, claims the love and service of our lives, and guarantees our eternal security.

This faith was Gellert's own assurance as he lay dying at the age of forty-four. When told that he had only about an hour to live, he lifted his hands and cried, 'Now God be praised, only an hour!'

TUNE: *St Albinus* (H. J. Gauntlett, 1805–76).

100 The strife is o'er, the   *Latin, 17th century*
battle done   *Tr. F. Pott*, 1832–1909*

When sung to the tune *Victory* this hymn begins with a trio of Alleluias. If the alternative tune *Vulpius* is used three Alleluias are sung at the end of each stanza. The Easter hymns abound in Alleluias – and there is a reason for this. The medieval Church ordained that Alleluia should be banished from worship during Lent in order to mark the penitential character of the season. But come Easter Day and Alleluias rang out again in the Church's praise and have become the dominant and characteristic note in the Easter hymns.

The present hymn serves as a good illustration. The Latin original, *Finita jam sunt praelia*, was thought by Dr Neale to have been of 12th century date, but in fact it cannot be traced back earlier than the year 1695. Its authorship is unknown.

The hymn views the death of Christ as a conflict between Christ and the powers of death and evil (*cf.* Col.2:15). The resurrection marks the end of the fight and demonstrates its decisive outcome: 'Now is the Victor's triumph won.' For:

> On the third morn he rose again
> Glorious in majesty to reign;
> O let us swell the joyful strain:
>   Alleluia!

The translation by Francis Pott was published in his collected *Hymns*, 1861, in five stanzas. The fourth is omitted from most hymnals.

TUNES: *Victory*, an adaptation by W. H. Monk of a tune by Palestrina; or *Vulpius*, a melody by Melchior Vulpius (*c.*1560–1616), harmonised by Henry G. Ley.

101 Christ the Lord is risen today   *C. Wesley**, 1707–88

Charles Wesley's 'Hymn for Easter Day' was published in his *Hymns and Sacred Poems*, 1739. It is thus one of his early hymns, written soon after his conversion. It consisted of eleven stanzas, without the Alleluias which some editors added later. Somewhat strangely, John Wesley omitted it from his famous *Collection*, 1780, and as a result it did not gain currency in Methodist circles till fifty years later.

As Wesley wrote it the hymn began:

> Christ the Lord is risen today,
> Sons of men and angels say;
> Raise your joys and triumphs high:
> Sing, ye heavens; thou earth reply.

When the hymn was included in the *English Hymnal*, 1906, this verse was omitted, because the editors thought its opening line caused it to be confused with other Easter hymns. It therefore began with the second stanza, 'Love's redeeming work is done.' Other hymnals later adopted this pattern, including *A&M*. The five verses usually printed are from the first part of the entire hymn.

Wesley incorporates into the hymn a number of the familiar Easter themes: the completed work of redemption, the empty tomb, the battle with evil fought and won, death vanquished, Paradise regained, the new risen life in Christ a glorious possibility *now*. So Wesley rounds it off with the words:

> King of glory! Soul of bliss!
> Everlasting life is this,
> Thee to know, thy power to prove,
> Thus to sing, and thus to love.

TUNES: *Savannah* (from J. Wesley's *Foundery Collection*, 1742); or in eight-line form, *St George's, Windsor* (G. J. Elvey,

1816–98); or with Alleluias, *Easter Hymn* (from *Lyra Davidica*, 1708).

102 Christ Jesus lay in death's strong bands
M. Luther*, 1483–1546
Tr. R. Massie, 1800–87

Coleridge declared that Luther did as much for the Reformation by his hymns as by his translation of the Bible. His fine Easter hymn *Christ tag in Todesbanden* is unfortunately little known in Britain outside Free Church circles. Anglican hymnals find no place for it. Luther published it in 1524 as an improved version of a medieval German hymn; but *Julian* states that only slight traces of the latter are retained by Luther and that his working out of the material is entirely original. Richard Massie's translation appeared in his *Martin Luther's Spiritual Songs*, 1854.

The hymn has as its theme the risen Christ's conquest of death, the breaking of its power, the ending of its reign. Now, exalted at God's right hand, he brings us life from heaven:

> So let us keep the festival
>   Whereto the Lord invites us;
> Christ is himself the joy of all,
>   The sun that warms and lights us;
>   By his grace he doth impart
> Eternal sunshine to the heart;
>   The night of sin is ended.
>   Alleluia!

Such is the third stanza. The fourth and final one has a sacramental reference and bids us on this high festival to feed on Christ, 'the true Bread of heaven'.

TUNE: *Christ tag in Todesbanden*, a German melody adapted by Luther for this hymn.

103 Ye choirs of new Jerusalem
St Fulbert of Chartres, d.1028
Tr. R. Campbell, 1814–68

As St Fulbert died in 1028, his Easter hymn *Chorus novae Jerusalem* must date from the beginning of the 11th century. A

man renowned for his wisdom, he was consecrated Bishop of
Chartres in 1007. The hymn circulated chiefly in Britain and
soon became one of the office hymns in the Sarum, York and
Hereford breviaries for the Sundays after Easter. The Latin
text was translated by Robert Campbell and published in
1850. As his name indicates, he was a Scotsman, a lawyer
by profession. He found relaxation from his professional
duties by making translations of Latin hymns. Another
Easter hymn, 'At the Lamb's high feast we sing', is also his
work.

This hymn stresses the triumphal character of Christ's
resurrection – 'his pascal victory' (v.1) – and his kingly rule.
The opening words of the second stanza must puzzle a good
many churchgoers:

> For Judah's Lion burst his chains,
> And crushed the serpent's head.

'The lion of the tribe of Judah' is a title given to Christ in
Revelation 5:5. His crushing of the serpent's head refers to
God's promise of redemption in Genesis 3:15, to the effect that
the seed of the woman (Christ) would win the final victory
over the serpent (Satan).

TUNE: *St Fulbert* (H. J. Gauntlett, 1805–76).

104 Alleluia! Alleluia! hearts   *C. Wordsworth**, 1807–85
to heaven

It is unlikely that Bishop Wordsworth's Easter hymn would
have retained its place in our hymnals for over a century (it was
published in 1862) had it not been associated with the fine tune
Lux Eoi by Sir Arthur Sullivan (1842–1900). The words are
not particularly distinguished. Like so many of the bishop's
hymns, it takes the form of a sermon in verse.

The second stanza views the resurrection in the light of the
life to come and is based on the words, 'Now is Christ risen
from the dead, and become the first-fruits of them that slept'
(1 Cor.15:20 *AV*). The third relates the resurrection to our
present life:

> Christ is risen, we are risen;
> Shed upon us heavenly grace . . .

And this develops into a prayer that we who have died and
risen with Christ may be nurtured by his grace, so that we may
bear much fruit (*cf.* John 12:24). The final stanza with its
sixfold Alleluia lifts the hymn to a high level of praise.

TUNE: *Lux Eoi* (see above).

105 O sons and daughters,　　　*J. Tisserand, d.*1494
　　　let us sing　　　　　　*Tr. J. M. Neale*★, 1818–66

Nothing is known of Jean Tisserand except that he was a
Franciscan friar who died in Paris in 1494. His poem *O filii et
filiae* was found in an untitled booklet printed in Paris in the
early part of the 16th century. Consisting of nine stanzas, it
began with a threefold Alleluia and had a single Alleluia as a
refrain.

After the opening stanza, with its call to praise, the poem
follows a narrative form, like certain Christmas carols. In fact
it might better be called an Easter carol. It puts into triple
rhyme several incidents from the resurrection narratives in the
Gospels: the visit of the faithful women to the tomb and
the angels' message to them, the Lord's appearance to the
disciples at the evening hour, and the story of doubting
Thomas.

Dr Neale's translation, as amended by the editors of *A&M*
1861, reproduces six of Tisserand's original verses and three
others which were incorporated later. Among these latter
is:

> How blest are they who have not seen,
> And yet whose faith hath constant been,
> For they eternal life shall win.
> 　　　　　Alleluia.

TUNE: *O filii et filiae*, a French melody of the 17th century.

106 Thine be the glory,   *Edmund L. Bundry, 1854–1932*
risen conquering Son   *Tr. R. B. Hoyle,* 1875–1937

The popularity of this hymn doubtless owes a good deal to its
splendid tune, an arrangement of the celebrated chorus from
Handel's *Judas Maccabaeus*, 1746. The original words were
written by Edmund Bundry, who for thirty-five years was
pastor at Verney, Switzerland. He composed the hymn in
1896, following the death of his first wife. It was published
in the YMCA *Hymn Book*, Lausanne, 1904, in its French
form:

> A toi la gloire, O Ressuscite,
> A toi la victoire pour l'éternité.
> Brillant de lumiêre, l'ange est descendu,
> Il roule la pierre du tombeau vaincu.

The English translation was made by Richard Hoyle, a Baptist
minister whose last pastorate was at Kingston-upon-Thames.
A man of considerable scholarship, he translated hymns from
various sources, being conversant with twelve languages.

The hymn has close links with the resurrection narratives in
the Gospels: v.1 with the angels and the rolling away of the
stone (Matt.28:2); v.2 with the Lord's greeting to the women
he met as they hurried from the tomb (Matt.28:8,9); v.3 with
the dispelling of Thomas's doubts (John 20:24*f.*).

TUNE: *Maccabaeus* (see above).

ASCENSIONTIDE

107 Hail the day that sees him rise   *C. Wesley★*, 1707–88

This, the most popular of Ascensiontide hymns, is not pure
Wesley. Since it appeared in his *Hymns and Sacred Poems*, 1739,
in ten verses, it has been considerably revised by different
editors. For example, the original opening stanza was:

> Hail the day that sees him rise,
> Ravished from our wistful eyes!
> Christ awhile to mortals given,
> Re-ascends his native heaven.

The *Methodist Hymn Book* retains this and loyally adheres to
Wesley throughout; but most hymnals adopt an altered version of the hymn by Thomas Cotterill, published in 1820. The
Alleluias were not added until 1852 in White's *Introits and
Hymns*. They give the hymn a festive touch but also considerably lengthen it. Consequently few hymnals include more
than five or six stanzas.

The hymn is full of biblical teaching on the significance of
the ascension. It celebrates the accomplishment of Christ's
work on earth, his triumphal entry into glory, his heavenly
reign and his priestly intercession. It also reminds us of his
continuing kinship with his people on earth:

> See! the heaven its Lord receives,
> Yet he loves the earth he leaves;
> Though returning to his throne,
> Still he calls mankind his own.

TUNES: *Ascension*, composed by W. H. Monk (1823–89)
for *A&M* 1861; or the Welsh melody *Llanfair* by Robert
Williams (1781–1821).

108 The head that once was crowned with thorns   *T. Kelly**, 1769–1855

This might be called the hymn of Christ's two coronations,
the one on earth, the other in heaven. When the Roman
soldiers led him away to be crucified they placed a crown of
thorns on his head and offered him mock homage as a king
(Mark 15:17–19). Years later the apostle John was given a
vision of him in his celestial glory and saw that on his head
were many crowns (Rev. 19:12). So:

> The head that once was crowned with thorns
>   Is crowned with glory now.

Thomas Kelly has given us an excellent hymn on this theme, particularly suited for Ascensiontide. Dr Erik Routley had a special affection for it and described it as all that a hymn should be: 'Not the greatest author could have written better, and not the most skilful could have expounded so much scripture with so little ostentation.'

A feature of the hymn is the way in which Kelly links Jesus' crucifixion, 'with all its shame', with his exaltation to 'the highest place that heaven affords', and sees in this the pattern of Christian discipleship. Those who bear the cross will also wear the crown:

> They suffer with their Lord below,
>   They reign with him above;
> Their profit and their joy to know
>   The mystery of his love.

TUNE: *St Magnus* (J. Clarke, *c.*1659–1707).

109 Where high the heavenly   M. Bruce, 1746–67
       temple stands

There has been a good deal of controversy about the authorship of this hymn. It is a rather curious and unhappy story. On the evidence provided by *Julian*, scholars now generally recognise the hymn as being originally the work of Michael Bruce, the son of a Scottish weaver, who died while a student for the ministry at the age of twenty-one. After his death the notebook containing the hymns he had written was entrusted to his friend John Logan (1748–88), who fourteen years later published the hymn in his book of *Poems* and claimed it – wrongly, it seems – as his own. In the same year it was included in the Scottish *Paraphrases*, 1781, and from that source it soon found its way into many hymnals.

The hymn is a paraphrase of Hebrews 4:14–16(*RSV*):

Since we have a great high priest who has passed through the heavens, Jesus, the Son of God, let us hold fast our confession. For we have not a high priest who is unable to sympathise with our weaknesses, but one who in every respect has been tempted as we are, yet without sin. Let us then with confidence draw near to the throne of grace, that we may receive mercy and find grace to help in time of need.

On the basis of this passage the hymn dwells in particular on the sympathetic character of Christ's heavenly priesthood as one who is 'partaker of the human frame' and who 'yet retains a fellow-feeling of our pains':

> In every pang that rends the heart
> The Man of Sorrows had a part;
> He sympathises with our grief,
> And to the sufferer sends relief.

TUNES: *Soldau* (adapted from J. Walther's *Gesangbuch*, Wittenberg, 1524); *Warrington* (R. Harrison, 1748–1810); and others.

110 At the name of Jesus   C. M. Noel, 1817–77

It comes as something of a surprise to learn that this strong, vigorous, extrovert hymn was written by a frail Victorian lady, Caroline Maria Noel, who was very much an invalid for a large part of her life. She was a niece of the Honourable Baptist Noel, a well known evangelist who wrote hymns and edited hymn books.

Intended for use as a processional hymn for Ascension Day it was published in the author's *The Name of Jesus and Other Poems*, 1870. It is based on the famous passage in Philippians 2:5–11, which was probably an early Christian hymn or poem in celebration of Christ's incarnation, passion and exaltation. The passage reaches its climax in the words, 'God gave him the name which is above every name, that at the name of Jesus every knee should bow.'

Miss Noel's hymn begins with these words, that is with the Lord's triumph and enthronement; but subsequent verses look back to his humiliation and suffering, while the final verse points forward to his coming again 'with his Father's glory'.

TUNES: *Evelyns* (W. H. Monk, 1823–89); *Cuddesdon* (W. H. Ferguson, 1874–1950); *Camberwell* (J. M. Brierley, b.1932). In USA *Kings Weston* (R. Vaughan Williams, 1872–1958) is popular.

111 Rejoice! the Lord is King   C. Wesley*, 1707–88

Wesley's hymn is usually associated with the ascension, but it appeared in his *Hymns for our Lord's Resurrection*, 1746. The resurrection and ascension are closely linked in the New Testament, especially in the fourth Gospel, and both bear witness to Christ's sovereignty. He who was raised from the dead as the Prince of Life was also raised to the throne of heaven as the King of Glory. As the hymn states, 'Jesus the Saviour *reigns*' – victorious over sin and death and all his foes. That is why we *Rejoice* – the opening word and the keynote of the hymn. It rings out in the refrain, which is based on Philippians 4:4 *AV*: 'Rejoice in the Lord always; again I say, rejoice.'

The original hymn consisted of six verses. Some hymnals print only the first four. Many include the fifth, beginning, 'Rejoice in glorious hope.' The final stanza has now dropped out of use.

The hymn has the distinction of being one of three of Wesley's hymns for which Handel composed tunes. His tune for this one is *Gopsal*, the name of the house near Ashby-de-la-Zouche where his friend Charles Jenner resided. It was Jenner who compiled the words for *Messiah*.

TUNES: *Gopsal* (see above). An alternative is *Darwall*, composed by J. Darwall for the *New Version* of Psalm 148.

112 Hail, thou once despisèd Jesus   J. Bakewell, 1721–1819

Here is an example of a hymn which is far more widely known in the Free Churches than in the Church of England. Its authorship is in some dispute. Though ascribed to John Bakewell, it is considered unlikely that he wrote the whole of it. Others, including Augustus Toplady of 'Rock of ages' fame, seem to have had a share in shaping its final form, comprising five stanzas in all. Most hymnals include no more than four of these, some only three.

Bakewell was a Derbyshire man who in his late twenties came to London, where he fell under the spell of the Wesleys and in due course became a Methodist preacher. It was in his house that Thomas Olivers wrote 'The God of Abraham praise' (7). He lived to the great age of ninety-eight.

The hymn begins by concentrating attention on the suffering Christ, the 'bearer of our sin and shame', whose death 'full atonement made' and thus opened the gate of heaven. Then in complete contrast the picture changes:

> Jesus, hail! enthroned in glory,
>   There for ever to abide;
> All the heavenly host adore thee,
>   Seated at thy Father's side:
> There for sinners thou art pleading,
>   There thou dost our place prepare;
> Ever for us interceding,
>   Till in glory we appear.

The hymn is thus specially suitable for Ascensiontide.

TUNES: *Bethany* (H. Smart, 1813–79); *Ebenezer* (T. J. Williams, 1869–1944); and others.

PENTECOST

113 Come, Holy Ghost, our souls inspire *Latin, 9th century*
Tr. J. Cosin, 1594–1672

The ancient Latin hymn *Veni Creator Spiritus* is best known to most of us by the translation of John Cosin, Bishop of Durham. Other English versions are available, notably those by the 17th century poet John Dryden, 'Creator Spirit, by whose aid', and Robert Bridges, 'Come, O Creator Spirit, come'.

The merit of Cosin's translation is its conciseness; its weakness is that it is not a complete rendering of the Latin text. He wrote it quite early in his ministry and published it in his *Private Devotions*, 1627, for personal use each day at 9 a.m. in commemoration of Pentecost (Acts 2:15). Much later it was included in the Ordinal of the *BCP*, 1662.

The original hymn dates back to at least the 9th century. There is no clear evidence as to its authorship and it must be regarded as anonymous. From the 11th century onwards it has been sung, in one version or another, at ordinations, coronations, church synods and confirmation services.

The key to the hymn lies in the title *Creator Spirit* in its opening line. Cosin does not actually use the title, as do Dryden and Bridges; but his version faithfully reflects the creative and energetic activity of the Holy Spirit in the life of God's people. It is he who inspires the soul, lightening it with 'celestial fire' and imparting his 'sevenfold gifts' (see Isa. 11:2; Rev. 1:4). He is the anointing Spirit whose unction is 'comfort, life, and fire of love'. He illuminates 'our blinded sight', cheers 'our soilèd face', guards us from our spiritual foes, guides our future way. This sums up the first three stanzas. The final one is a prayer to the Spirit to impart to us the knowledge of God in the mystery of his Being, followed by an ascription of praise to the Holy Trinity.

TUNE: *Veni, creator Spiritus* (medieval melody from *Vesperale Romanum*, Mechlin, 1848).

114 Come, thou holy   *Latin, 13th century*
Paraclete   *Tr. J. M. Neale*, 1818–66,*
                          and E. Caswall*, 1814–78

This Latin hymn *Veni, sancte Spiritus* is sometimes confused with the *Veni, Creator Spiritus* (113); yet not only is it quite distinct: it also belongs to a later period, not earlier than the 13th century. Its authorship is uncertain, but the available evidence supports the claims of Stephen Langton, Archbishop of Canterbury, 1217–28. In medieval times its fine qualities earned it the title of the 'Golden Sequence'. Archbishop Trench regarded it as 'the loveliest of all the hymns in the whole circle of Latin sacred poetry'.

The hymn is best known to us in two English translations, the one by Neale beginning 'Come, thou holy Paraclete' and Caswall's much altered version in *A&M*, 'Come, thou Holy Spirit, come'. Compare this with Caswall's original first verse:

> Holy Spirit, Lord of Light,
> From thy clear celestial height
>   Thy pure beaming radiance give;
> Come, thou Father of the poor,
> Come, with treasures that endure,
>   Come, thou Light of all that live.

Other translations are in use, including one by the American Dr Ray Palmer, 'Come, Holy Ghost, in love' (*CP* 202), and a modern one by the Jesuit hymn-writer James Quinn, 'Come, O Spirit, from on high' (*WOV* 326). The respective merits of the different versions can best be judged by examining and comparing them. But a purely critical approach to a glorious hymn like this is not likely to yield the most profit. It is one of the Church's great devotional treasures and provides rich and rewarding material for personal meditation and prayer.

TUNE: *Veni sancte Spiritus* (S. Webbe the elder, 1740–1816).

115 Come down, O Love divine
Bianco da Siena, d. 1434
Tr. R. F. Littledale, 1833–90

The popularity of this hymn probably owes as much to the tune as to the words. Dr R. Vaughan Williams composed *Down Ampney* – named after his birthplace – for the hymn when it appeared in the *English Hymnal*, 1906. It makes an immediate appeal and perfectly matches the words.

Little is known of Bianco, the author of the Italian *Discendi, Amor santo*. He joined a religious order in 1367, wrote a number of hymns, and spent the latter part of his life in Venice.

Dr Richard Littledale, a distinguished liturgical scholar, translated four of Bianco's original eight stanzas and included the work in his *People's Hymnal*, 1867.

The Holy Spirit is addressed as 'Love divine' – an unusual designation but not inappropriate; for at Pentecost the Spirit came in semblance of *fire*, and in the first two stanzas the love of the Spirit is represented as love aglow: warm, ardent, burning, a 'holy flame' consuming our earth-bound passions and illuminating our path. And since the Spirit is holy Love, we pray in the third stanza that he will clothe us with the same character, along with 'true lowliness of heart' (cf. Col. 3:12–14).

TUNE: *Down Ampney* (see above).

116 Our blest Redeemer, ere he breathed   *H. Auber,*
1773–1862

There has long been a story, which still persists in some quarters, that Miss Harriet Auber wrote this hymn with a diamond ring on a window pane of her house at Hoddesdon, Herts – the reason given being that the words came to her in a sudden inspiration when she had no writing materials ready to hand. That such a pane existed at one time – probably with no more than the first line of the hymn scratched on it – seems reasonably likely to be true, but there is no evidence that it was her work. The story must be dismissed as pure legend.

First published in her book *The Spirit of the Psalms*, 1829, the hymn begins on the theme of the Spirit as Christ's promised gift to his Church, a promise fulfilled in dramatic fashion on the Day of Pentecost:

> He came in tongues of living flame,
>   To teach, convince, subdue;
> All-powerful as the wind he came,
>   As viewless too.

The remaining stanzas speak of the Spirit in gentler, quieter ways and focus on his indwelling presence. He is the soul's 'gracious, willing guest' – again in accordance with our

Lord's promise (John 14:17) – who speaks peace to the heart and is the source of 'every virtue we possess'. In keeping with this is the hymn's closing prayer:

> O make our hearts thy dwelling-place,
> And worthier thee.

TUNE: *St Cuthbert* (J. B. Dykes, 1823–76).

117 Away with our fears   *C. Wesley**, 1707–88

> Away with our fears,
> Our troubles and tears,
> The Spirit is come,
> The witness of Jesus returned to his home.

A hymn in the unusual metre of 5.5.5.11 – which to the initiated at once identifies its authorship. The metre was used only by Charles Wesley, who seemingly invented it. Another example is to be found in his hymn for the New Year, very dear to Methodist people, 'Come, let us renew'.

The present hymn is the last of Wesley's thirty-two hymns for Whit-Sunday, published in Bristol in 1746. It consisted of five (double) verses of eight lines. In its entirety, and even in its usual shortened form, it is rich in biblical teaching about the gift of the Spirit as a witness to the Lord's ascension, the pledge of his accomplished work on earth, and the earnest of our eternal inheritance above. The hymn, as it has been said, 'spans the whole history of Christ's Church from the day of Pentecost to the end of the world – from the hour of conversion to that victory by which the last enemy shall be destroyed. And it is a statement at once of divine fact and of the believer's experience' (A. S. Gregory).

TUNE: *Ardwick* (H. J. Gauntlett, 1805–76).

118 Come, gracious Spirit,   *S. Browne*, 1680–1732,
heavenly dove   *and others*

Come, gracious Spirit! It is noteworthy how many of the familiar hymns of Whitsun or Pentecost begin with that word of invocation. To use it in this connection is not to deny that the Holy Spirit has already come as the abiding gift of the glorified Christ to his Church. It is rather to avail ourselves of that fact and to open our lives afresh to his comfort and strength.

In its original form this hymn was written by Simon Browne, an Independent (Congregational) minister and a contemporary of Isaac Watts. He published it with a great many other hymns, now all forgotten, in his *Hymns and Songs*, 1720. In its present form the hymn has been greatly altered. Not only have its seven stanzas been reduced to four; its language has also been considerably improved. But Browne's main idea remains. He laid particular stress on the *leading* of the Spirit (cf. Rom.8:14; Gal.5:18), and this note is still prominent, as in the third stanza:

> Lead us to Christ, the living Way,
> Nor let us from his pastures stray;
> Lead us to holiness, the road
> That we must take to dwell with God.

TUNE: *Hawkhurst* (H. J. Gauntlett, 1805–76), or *Galilee* (P. Armes, 1836–1908).

119 Spirit divine, attend our prayers   A. Reed, 1787–1862

This hymn is usually, and rightly, associated with the season of Pentecost; yet strangely enough it was actually sung for the first time on a Good Friday. Its author, Dr Andrew Reed, a prominent Congregational minister and philanthropist in London's East End, wrote it in 1829 for a 'Day of Solemn Prayer and Humiliation' organised by the London Board of Congregational Ministers. This was arranged to take place on the Good Friday of that year, its purpose being 'to promote, by the divine blessing, a revival of religion in the British Churches'. Hence the particular character of the hymn. It takes up various symbols of the Spirit and makes them the basis of urgent prayer, as follows:

'Come as the light' – a prayer for illumination.
'Come as the fire' – a prayer for cleansing.
'Come as the dew' – a prayer for refreshment.
'Come as the dove' – a prayer for peace.
'Come as the wind' – a prayer for renewal.

The final stanza sums up these fervent longings for wide-spread spiritual awakening:

> Spirit divine, attend our prayers,
> And make this world thy home;
> Descend with all thy gracious powers,
> O come, great Spirit, come!

TUNES: Various, including *Emmaus* (anonymous); *Grafenberg* (melody by J. Crüger, 1598–1662); and *Störl* (J. G. Störl, 1675–1719).

120 Filled with the Spirit's power

J. R. Peacy,
1896–1971

Hymns about the Holy Spirit tend to be of a personal and subjective character, concerned primarily with his work in the life of the individual believer. John Raphael Peacy, who after long service in India became a canon residentiary of Bristol Cathedral (1954–66), felt the need for a contemporary hymn touching on the wider aspect of the Spirit's ministry in the life of the Church. After his retirement he found the opportunity to write it, in 1967, and it first appeared in the *A&M* supplement *100 Hymns for Today*, 1969.

It begins by pointing to the pattern of the Church in apostolic days, the Spirit-filled community of Christ's people who 'with one accord' confessed him before the world. Then follows the petition:

> O Holy Spirit, in the Church today
> No less your power of fellowship display.

Here is the key to the hymn's message. Reference is to the

Church rather than to the individual, and stress is laid on the 'power of fellowship' – i.e. the fellowship of the Holy Spirit (2 Cor. 13:14). This is something more than comradeship, 'chumminess', 'all good pals together'. It goes far deeper, for it is God's creation; and the burden of the prayer that follows in the last two stanzas is that we, as Christ's people, may experience and demonstrate it in genuine unity, corporate service and all-embracing love.

TUNE: *Farley Castle* (H. Lawes, 1596–1662), and others.

SECTION THREE
THE CHURCH OF GOD

THE CHURCH'S FELLOWSHIP

121 The Church's one foundation   *S. J. Stone*, 1839–1900

This famous hymn arose out of a theological controversy in the mid-19th century known as the Colenso affair. John Colenso, Bishop of Natal, published some works which adopted a 'critical' view of the Bible and questioned certain articles of the Christian faith. The result was a storm of protest, in Britain as well as in South Africa; and it was in the role of defender of the faith that a zealous young clergyman, Samuel John Stone, then curate of Windsor, wrote this hymn in the year 1866.

Whatever may be said of the circumstances that called it forth, this is a fine hymn. Its portrayal of the Church of God is clear, positive, biblical. Christ himself is its one foundation (1 Cor. 3:11). Its members are his 'new creation' (2 Cor. 5:17) through the water of baptism and the word of the gospel. They are also his 'holy bride' for whom he gave his life (Eph. 5:25). All this teaching is packed into the opening stanza. The second asserts further truths: the Church's catholicity ('elect from every nation') and its unity ('yet one o'er all the earth').

The third stanza recognises the presence of the Church's enemies and the perils that beset it. This is the only direct reference to the Colenso dispute:

> Though with a scornful wonder
> Men see her sore oppressed,

By schisms rent asunder,
By heresies distressed.

But the stanza ends on the note of hope, and this is taken up
and developed in the final verses. Here we see the Church as at
last it will be, triumphant, glorified and at rest.

TUNE: *Aurelia* (S. S. Wesley, 1810–76).

122 Glorious things of thee are spoken   J. Newton*,
1725–1807

As *Julian* remarks, this ranks with the finest hymns in the
English language. It is certainly one of the great hymns about
the Church, the Evangelical equivalent of the more Catholic-
orientated 'The Church's one foundation' (121). It comes from
the *Olney Hymns*, 1779, entitled 'Zion; or the City of God'.
The text attached to it is Isaiah 33:20,21, but clearly the
opening line echoes Psalm 87:3. Zion is the poetic name for
Jerusalem, which is regarded here as symbolic of the Church
of Christ, the heavenly Jerusalem (Gal.4:26).

As Newton wrote it the hymn consists of five stanzas.
Editors of hymnals vary in the selection they make. All
include, in addition to the first stanza, the second ('See the
streams of living water' – a reference to Psalm 46:4 and the
story of the smitten rock in Exodus 17) and the final one
('Saviour, if of Zion's city'). Others add the third stanza
beginning 'Round each habitation hovering' – another OT
allusion, this time to the pillar of cloud and fire which guided
the Israelites in their wilderness journey (Num.9:15). Most
hymnals omit Newton's fourth:

Blest inhabitants of Zion,
   Washed in the Redeemer's blood;
Jesus, whom their souls rely on,
   Makes them kings and priests to God.
'Tis his love his people raises,
   Over self to reign as kings;
And as priests, his solemn praises
   Each for a thankoffering brings.

The final stanza makes a splendid finish to the hymn. Newton wrote, as quoted above, 'Saviour, *if* of Zion's city', the 'if' reflecting his Calvinistic creed. Surely it is not presumptuous to change this to *since*, as most books do, for we acknowledge that it is 'through grace' that we belong to the City of God and accordingly give glory to him.

TUNES: *Abbot's Leigh* (C. V. Taylor, *b*.1907), or *Austria* (F. J. Haydn, 1732–1809).

123 Thy hand, O God, has guided   *E. H. Plumptre,*
                                                        1821–91

It has been suggested that when Dr Edward Plumptre, Dean of Wells, wrote this hymn he had the Church of England in mind. That may be so; but surely the learned dean – one of the foremost biblical scholars of his day – had a bigger view of God's Church than that. He entitled the hymn 'Church Defence' and it was published in the 1889 Supplement to *A&M*.

The hymn is something in the nature of an historical survey. It acknowledges God's guiding hand in the story of the Church's life and witness 'from age to age', but at the same time makes clear that the story has not been altogether a rosy one. There have been dark days 'when shadows thick were falling'; there have been troubled times and 'many a scene of strife'. But God has never failed his Church or left himself without witness. He has always had his good and faithful servants, and these throughout the centuries have proclaimed the same unchanging truth – *One Church, one Faith, one Lord*. This refrain, which comes with fine effect at the end of each stanza, is derived from Ephesians 4:4,5: 'There is one body (viz. the body of Christ) . . . one Lord, one faith.'

The story of the Church's past is a challenge to us who are the Church of today and encourages us to believe that God's mercy will not fail us or leave his work undone – the cheerful and optimistic note on which the hymn ends.

TUNE: *Thornbury* (Basil Harwood, 1859–1949).

124 City of God, how broad and far   *S. Johnson*, 1822–82

It has often been pointed out, and readily acknowledged, that
'City of God' is not a distinctively Christian hymn. This
is understandable since its author, the American Samuel
Johnson, was not attached to any of the recognised religious
denominations but was if anything a Unitarian. He established
his own Free Church at Lynn, Massachusetts, and it was while
he ministered there that he published this hymn in 1864.

From a literary point of view it is an admirable piece of
writing and makes a fine, inspiring song. From the Christian
viewpoint it is far from being an adequate description of the
Church. By an odd coincidence it was written in the same year
as 'The Church's one foundation' (see 121), but the contrast
between the two works could scarcely be more marked. The
latter is strongly doctrinal and represents the biblical Catholic
Faith. Johnson's hymn expresses the humanistic outlook of
19th century liberalism.

Nevertheless the hymn is not to be written off because of its
lack of dogma. Erik Routley defended it not only for its
masterly craftsmanship and generous breadth of thought but
as providing 'a unique point of sympathy' between traditional
Christian worship and the intelligent seeker after truth. And
whatever may be said, it is certainly open to a fully Christian
interpretation.

TUNE: *Richmond* (T. Haweis, 1734–1820).

125 Lord of our life, and God   *Based on M. von Löwenstern*,
of our salvation   1594–1648
Tr. P. Pusey, 1799–1855

Philip Pusey's hymn is a paraphrase rather than a translation
of the German *Christe, du Beistand deiner Kreuzgemeine* by
Matthäus von Löwenstern, written in 1644 during the last part
of the Thirty Years War. The hymn bears the marks of those
disturbed and distressing times. The author, writing of it to his
famous brother, Dr E. B. Pusey, said: 'It refers to the state of
the Church – that is to say, the Church of England in 1834 –
assailed from without, enfeebled and distracted within, but on

the eve of a great awakening.' The description of the Church then as being enfeebled and distracted was something of an exaggeration. The 'great awakening' was of course the Oxford Movement.

Be all that as it may, this is admittedly a hymn for troubled times. And throughout its long history the Church of Christ has had to face such times. In various parts of the world it is facing them today. So this is not a hymn to be dismissed as irrelevant or out of date; and its prayer for peace is particularly meaningful:

> Peace in our hearts, our evil thoughts assuaging;
> Peace in thy Church, where brothers are engaging;
> Peace, when the world its busy war is waging:
>> Calm thy foes' raging.

TUNES: *Iste Confessor* (Rouen Church melody), or *Cloisters* (J. Barnby, 1838–96).

126 We come unto our fathers' God
T. H. Gill,
1817–1906

Thomas Hornblower Gill was regarded as one of the leading hymn-writers of his day. Early in life he abandoned the Unitarian faith in which he had been brought up and became an ardent Evangelical in the Puritan tradition. This hymn, published in his *Golden Chain of Praise*, 1869, and entitled 'The People of God', was inspired by what he called 'my lively delight in my Protestant forefathers'. Hence the reference to 'our fathers' God' in the first line.

Whatever our church allegiance we can all readily enter into the spirit of this hymn and rejoice in the rich legacy bequeathed to us by our Christian forebears. Their God is still *our* God: our rock, our salvation, our dwelling-place, our guide, our strength. And their joy is ours too:

> Their joy unto their Lord we bring,
>> Their song to us descendeth;
> The Spirit who in them did sing

To us his music lendeth;
His song in them, in us, is one;
We raise it high, we send it on,
The song that never endeth.

TUNES: *Luther's Hymn* (from *Geistliche Lieder*, Wittenberg, 1535); *Irvine Waterside* (K. G. Finlay, 1882–1974); and others.

127 Blest be the tie that binds   *J. Fawcett*, 1740–1817

Round this hymn lies the story of John Fawcett and the devoted members of his flock when at the age of thirty-two he was minister of a small Baptist chapel near Hebden Bridge in Yorkshire. He found it almost impossible to support his wife and growing family on his tiny stipend; so when invited to become minister of an important London chapel he felt it right to accept. He had preached his farewell sermons and the day of departure had come. But while the wagons were being loaded with his furniture many of his congregation stood around in tears and implored him not to leave them. So overcome was the young minister by the scene that he decided he must remain with them and sacrifice the London pulpit. This he did, and stayed with his loving Yorkshire people for the rest of his life. Well might he have written then, as his biographer states:

Blest be the tie that binds
Our hearts in Jesu's love;
The fellowship of Christian minds
Is like to that above.

It need only be added that by his outstanding gifts as pastor, preacher and scholar he built up the little congregation and before long a new and larger chapel was erected. He wrote many books and numerous other hymns, including 'Lord, dismiss us with thy blessing'.

TUNES: Various, of which *Dennis* (J. G. Nagell, 1773–1836) would appear to be the favourite.

128 Ye that know the Lord is gracious   C. A. Alington, 1872–1955

Dr Cyril Alington is remembered as a distinguished Head-master of Eton, 1916–33, and then as Dean of Durham for the remainder of his life. He was the author of a number of hymns, including the Easter hymn 'Good Christian men rejoice and sing', written while at Eton for *SP* in 1931; but none is finer than this, which he composed for a service at Durham Cathedral and was first published in *A&M* 1950.

A paraphrase of 1 Peter 2:3–10, it provides a splendid and thoroughly biblical hymn about the Church. In the scripture passage the Church is represented figuratively as 'a spiritual house' or temple of which Christ is the chosen and precious cornerstone and Christian believers are 'living stones' in-corporated into him. They are also seen to be (by a swift transition of thought) 'a holy priesthood' who minister within the temple and 'offer spiritual sacrifices acceptable to God through Jesus Christ.' The passage ends (v.9) with 'a magnifi-cent statement of the nature and function of the Church, wherein all the faithful, in living union with their Lord and with one another, serve God and proclaim his glories' (F. W. Beare).

All these ideas find expression in the hymn. It makes clear that the main thing about the Church is that it is Christ's and that membership of it involves both privilege and re-sponsibility.

TUNE: *Hyfrydol* (R. H. Prichard, 1811–87), or *Abbot's Leigh* (C. Taylor, b.1907).

129 May the grace of Christ our Saviour   J. Newton*, 1725–1807

The value of a hymn cannot be assessed by its length. Some of the most satisfying hymns are quite short. Here is a good example in John Newton's two-verse hymn to be sung 'After Sermon'. It is essentially a benediction for use at the end of divine service, based on the words with which the apostle Paul concluded his second letter to the Corinthians (13:14):

The grace of the Lord Jesus Christ, and the love of God, and the fellowship of the Holy Spirit be with you all. Amen.

This is the only Trinitarian form of benediction in the New Testament. The order in which the persons of the Trinity are named is not the traditional theological order (Father, Son and Holy Spirit) but the order of Christian experience. It is through the saving *grace* of Jesus Christ that we come to believe in the *love* of God the Father and enter into that *fellowship* of the Spirit which finds its expression in the Church. Newton follows this order in the prayer which makes up the first stanza. In the second he indicates the spiritual union and communion which result when the prayer is answered.

TUNES: Various, including *Waltham* (H. Albert, 1604–51) and *Sharon* (W. Boyce, 1710–79).

130 Christ is the King! O friends rejoice   *G. K. A. Bell, 1883–1958*

George Kennedy Bell is remembered and honoured as one of the outstanding leaders of the English Church during the present century. Successively Dean of Canterbury and Bishop of Chichester, he devoted his life to the ecumenical movement and the cause of Christian unity. These concerns are reflected in this hymn, which was written for *Songs of Praise*, 1931. It then consisted of four six-line stanzas and was set to the Welsh melody *Llangoedmor*. When included in *100 Hymns for Today*, 1969, it appeared in a new form. The verses were broken up to three lines apiece, plus an Alleluia, and given the fine tune *Vulpius* (see 100).

The theme of the hymn is clearly Christ the King, but it is also about the King's subjects. Beginning on an exultant note of joy it gives praise to God 'for Christ's saints in ancient days':

> They with a faith for ever new
> Followed the King, and round him drew
> Thousands of faithful men and true.

From the past the hymn moves into the present and challenges Christ's people today to follow in the path of his first disciples, in the assurance that:

> Christ through all ages is the same:
> Place the same hope in his great name,
> With the same faith his word proclaim.

The final appeal is for unity: for the Church's 'scattered companies' to work together in the Lord's service and so to further his kingdom in the world.

TUNES: See above.

131 Lord Christ, the Father's mighty Son   B. Wren, b.1936

'A most valuable and welcome hymn on Christian Unity,' writes Canon Cyril Taylor, 'reinforced by the delightful and unconventional tune written for it by Peter Cutts.' The words and tune were written when the author and the composer were fellow students at Mansfield College, Oxford, in the early sixties, and first appeared in *100 Hymns for Today*, 1969. The tune is called *Hampton Poyle*, the name of a village near Oxford.

The hymn, as stated, is about Christian unity; but its main concern is with the scandal and tragedy of the Church's disunity in the eyes of the world. Jesus' prayer for his people was: 'That they all may be one, as thou, Father, art in me, and I in thee, that they also may be one in us: *that the world may believe* that thou hast sent me' (John 17:21 *AV*). The Church's visible unity is part of its witness:

> To make us one your prayers were said,
> To make us one you broke the bread
>   For all to receive;
> Its pieces scatter us instead:
>   How can others believe?

How indeed! So in penitence we are bound to pray, 'Lord Christ, forgive us, make us new!' and to ask that his love may

achieve what we cannot do, by reconciling our differences –
'that the world may believe'.

TUNE: See above.

132 Forth in the peace of Christ we go   *J. Quinn, b.*1919

The Revd James Quinn, S. J., one of the most distinguished
Roman Catholic hymn-writers of our time, published this
work in his *New Hymns for All Seasons*, 1969. Its theme is that,
as members of the Church, we are sent forth by Christ into the
world in the threefold role of prophets, priests and kings.

In the hymn the order of the roles is reversed. Our kingship
is expressed, like Christ's, in the royalty of service: 'Christ's
world we serve to share Christ's reign.' By our priesthood – a
priesthood we share with the whole Church – we consecrate
the world for Christ and minister his healing grace; and as
prophets we proclaim Christ's truth by word and deed and so
spread his name in the world. Hence:

> We are the Church; Christ bids us show
>   That in his Church all nations find
> Their hearth and home, where Christ restores
>   True peace, true love, to all mankind.

TUNES: *Llenrod* (traditional Welsh melody), or *Duke Street*
(J. Hatton, *d.*1793).

WORSHIP AND PRAYER

133 Angel voices ever singing   *F. Pott*★, 1832–1909

The dedication of a new organ in Wingates church,
Lancashire, in 1861, was the occasion for the writing of this
hymn. The vicar, the Revd W. K. Macrorie (later to become
Bishop of Maritzburg in S. Africa) invited Francis Pott to
write a hymn to be sung at the dedication service. Having

secured the hymn he next requested Dr E. G. Monk, musical editor of *A&M*, to provide a suitable tune. Thus *Angel Voices* came into being, and words and music have remained wedded ever since.

Its origin furnishes the clue to the hymn. It begins by asking, Is it possible that Almighty God, worshipped unceasingly by the angelic hosts in heaven, has any regard for the 'songs of sinful man' on earth? The answer is (v. 3):

> Yea, we know that thou rejoicest
>   O'er each work of thine;
> Thou didst ears and hands and voices
>   For thy praise design;
> Craftsman's art and music's measure
>   For thy pleasure
>   All combine.

The reference to 'craftsman's art and music's measure' made the hymn particularly appropriate for the service at which it was first sung. But it is equally suitable for any act of worship in which organist, choir and congregation join in offering their 'choicest psalmody' to God with 'hearts and minds and hands and voices' (v. 4) – words which remind us that true worship demands the best we have to give and involves the use of all our faculties.

TUNE: *Angel Voices*. See above.

134 Christ is made the sure   *Latin, 7th century*
**   foundation   *Tr. J. M. Neale*, 1818–66***

The Latin original, *Urbs beata Jerusalem* (Blessèd city, heavenly Salem) from which this hymn is taken dates back to at least the 7th century. The entire work consists of nine stanzas, the last being a doxology. It is usually divided into two sections of four stanzas each. Dr Neale's translation was published in his *Medieval Hymns*, 1851, but it has been considerably altered since then.

Our hymn is the second part of the work, *Angularis funda-mentum*. It is based largely on St Paul's description of the

Church in Ephesians 2:20,21: '. . . built upon the foundation of the apostles and prophets, Christ Jesus himself being the chief cornerstone, in whom the whole structure is joined together and grows into a holy temple in the Lord.' The emphasis here is on the Church's unity in Christ, its members being 'living stones' built into him and thus joined together to form 'a spiritual house' (1 Pet.2:5). There is also reference, as in the first part, to the 'dedicated city', the heavenly Jerusalem, an image derived from Revelation 21.

Another version of the same hymn is 'Christ is our cornerstone', by John Chandler (1806–76), published in 1837. It is a freer rendering of the Latin text and is more in the nature of a paraphrase.

TUNE: *Westminster Abbey* (adapted from an anthem of Henry Purcell, 1659–95).

135 Lo! God is here! let us adore

G. Tersteegen, 1697–1769
Tr. J. Wesley, 1703–91

John Wesley's keen interest in hymnody began on his voyage to the American colony of Georgia in 1736. With him on board ship was a group of Moravian emigrants who deeply impressed Wesley not only by their assured and indomitable faith but also by their hymn-singing. He quickly made it his business to learn the German language so that he could converse with these godly folk and study their hymnal – Count Zinzendorf's *Gesangbuch*, published the previous year. One immediate result was that he made translations of five of the hymns and included them in the hymn book he compiled while still in Georgia. In later years he made further translations, which number thirty-three in all and demonstrate his skill as a translator and poet.

The present hymn, *Gott ist gegenwartig*, was written by Gerhard Tersteegen, a mystical poet who led a solitary life, unconnected with any of the Churches, and yet exercised an influential ministry through personal counselling as well as by his numerous hymns. He entitled this hymn 'Remembrance of the glorious and delightful Presence of God'; and that assuredly is the right approach to worship.

When as Christians we meet together for worship we do not have to seek God's presence. We are already in his presence. 'Lo, God is here!' It is a fact, the realisation of which leads at once to adoration and produces a sense of awe. 'How dreadful is this place!' – the words of Jacob after his night of dreaming at Bethel (Gen. 28:16,17). Wesley recognised this to be the biblical basis of the hymn. In his famous *Collection* of 1780 it has six stanzas. Modern hymnals reproduce no more than three or four.

TUNES: *Vater Unser* (from V. Schumann's *Gesangbuch*, 1539); *Old 117th* (from *Genevan Psalter*, 1551); and others.

136 Lord of the worlds above   I. Watts*, 1674–1748

The 84th Psalm has been a special favourite with the hymn-writers and paraphrasers. Different versions abound. John Milton's, beginning 'How lovely are thy dwellings fair', comes from his *Nine Psalms done into Metre*, 1648. The metrical version in the *Scottish Psalter*, 1650, begins in a somewhat similar way: 'How lovely is thy dwelling-place.' Henry Francis Lyte also made a version for his *The Spirit of the Psalms*, 1833, the once popular 'Pleasant are thy courts above'.

Isaac Watts included three paraphrases of the psalm in his *Psalms of David Imitated in the Language of the New Testament*, 1719. 'Lord of the worlds above', in seven stanzas, is the third. Entitled 'Longing for the House of God', it provides a good illustration of Watts's great gift as a paraphraser and also of the freedom he allowed himself in his treatment of the Psalms. He is not concerned to produce yet another metrical version or to adhere strictly to the Bible text. His aim here, as in all his paraphrases, 'is to introduce reality and emotional warmth into this part of divine service for the *whole* Church'. (Harry Escott) And undoubtedly the whole Church is indebted to him for his achievements.

TUNES: *Darwall's 148th* (J. Darwall, 1731–89), or *Croft's 136th* (W. Croft, 1678–1727).

137 We love the place, O God

W. Bullock, 1798–1874
W. H. Baker*, 1821–77

In the early part of the 19th century William Bullock, as a young naval officer, was a member of a party ordered to survey the coast of Newfoundland. He was so horrified at the condition of the settlers he met with – their poverty, isolation, lack of religious worship – that he resigned his commission, was ordained and returned to Newfoundland as a missionary. At Trinity Bay he built a small mission church and for its dedication in 1827 he wrote the original version of this hymn. Consisting of six stanzas, it was based on Psalm 26:8: 'Lord, I have loved the habitation of thy house.' Years later, when he was Dean of Nova Scotia, Bullock published the hymn in his *Songs of the Church*, 1854.

In this form it came to the notice of Sir Henry Baker, who revised it and included it in the first edition of *A&M*. It now had seven stanzas. Of these, the first three were by Bullock with only minor alterations. His fourth ran:

> We love our Father's board,
>   Its altar steps are dear;
> For there in faith adored,
>   We find his presence near.

Baker recast this in the now familiar form, and then added the last three stanzas, which were entirely his own. Doubtless he greatly improved the original version and produced a hymn suitable for use at dedication festivals and on similar occasions.

TUNE: *Quam dilecta* (Bishop H. L. Jenner, 1820–98).

138 Jesus, stand among us

W. Pennefather, 1816–73

> Jesus, stand among us
>   In thy risen power;
> Let this time of worship
>   Be a hallowed hour.

When he wrote these words William Pennefather, vicar of St Jude's, Mildmay Park, London, clearly had in mind the story of the first Easter Day in John 20:19–23. It was the evening hour and the disciples had met together behind closed doors. And then . . .

. . . Jesus came and stood among them and said to them, 'Peace be with you . . . As the Father sent me, even so I send you.' And when he had said this, he breathed on them and said, 'Receive the Holy Spirit . . .'.

As he reflected on these words Mr Pennefather turned them into prayer and poetry. The three stanzas of his hymn were intended to be sung as a prelude to Sunday worship and they admirably fulfil this purpose. They are specially suitable for use at Eastertide. But since every Sunday is a 'little Easter' in celebration of the Lord's resurrection on the first day of the week the hymn is not restricted to any particular season. The second stanza ('Breathe the Holy Spirit into every heart') is a further echo of Jesus' words and actions. It thus unites the resurrection with the gift of the Spirit, as is commonly done in the fourth Gospel.

TUNES: Various, including *Quietude* (H. Green, 1871–1931) and *Gott ein Vater* (F. Silcher, 1789–1860).

139 Jesus, where'er thy people meet   W. Cowper*, 1721–1800

An unusual thing happened in the parish of Olney, Bucks, under John Newton's vigorous ministry. Attendance at the weekly prayer meeting grew to such an extent that a larger meeting-place had to be sought. Accordingly, a move was made to a commodious room (seating 130 people) in the Great House, owned by Lord Dartmouth, the patron of the living; and to mark the occasion both Newton and his poet-friend William Cowper wrote a special hymn. Newton's was our 'Great Shepherd of thy people, hear'; this one was Cowper's contribution.

The hymn becomes especially meaningful when we bear in mind the circumstances that called it forth. Were some of the faithful Olney folk a bit hesitant about moving to the new meeting-place? Were they afraid that everything would be different in the larger and grander building? The hymn supplies a reassuring answer to any such questions. One thing, the all-important thing, would be the same, namely the Lord's presence. He is with his people 'where'er they meet', for:

> Where'er they seek thee, thou art found,
> And every place is hallowed ground.

The next stanza develops this thought. God is 'within no walls confined'. Not consecrated places but consecrated people are the essence of Christian worship, as Jesus taught (John 4:21–24). In the end it matters little *where* people worship. *How* they worship, 'in spirit and truth', is everything. This is the fundamental fact the hymn affirms. In its later part it becomes a prayer: first, earnest petition for God's 'chosen few' as they meet to pray, and then intercession for those outside the Church's fellowship.

TUNES: *St Sepulchre* (G. Cooper, 1820–76); *Festus* (from Frylinghausen's *Gesangbuch*, 1704); and others.

140 Lord, teach us how to pray aright   *J. Montgomery**, 1771–1854

Good hymns on prayer are not too numerous. Here Montgomery has given us one of the best. It begins by echoing the request of the disciples to Jesus, 'Lord, teach us to pray, as John also taught his disciples' (Luke 11:1); and the words that follow provide the teaching we seek. To pray aright we need:

> Reverence and godly fear;
> Due preparation of the heart;
> Penitence, sincerity, and humility;
> Faith in Christ's atoning sacrifice;
> Patience and courage to persevere.

These are the marks of true prayer. What remains?

> Give these – and then thy will be done!
> Thus strengthened with all might,

> We by thy Spirit, and thy Son,
> Shall pray, and pray aright.

Mention here should be made of Montgomery's other fine hymn on the subject, written and published at the same time (1818), 'Prayer is the soul's sincere desire'. Admittedly it is really a religious poem rather than a hymn; but its teaching is of the first importance, stressing as it does the *inwardness* of genuine prayer.

TUNE: *St Hugh* (E. J. Hopkins, 1818–1901), and others.

141 What a Friend we have in Jesus   *Joseph M. Scriven, 1819–86*

Joseph Scriven was an Irishman, born near Banbridge, Co. Down, and a graduate of Trinity College, Dublin. At the age of 25 he suffered a terrible loss. The girl to whom he was engaged was accidentally drowned shortly before their wedding day. Overcome by grief, the young man decided to emigrate to Canada, where he settled in the province of Ontario and took up school teaching. He devoted his spare time to evangelism and to helping the poor and infirm. He was a member of the Brethren.

Scriven was certainly a man who knew the meaning of trouble; and it was to console his mother in Ireland at a time of special sorrow that he wrote the hymn. He entitled it 'Pray without ceasing'. When asked by a friend how he had managed to write it, he replied, 'The Lord and I did it between us.' Clearly it is a hymn born of experience. Scriven was no poet and his hymn is not great poetry. But who can deny its spiritual appeal or the effectiveness of the repeated phrase 'Take it to the Lord in prayer'? And when you come to think of it, how few hymns there are about Jesus as our unfailing friend in time of trouble.

TUNE: *Converse* (Charles C. Converse, 1832–1918), or *Blaenwern* (W. P. Rowlands, 1860–1937).

HOLY COMMUNION

142 Now, my tongue, the mystery telling

St Thomas Aquinas, 1227–74
Tr. J. M. Neale*, 1818–66,
and E. Caswall*, 1814–78

St Thomas Aquinas, a Dominican monk, won renown not only as a great theologian but as one of the few Italian sacred poets. His *Pange lingua gloriosi corporis mysterium* has been described as the greatest of all communion hymns: 'A wonderful union of sweetness of melody with clear-cut dogmatic teaching,' as *Julian* remarks. It was written in 1263 for the office of Corpus Christi which St Thomas drew up at the request of Pope Urban IV.

The hymn consists of two parts. The first four stanzas were intended to be sung at the daily offices of Matins or Vespers. The last two, beginning 'Therefore we, before him bending', were for use at the office of Benediction or during mass at the elevation of the Host. Our English versions, based on the translations of Neale and Caswall, vary from book to book. In some hymnals (e.g. *EH* and *WOV*) the hymn begins, 'Of the glorious body telling'. Dr Neale was particularly exercised about the rendering of the fourth stanza. He was critical of the way others had treated the Latin text and insisted that his own translation was the most accurate:

> Word made flesh, by word he maketh
>   Very bread his flesh to be;
> Man in wine Christ's blood partaketh;
>   And if senses fail to see,
> Faith alone the true heart waketh
>   To behold the mystery.

Another of Aquinas's communion hymns is almost equally well known, 'Thee we adore, O hidden Saviour', translated by Bishop J. R. Woodward, 1820–85.

TUNE: *Pange lingua* (proper plainsong melody, Sarum version).

143 And now, O Father, mindful of the love   *W. Bright,*
1824–1901

The Revd William Bright was an eminent scholar, Regius
Professor of Ecclesiastical History at Oxford from 1868 till his
death, and the author of numerous works, including many
poems and hymns. But of the latter only two are now widely
used, both communion hymns: 'Once, only once, and once
for all' and the present one, his abiding memorial.

It may be asked why the hymn should begin with the word
And. Many hymns in fact do this, often for no apparent reason.
In this instance however there is a simple explanation. The
four stanzas form the latter part of a longer poem, published in
1873, and the copulative links up with what has gone before.

The stanzas follow a clear pattern of thought. At the beginning we are reminded of the love of Christ and his sacrificial
work, represented by the sacramental elements of bread and
wine. In the second we acknowledge our unworthiness
and seek the Father's acceptance and forgiveness for Jesus'
sake:

> For lo, between our sins and their reward
> We set the Passion of thy Son our Lord.

In the third stanza we pray for others, 'our dearest and our
best', asking that God may keep them close to him and do the
'utmost for their souls' true weal'. Finally we pray that our
Lord may deliver us from all evil and make us 'glad and free' in
his service.

TUNES: *Song 1* (Orlando Gibbons, 1583–1625), or *Unde et
Memores* (W. H. Monk, 1823–89).

144 Deck thyself, my soul,   *J. Franck*, 1618–77
  with gladness   *Tr. C. Winkworth*★, 1829–78

To Miss Winkworth we owe the translation of what is gener-
ally recognised to be the finest of all German hymns for Holy
Communion, *Schmucke dich, o liebe Seele*. Written by Johann
Franck, burgomaster of his native town Guben, Brandenberg,

it was first published in a collection of hymns made by the distinguished musician Johann Crüger (1598–1662), precentor of the Lutheran Cathedral of St Nicholas in Berlin. It was he who composed for it the tune *Schmucke dice* to which it is always sung. Miss Winkworth translated six of its nine stanzas in 1858 and later rewrote them in the original metre for her *Chorale Book for England*, 1863.

Julian says of this hymn, 'It is an exhortation to the soul to arise and draw near to partake of the heavenly food and to meditate on the wonders of the heavenly love.' In its stanzas many notes are blended: joy and praise, wonder and awe, worship and homage. Its concluding prayer is especially memorable:

> From this banquet let me measure,
> Lord, how vast and deep its treasure;
> Through the gifts thou here dost give me,
> As thy guest in heaven receive me.

The hymn, still used in many German churches, has gained general acceptance in British churches of all denominations. TUNE: See above.

145 Alleluia, sing to Jesus   *W. Chatterton Dix**, 1837–98

William Chatterton Dix is probably best known for his Epiphany hymn 'As with gladness men of old' (66), but Church of England people are almost as familiar with his communion hymn. It was published in his *Altar Songs*, 1867, under the title 'Redemption by the Precious Blood' and appointed especially for Ascensiontide. There is a general allusion to the Lord's ascension in the first stanza – 'His the sceptre, his the throne' – and another in the final one: 'Thou within the veil hast entered.' The second stanza is more specific:

> Though the cloud from sight received him
> When the forty days were o'er,

> Shall our hearts forget his promise,
> 'I am with you evermore'?

Though the Lord ascended to heaven in his resurrection body, the Church still enjoy his spiritual presence. The whole hymn is accordingly of a joyful and triumphal character and each stanza begins with an Alleluia.

A point of interest is the number of titles given to Jesus in the last two stanzas. The first is 'Bread of angels' – a reference to the manna in Psalm 78:25 and so to Jesus as 'the true bread from heaven' (John 6:32). Hence he is 'our Food' as well as 'our Stay' or strength. Three other titles follow: 'Intercessor, Friend of sinners, earth's Redeemer'. In the final stanza he is 'King eternal', 'Lord of lords' and our 'great High Priest'.

TUNES: *Alleluia* (S. S. Wesley, 1810–76) or *Hyfrydol* (R. H. Prichard, 1811–87).

146 Jesus, we thus obey   *C. Wesley*★, 1707–88

Charles Wesley wrote a great many eucharistic hymns. His *Hymns on the Lord's Supper*, published in Bristol, 1745, contains no less than 165 of them: a reminder of the fact that the Evangelical Revival was also in the nature of a sacramental revival. The hymns set forth the Wesleys' teaching on the sacrament. That teaching they had inherited from their father the Revd Samuel Wesley, who was a High Churchman, and they saw no reason to abandon it after their evangelical conversion. To them the Lord's Supper was more than a bare memorial meal. It was a divine means of grace in which the Lord himself is spiritually present and by which he conveys the benefits of his sacrificial death to each faithful worshipper.

The present hymn provides an illustration of this teaching. When we obey Christ's 'last and kindest word' (by which Wesley meant 'Do this in remembrance of me') we come with confidence to meet our risen and living Lord:

> Our hearts we open wide
> To make the Saviour room;
> And lo! the Lamb, the Crucified,
> The sinner's Friend is come.

Thy presence makes the feast;
Now let our spirits feel
The glory not to be expressed,
The joy unspeakable.

Many other of Wesley's sacramental hymns will be found in the Methodist hymnals.

TUNES: Various. The hymn has no 'set' tune.

147 Let all mortal flesh
**   keep silence**

Liturgy of St James
Tr. G. Moultrie, 1829–85
and P. Dearmer★, 1867–1936

In the Greek Orthodox Church various liturgies existed in early times, providing the eucharistic rites and named after apostles. The Liturgy of St James, connected with the Syrian Church and dating from the 4th century, was rendered from the Greek into English by J. M. Neale and R. F. Littledale in their *Primitive Liturgies*, 1868–9, and a part of it entitled 'Prayer of the Cherubic Hymn' was versified by the Revd Gerard Moultrie to form this hymn.

Its teaching as thus rendered is not altogether satisfactory. The language is ambiguous and comes near to identifying the sacramental presence of Christ in the eucharist with his physical presence in his incarnate life. It was presumably to remove this difficulty that Dr Percy Dearmer made a fresh version of the hymn, on the lines of Moultrie's, for inclusion in *Songs of Praise*, 1931. In this form the hymn – which thus loses something of its sacramental character – finds acceptance in the *Baptist Hymn Book*, 1962, where it is placed in the Christmas section. Dearmer retained the original metre so that the same tune could be used: the attractive French carol melody *Picardy*, probably dating from the 17th century.

Another hymn derived from the Liturgy of St James is the joyful 'From glory to glory advancing'.

TUNE: See above.

148 Strengthen for service, Lord, the hands *Liturgy of Malabar Versified by C. W. Humphreys, 1841–1921*

The history of this hymn covers a period of fifteen centuries. It is based on a 5th century prayer in the liturgy of the ancient Church of St Thomas in Malabar, South India. The prayer was said by the deacon while the people were receiving communion. Dr J. M. Neale made a translation of the prayer which he printed in a volume of early liturgies in 1859. Mr Charles Humphreys turned Neale's prose into verse and so created this hymn in its basic form. As such it was chosen for inclusion in the *English Hymnal*, 1906. Dr Vaughan Williams, the musical editor, wished it to be set to the German melody *Ach Gott und Herr* (Leipzig, 1682, adapted by J. S. Bach), and certain alterations were then made to the text by Percy Dearmer to enable it to fit the tune.

It makes an excellent post-communion hymn. The prayer stresses the fact that the sacrament, far from separating us from the life of the world, is a preparation for it and sanctifies the whole of life: the work we do, the words we speak, the things we listen to and see – all summed up in the last two lines:

> The bodies by thy Body fed
> With thy new life replenish.

TUNE: See above.

149 According to thy gracious word *J. Montgomery*, 1771–1854*

First published in Montgomery's *Christian Psalmist*, 1825, the hymn was entitled with the words of Jesus, 'Do this in remembrance of me' (Luke 22:19). It consists of six stanzas, which happily are usually printed in their entirety. The word 'remember' occurs in each of them and forms the theme of the hymn, which thus celebrates the memorial aspect of the Lord's Supper. It is one of the most widely used communion hymns and finds a place in nearly every book.

One or two textual matters are worth noting. In Montgomery's original manuscript the word 'will' at the end of the first stanza is underlined, so as to read 'I *will* remember thee'; and similarly the word 'me' in the last line of all, so as to read 'Jesus, remember *me*' – an echo of the words of the penitent thief (Luke 23:42). Again, the second stanza as written is:

> Thy body, broken for my sake,
>   My bread from heaven shall be;
> Thy testamental cup I take,
>   And thus remember thee.

Some books unnecessarily change the third line to 'The cup, thy precious blood, I take'; but *testamental* is perfectly scriptural here and refers to the words of Jesus, 'This cup is the new covenant [testament] in my blood' (1 Cor. 11:25).

TUNES: *Bangor* (W. Tans'ur in *The Harmony of Zion*, 1734); *Tallis's Ordinal* (T. Tallis, *c*. 1510–85); and others.

150 The King of love my Shepherd is   *Henry W. Baker**, 1821–77

Sir Henry Baker's popular hymn, first published in 1861, is not simply another metrical version of the 23rd Psalm (see 213). While making the psalm his basis he treats it with a large degree of freedom and gives it a distinctively Christian interpretation. Thus at the outset the sacred name 'The Lord' (viz. Jehovah) is invested with a new tenderness and becomes 'The King of love' – a recognition of his sovereign grace. In the next stanza the 'still waters' of the psalm are transformed into 'streams of living water' (a phrase used by Jesus himself: see John 7:37–9). The fourth stanza introduces the Cross, the symbol of sacrificial love, for the Good Shepherd lays down his life for the sheep; and the stanza that follows takes on a sacramental character, relating the psalmist's words to the Lord's table and the eucharistic chalice.

Of particular interest is the third stanza:

Perverse and foolish oft I strayed,
But yet in love he sought me,
And on his shoulder gently laid,
And home, rejoicing, brought me.

Here the words of the psalm, 'He restoreth my soul', are given
a pictorial explanation, borrowed from our Lord's parable in
Luke 15:3–7. The Shepherd 'in love' seeks and finds the sheep
that has gone astray and 'restores' it to himself and the flock.
The stanza meant much to Sir Henry himself and was his
comfort at the end. As he lay dying at the age of fifty-six he
was heard quietly repeating these words.

TUNE: *Dominus regit me* (J. B. Dykes, 1823–76).

151 Jesus, thou joy of   *Latin, 12th century*
**   loving hearts**   *Tr. R. Palmer*, 1808–87*

Dr Ray Palmer, the author of 'My faith looks up to thee' (200),
was one of America's leading Congregationalist ministers as
well as one of its finest hymn-writers.

This hymn is a translation (or, better, paraphrase) of five
stanzas of the famous medieval hymn often attributed to St
Bernard of which 'Jesu, the very thought of thee' (see 249) is a
part. Palmer's hymn is dated 1858 in his *Poetical Works*, 1876,
and given the title 'Jesus the Beloved'. It is a devotional hymn
of considerable merit. Christ is its focal point as the fountain of
life and light of mankind, the answer to the quest for spiritual
fulfilment in a restless and changing world.

It is not strictly or specifically a communion hymn, but its
third stanza makes it particularly suitable for the eucharist:

We taste thee, O thou living bread,
And long to feast upon thee still;
We drink of thee, the fountain-head,
And thirst our souls from thee to fill.

TUNES: *Maryton* (H. P. Smith, 1825–98); *Hereford* (S. S.
Wesley, 1810–76); *Quebec* (Henry Baker, 1835–1919).

152   My God, and is thy table spread   *P. Doddridge*,*
                                                          1702–51

As a hymn-writer Dr Doddridge tends to be overshadowed by his contemporary and friend Isaac Watts; but here he shows himself to be, according to *Julian*, the equal of Watts and even his superior in certain respects. His communion hymn certainly represents Doddridge at his best and 'towers above all the rest of his work in sheer excellence' (Erik Routley). It became widely known to members of the C of E by its inclusion among the hymns in the Supplement (1700) to the *New Version* of the Psalms which was commonly bound up with the *BCP*.

When it was published posthumously with Doddridge's hymns in 1755 it was given in six stanzas. Most hymn books now print no more than three or four, which even so make a quite satisfactory hymn. They are sufficient to reveal the 'high' view of the sacrament which Doddridge shared with Watts. Another point to be noted is that when the hymn was first published it bore the heading, 'God's Name profaned, when his Table is treated with contempt, Malachi 1:12. Applied to the Lord's Supper.' The words refer to the sermon Doddridge had preached before the hymn was sung in his Northampton chapel. He doubtless pointed out that one of the ways in which the Lord's table is treated with contempt is by neglect, and this may account for the stanza beginning:

> O let thy table honoured be,
>   And furnished well with joyful guests.

Another way is by lack of due preparation, hence the stanza omitted by most hymnals:

> Let crowds approach with hearts prepared,
>   With hearts inflamed let all attend;
> Nor when we leave our Father's board,
>   The pleasure or the profit end.

TUNE: *Rockingham* (adapted by E. Miller, 1731–1807).

153 Here, O my Lord, I see thee face to face   H. Bonar*, 1808–89

Once a year Dr Horatius Bonar visited his elder brother Dr John Bonar, minister of St Andrew's Free Church, Greenock, to share with him in a communion service. On the occasion of his visit on the first Sunday of October 1855 Horatius Bonar supplied this hymn, at his brother's request, for the printed order of service, and it was then used for the first time. With some alterations it was reprinted in Bonar's *Hymns of Faith and Hope*, 1857, in ten verses. It is inevitably shortened in all hymnals.

Bonar views the sacrament as a meeting point between the worshippers and their living Lord. By faith they see him 'face to face' and 'touch and handle things unseen'; they 'feed upon the bread of God' and 'drink the royal wine of heaven'. Such language is characteristic of the tenor of the hymn. One of the stanzas sometimes missing from the hymn books is:

> This is the hour of banquet and of song,
>   This is the heavenly table spread for me;
> Here let me feast, and, feasting, still prolong
>   The brief bright hour of fellowship with thee.

TUNES: Various, including *Song 22* (Orlando Gibbons, 1583–1625); *Farley Castle* (H. Lawes, 1596–1662); and *Sursum Corda* (Alfred M. Smith, b. 1879).

154 Lord, enthroned in heavenly splendour   G. H. Bourne, 1840–1925

George Hugh Bourne is one of the many Victorian hymn-writers who are remembered by only one hymn. Ordained in 1863, he spent much of his life in educational work and was for many years headmaster of St Edmund's School, Salisbury. The hymn is one of his *Seven Post-Communion Hymns* printed privately for use at St Edmund's. It first appeared in the supplement to *A&M* 1889, when Sir George Martin (1844–

1916) supplied for it the fine tune *St Helen* which has undoubtedly contributed to its popularity.

Six of the original ten stanzas are to be found in *WOV*. *A&M*
and *EH* use five of these but omit Bourne's original seventh:

> Great High Priest of our profession,
>> Through the veil thou enteredst in;
> By thy mighty intercession
>> Grace and mercy thou canst win:
>>> Alleluia! Alleluia!
>> Only sacrifice for sin.

As in other communion hymns, much of the imagery is
drawn from the Old Testament (e.g. Jesus the Pascal Lamb,
great High Priest, heavenly Manna). There is a healthy
emphasis on Christ's complete and victorious redemption,
and the note of praise is prominent, reaching its climax in the
splendid last line: 'Risen, ascended, glorified!'

TUNE: See above.

155 By Christ redeemed, in Christ restored   *G. Rawson,*
1807–89

George Rawson was a Congregationalist who practised as a
solicitor in Leeds. He assisted in producing the so-called *Leeds
Hymn Book* in 1853 for the Congregational churches, and later
earned the gratitude of the Baptists by aiding in the compilation of their *Psalms and Hymns*, 1858, to which he contributed
this hymn and twenty-six others.

The hymn is well known and widely used in the Free
Churches of Britain and also in America. It is based on the
words which St Paul adds to his account of the institution of
the Lord's Supper in 1 Corinthians 11:26 *AV*: 'For as often as ye
eat this bread and drink this cup, ye do shew the Lord's death
till he come.' The hymn takes up these last words and the phrase
'Until he come' is made the refrain at the end of each stanza.
The sacrament is thus seen to have a twofold significance. It is
not only a commemoration of his sacrificial death; it is also a
pledge of his future glory and heavenly kingdom. Two stanzas
sum up the message:

The streams of his dread agony,
His life-blood shed for us, we see;
The wine shall tell the mystery,
      Until he come.

And thus that dark betrayal night
With the last advent we unite,
By one blest chain of loving rite,
      Until he come.

TUNE: *St Gabriel* (F. A. G. Ouseley, 1825–89), or *Ripponden* (Norman Cocker, 1889–1953).

156 Lord Jesus Christ, you have come to us

P. Appleford, b.1924

Patrick Appleford wrote this hymn or spiritual song about the year 1957 when he was a curate in Poplar. Entitled 'Living Lord' it was published by the Twentieth Century Church Light Music Group in 1960. The initial aim of the group was to provide modern-style tunes for some of the standard church hymns, in the belief that 'the ordinary and transient music of today – which is the background to the lives of so many – has a rightful place in our worship.'

In the case of the present hymn the words as well as the tune, *Living Lord* (also by Mr Appleford), were new. It was intended for use as a communion hymn, but in fact it contains only one allusion to the sacrament, viz. in the second stanza:

You have commanded us to do
This in remembrance, Lord, of you.

With the omission of this stanza the hymn can be sung on any occasion.

From beginning to end it brings us face to face with the person of Christ, the Christ who has come to us: 'Mary's Son' but also 'Son of God'; born for us but also crucified for us (v. 3); the living Lord who pours his love and power into our lives (vv. 1,4). So the song ends appropriately with a prayer of

dedication as our personal response to his coming and his
lordship.

TUNE: See above.

157 Come, risen Lord, and deign   G. W. Briggs*,
         to be our guest   1875–1959

In Canon Briggs's *Songs of Faith*, 1945, this hymn is entitled
'The Upper Room'. The opening stanza describes the Last
Supper when Jesus presided as host at the sacramental meal
while the disciples gathered round him as his guests. In the
same way, as the second stanza suggests, Christ is the cele-
brant at every communion: 'Thou at the table blessing still
dost stand,' and we receive the bread and cup as from him.
Thus we are united as 'one body' with all Christ's people: 'One
with each other, Lord, for one in thee' (4th stanza).

The final two lines refer to the supper at Emmaus when the
disciples recognised their risen Lord in the breaking of the
bread (Luke 24:28–35). Perhaps the opening line of the hymn
also looks back to this story and the disciples' invitation to
Jesus to abide with them for the night. They were asking him
to be their guest; but when he entered their home he took his
place as host at the table and they became his guests.

TUNES: Various, including *Song 24* (Orlando Gibbons,
1583–1625); *Holborn* (Eric H. Thiman, 1900–75); and *Blackbird
Leys* (Peter Cutts, *b*.1937).

158 An upper room did our Lord   F. Pratt Green*, b.1903
         prepare

This hymn is written in the unusual metre of 9.8.9.8 and it was
done for a purpose. In the summer of 1973 John Wilson, one of
the editors of the RSCM's *Hymns for Celebration*, asked Dr
Green to submit a text to fit the English folksong 'O Waly,
Waly'. This hymn was the result, and together with Mr
Wilson's setting of the melody it was published in the RSCM's
collection of communion hymns the following year.

The hymn brings us in spirit to the upper room where, on
the night in which he was betrayed, Jesus gathered with his

disciples – 'Those he loved until the end' (a quotation from John 13:1). To those disciples, and all his disciples since then, he gave 'a parting gift', the sacrament of his body and blood, as a perpetual memorial of his Passion. But that was not all:

> And after supper he washed their feet,
>   For service, too, is sacrament,
> In him our joy shall be made complete –
>   Sent out to serve, as he was sent.

The reference to the feet-washing in a communion hymn is unusual but wholly appropriate as a symbol of the service that follows worship. The final stanza begins, 'No end there is!', for the fellowship with Christ which we enjoy here and now will have its consummation in heaven:

> In every room in our Father's house
>   He will be there, as Lord and Host.

TUNE: See above.

159 I come with joy to meet my Lord   B. Wren, b.1936

Like several of his hymns, this was written by Dr Brian Wren when he was minister of the Congregational Church of Hockley and Hawkwell, Essex. It was first published in *The Hymn Book*, Canada, 1971. He explains that the hymn was intended to follow a sermon on the presence of Christ in Holy Communion and to do this 'as simply as possible, in a way that would take the worshipper (probably without his recognising it) from the usual individualistic approach to communion ("I come") to an understanding of its essential corporateness ("we'll go")'.

This thought of corporate worship finds expression in the second stanza: 'I come with Christians far and near . . .' and still more in the third:

> As Christ breaks bread for men to share
>   Each proud division ends.

> The love that made us, makes us one,
>   And strangers now are friends.

Our fellowship with others at the Lord's table also deepens our fellowship with Christ and makes his presence more real (v.4), so that having been drawn together in worship we are then ready to separate and go out into the world to 'live and speak his praise' (v.5).

One of the welcome features of this hymn is its note of *joy*. Too often that note is missing – not only from our communion hymns but from our communion services. The eucharist, if it is true to its name, should always be a time of glad thanksgiving.

TUNES: *Winchcombe*, written for this hymn by Leonard Blake (*b*.1907); or *St Botolph* (Gordon Slater, 1896–1979).

160 Now let us from this table rise   *F. Kaan*, *b*.1929

The Revd Fred Kaan of the United Reformed Church wrote this post-communion hymn in 1964 when he was minister of the Pilgrim Church, Plymouth. It was published in his *Pilgrim Praise*, 1967, and has since become one of his best known hymns. He explains: 'The celebration of the Eucharist is – among other things – a preparation for service. This is a hymn which tries to say: the worship is now over, the service begins.'

The hymn is entitled 'The Sacrament of Care'. We rise from the Lord's table 'renewed in body, mind and soul' and:

> With minds alert, upheld by grace,
>   To spread the Word in speech and deed,
> We follow in the steps of Christ,
>   At one with man in hope and need.

The message is clear. Our participation in the sacrifice of Christ in the church must find expression in sacrificial love and service outside the church. Hence the hymn reflects the post-communion prayer in the URC order of Holy Communion: 'Most gracious God, now we give ourselves to you; and we ask that our daily living may be part of the life of your kingdom, and that our love may be your love reaching out into the life of the world.'

TUNES: *Niagra* (R. Jackson, 1840–1914), or *Solothurn*, Swiss traditional melody.

THE SCRIPTURES

161 Lord, thy word abideth   *H. W. Baker*, 1821–77*

Sir Henry Baker's well known Bible hymn appeared in the first edition of *A&M*, 1861. Its most notable feature is its sheer simplicity. Yet while it says nothing profound it is not trivial or commonplace. It rings true to experience and speaks directly to our condition.

Its opening affirmation gives immediate assurance. God's word *abides*, unchanged and unchanging in a world of flux (cf. 1 Pet. 1:23–25). It outlives all its assailants and critics. To the man or woman of faith it vindicates itself:

> Who its truth believeth,
> Light and joy receiveth.

The remaining stanzas continue this theme and dwell on the power of the scriptures to meet the need of the human heart in all life's varying moods, from beginning to end:

> Word of mercy, giving
> Succour to the living;
> Word of life, supplying
> Comfort to the dying.

An unusual feature of the hymn is its rhyme pattern. The rhyming syllable is not the last one in the line but the syllable preceding it.

TUNE: *Ravenshaw* (medieval German melody from M. Weisse's *Ein neu Gesengbuchlin*, 1531).

162　Father of mercies, in thy word　*Anne Steele, 1716–78*

Anne Steele was probably the first woman to write and publish any notable hymns. Her father, William Steele, a timber merchant, was lay pastor of the Baptist Church at Broughton, Hampshire, of which she was an active member. As a young woman she suffered a tragic blow. The man whom she was to marry was drowned only a few hours before the ceremony was to take place and she never fully recovered from the shock.

Her hymns were highly thought of in her time and ranked next to those of Watts and Doddridge. For the next century or so a large proportion of the 144 she wrote were to be found in all collections and were extensively used. Today she is remembered chiefly for this hymn about the Bible, published in 1760 among her collected poems.

She approaches the Bible with deep reverence and extols its worth. It is the word of God in which 'endless glory' shines. It gives sight to the blind, food to the hungry, consolation to the fainting, refreshment to the thirsty. Above all, in its pages 'the Redeemer's welcome voice' is heard, spreading peace and life and joy around. That being so, we do well to pray:

> O may these heavenly pages be
> 　My ever dear delight;
> And still new beauties may I see,
> 　And still increasing light.

TUNE: *Southwell* (H. S. Irons, 1834–1905) and others.

163　Break thou the bread of life　*Mary A. Lathbury, 1841–1913*

Mary Lathbury, a member of the American Methodist Episcopal Church, was a versatile woman. An artist by profession, she was also a gifted poet and wrote a lot of prose and verse for children. Her two hymns by which she is now remembered (see 283) were written in connection with the work of the Chautauqua Conference Centre in New York

State, founded by the Revd John Vincent. Miss Lathbury was one of his early assistants and her hymns were written at his request. This one, composed in 1877, was designed as a short hymn to be sung before Bible study. It consisted of two stanzas only, the first and the last. The middle one, 'O send thy Spirit Lord', was added in 1913 by an English Methodist, Alexander Groves (1842–1909).

Miss Lathbury's verses are based on the story of the feeding of the five thousand when Jesus broke the bread 'beside the sea', viz. the Sea of Galilee. Our prayer in the first stanza is that 'beyond the sacred page' of scripture we may seek and feed upon Christ, the 'living Word', so that our Bible study may bear fruit in our lives:

> Bless thou the bread of life
>   To me, to me,
> As thou didst bless the loaves
>   By Galilee;
> Then shall all bondage cease,
>   All fetters fall,
> And I shall find my peace,
>   My All in all.

TUNE: *Lathbury* (W. F. Sherwin, 1826–88).

164 Not far beyond the sea nor high

G. B. Caird,
1917–84

Suitable hymns about the Bible are scarce and it is good to have a new one by a leading biblical scholar. Dr George Caird, a former principal of Mansfield College, Oxford, wrote the hymn around 1945, but it was not published till some twelve years later. The opening stanza provides the key to its message:

> Not far beyond the sea nor high
> Above the heaven, but very nigh
>   Thy voice, O God, is heard.
> For each new step of faith we take

Thou hast more truth and light to break
Forth from thy holy Word.

The reference in the first three lines is to Deuteronomy
30:11–14, a passage quoted by St Paul in Romans 10:6–8 to
make the point that the word of the gospel is not remote from
us but readily accessible and open to all who have faith. Hence
the later allusion to the famous words of Pastor John Robinson
to the Pilgrim Fathers, that, 'The Lord has still more truth and
light to break forth out of his holy Word.'

The second stanza, omitted by some hymnals, assures us
that the scriptures provide spiritual food for 'the babe in
Christ' as well as 'stronger meat' for the mature believer (cf.
1 Cor.3:1,2; Heb.5:12–14). The third is based on Paul's
prayer in Ephesians 3:14–19 and points to Christ, the central
theme of all scripture.

TUNES: *Cornwall* (S. S. Wesley, 1810–76); or *Manna*
(melody by J. G. Schicht, 1753–1823).

165 Thanks to God whose Word was spoken   R. T. Brooks, b.1918

Thanksgiving for the Word of God is the theme of this hymn
by Reginald Thomas Brooks, a minister of the URC who has
worked for many years in the religious broadcasting department of the BBC. It was written in 1954 for the 150th
anniversary of the Bible Society.

The virtue of the hymn lies in its teaching character. It helps
us to understand what is meant by the 'Word of God'. We
begin by thanking God for his *creative* word 'spoken in the
deed that made the earth'. As the psalmist said, 'By the word
of the Lord the heavens were made . . . For he spoke, and it
came to be' (Ps.33:6,9). Next the *incarnate* Word:

Thanks to God whose Word incarnate
Glorified the flesh of man.

In the highest sense the Word of God is the historic Christ.
'God has spoken to us in his Son' (Heb.1:2). That revelation is
preserved for all time in the scriptures, the *written* word:

Thanks to God whose word was written
    In the Bible's sacred page,
Record of the revelation
    Showing God in every age.

The fourth aspect is the word of God *preached* in the gospel ministry. For what is preaching but – according to Bernard Manning – 'a manifestation of the incarnate Word, from the written word, by the spoken word'?

'God has spoken' – four times the phrase is repeated. But it is also true, as the final stanza says, that 'God is speaking,' speaking now, and it is for us to listen to what 'the Spirit's voice within' says to us.

TUNES: *Kingley Vale* (H. P. Allen, 1869–1946), or *Regent Square* (H. Smart, 1813–79).

MISSION AND WITNESS

166 Jesus shall reign where'er the sun *I. Watts*★, 1674–1748

This is probably the oldest, finest and most popular of all missionary hymns – published, be it noted, in 1719, well over fifty years before the birth of the modern missionary movement at the end of the 18th century. But Watts did not write it as a missionary hymn. It was part of his metrical version of Psalm 72, with its magnificent vision of an ideal king and his reign of righteousness extending throughout the earth. The Jews saw in it a foreshadowing of the coming Messianic King. Watts interprets it as such and gives it a fully Christian meaning. The psalmist did not name the king of whom he wrote, for he did not know his name. But Watts knows it well enough. '*Jesus* shall reign,' he begins, and proceeds to build up a glowing picture of Christ's universal kingdom.

The hymn as published consisted of eight stanzas and was entitled 'Christ's kingdom among the Gentiles'. A comparison with the psalm will show the verses from which Watts drew his inspiration (chiefly 5,8,12–15,17–19). But in our hymnals we do not have all that Watts wrote; most reproduce no more than five (possibly six) of the original stanzas. Even so, they are sufficient to illustrate the hymn's dominant theme, the worldwide nature of Christ's reign, extending 'from shore to shore' and embracing 'people and realms of every tongue.' The hymn also magnifies the beneficent effects of Christ's kingdom: 'Blessings abound where'er he reigns!' And in Watts's penultimate stanza – missing from most hymn books – it is said:

> Where he displays his healing power
> Death and the curse are known no more;
> In him the tribes of Adam boast
> More blessings than their father lost.

TUNES: The choice is plentiful, including *Galilee* (P. Armes, 1836–1908); *Duke Street* (J. Hatton, d.1793); *Truro*, from *Psalmodia Evangelica*, 1789; and *Rimington* (F. Duckworth, 1862–1941).

167 Thou, whose almighty word J. Marriott, 1780–1825

John Marriott was a humble Oxford scholar and rector of an obscure country parish in Warwickshire. His poetry was of sufficient merit to attract the attention of Sir Walter Scott; but of all he wrote only this hymn now remains. Its survival may be due in part to its association with the tune *Moscow*, by the Italian-born composer Felice de Guardini (1716–96).

The hymn is built around Genesis 1:3 *AV*: 'And God said, Let there be light: and there was light.' In its entirety it is a prayer that the light of the gospel may dissipate the darkness of the world and heal the spiritual blindness of mankind.

The stanzas follow the traditional Trinitarian pattern. The first adheres to the Genesis story, with its reference to the 'darkness upon the face of the deep' which was dispelled by the creative word of God the Father. The second recalls Malachi 4:2, 'To you who fear my name the sun of righteousness shall arise with healing in his wings,' now applied to the healing ministry of Christ. The third alludes to the Holy Spirit under the symbolism of the dove, as at the Lord's baptism (Mark 1:10); but it also reverts to Genesis 1 – 'The Spirit of God was moving over the face of the waters' (v.2). The fourth stanza is a doxology addressed to the Triune God as 'Wisdom, Love, Might'.

TUNE: *Moscow* (see above).

168 Thy kingdom come, O God   *L. Hensley*, 1824–1905

The author of this hymn, Lewis Hensley, was a Cambridge Senior Wrangler – that is to say, a graduate who won first class mathematical honours. Ordained in 1851, he later became vicar of Hitchin, Herts, and an honorary canon of St Albans. He published two volumes of hymns; this is the only one of them that has survived. It was written in 1867 for use in Advent.

The writer looks out upon a world which, well over a century back, looks remarkably like our own: a world dominated by the tyrannies of sin, hatred and war, of 'lust, oppression, crime'. And he sees no hope for the future except in the coming of Christ and his kingdom. The final stanza as he wrote it begins, 'O'er heathen lands afar'; but heathen lands are not only afar and some modern hymnals wisely change this to 'O'er lands both near and far'.

TUNE: *St Cecilia* (L. G. Hayne, 1836–83).

169 O Spirit of the living God *J. Montgomery**, 1771–1854

Dr Erik Routley gave it as his opinion that among Montgomery's great missionary hymns this 'takes the highest place for good doctrine, literary skill and general grace'. He wrote it in 1823 for a missionary rally in Salem Chapel, Leeds. Its subject makes it particularly suitable for use at Pentecost, since the gift of the Spirit and the mission of the Church are inseparable.

The hymn is a fervent prayer for a fresh outpouring of the Holy Spirit in order that the Church may be endued with love and power 'to preach the reconciling word' throughout the world. This leads up to the cry:

> Baptise the nations; far and nigh
>   The triumphs of the cross record;
> The name of Jesus glorify,
>   Till every kindred call him Lord.

Montgomery added a further verse which few modern hymnals reproduce, and which some might consider to be an anticlimax; but it does complete the doctrine of the Trinity with its reference to the love of God the Father and the atoning work of God the Son:

> God from eternity hath willed
>   All flesh shall his salvation see;
> So be the Father's love fulfilled,
>   The Saviour's sufferings crowned through thee!

TUNE: *Winchester New*, from *Gesangbuch*, Hamburg, 1690.

170 I cannot tell why he,   *W. Y. Fullerton,*
whom angels worship   1857–1932

A hymn written for the haunting melody of the *Londonderry Air*. Some purists might frown on the idea, but at least William Booth would have approved. He didn't see why the devil should have all the good tunes. And apart from the tune, the hymn itself is a worthy one. Not surprisingly it has a strong missionary flavour, for its author, Dr William Young Fullerton, was a man with a warm missionary heart. As a young Baptist minister he conducted evangelistic missions in many parts of the British Isles, and later in life (1912) he became home secretary of the Baptist Missionary Society.

The message of the hymn, composed in 1929, is that Jesus came to be the Saviour of the entire world. To this end he lived and died (vv.1,2); and now he claims the nations as his heritage, and at last all lands shall worship him (vv.3,4). Note how each stanza consists of two distinct parts. The 'I cannot tell' lines in the first half are followed by the confident 'But this I know' ones in the second, and this change of mood exactly matches the tune.

TUNE: *Londonderry Air*, traditional Irish melody.

171 In Christ there is no east or west   *J. Oxenham*, 1852–1941

John Oxenham was the pen-name of William Arthur Dunkerley, who under that pseudonym enjoyed a wide repu-tation as a poet and novelist. He was a deeply committed Christian, a deacon of Ealing Congregational Church, where he conducted a Bible class.

His hymn was written for a London Missionary Society pageant at the Agricultural Hall, London, in 1908. There is significance in this fact, for the theme of the hymn is Christian unity – and unity and mission are inextricably linked. Perhaps the most arresting thing in the hymn is its description of the Church as 'one great fellowship of love throughout the whole wide earth'. The phrase expresses an ideal rather than a fact; yet love for one another is Christ's own ideal for his people and the mark by which the world recognises them as his disciples (John 13:35). For love is visible. It is not sentiment but service – and 'His service is the golden cord, close binding all mankind.' Again:

> Who *serves* my Father as a son
> Is surely kin to me.

So 'In Christ now meet both east and west,' for he himself is the centre of all real unity and 'All Christlike souls are one in him.'

TUNES: Various, including *St Bernard* (adapted from *Tochter Sion*, 1741); *St Stephen* (W. Jones, 1726–1800); and *Kilmarnock* (N. Dougall, 1776–1862).

172 God is working his purpose out

A. C. Ainger,
1841–1919

This popular missionary hymn was written in 1894 for the boys of Eton College by Arthur Campbell Ainger. He himself had been educated at the school, and after winning a first class in the Classical Tripos at Cambridge he returned there as a master. He remained till his retirement in 1901. He has been described as one of Eton's most distinguished and useful masters.

In addition to his *Eton Songs* Ainger wrote a number of hymns. This one, which was dedicated to Archbishop Benson, is the best known of those that have survived. It has the vigorous and challenging character that would appeal to boys. One can imagine it being sung with gusto by a thousand voices in the college chapel to the rousing tune *Benson*:

> God is working his purpose out as year succeeds to year,
> God is working his purpose out and the time is drawing
> near;
> Nearer and nearer draws the time, the time that shall surely
> be,
> When the earth shall be filled with the glory of God as the
> waters cover the sea.

The last line of each stanza ends with the same words, derived from Isaiah 11:9.

The hymn still has value in reminding us that God has a purpose for his world and that amid the events of history that purpose is being worked out.

TUNE: *Benson* (Millicent D. Kingham, 1866–1927).

173 Christ is the world's true light

G. W. Briggs★,
1875–1959

Canon Briggs described this as 'essentially a missionary hymn'. He wrote it for the Advent section of *Songs of Praise*, 1931. Its missionary character and cosmic outlook are evident throughout, from the first line onwards. The light of Christ is

> The daystar clear and bright
> Of every man and nation.

But further: Christ is not only the world's true *light*. He is also the world's true *peace*, the one whose reconciling power unites nations and peoples long divided by colour, class and creed:

> In Christ all races meet,
> Their ancient feuds forgetting . . .

So that:

> When Christ is throned as Lord,
> Men shall forsake their fear.

This means that Christ is the war-torn world's true *hope*; and the Church – one body in union with one Lord – should be a visible demonstration of that hope. A united Church provides in miniature the pattern for a united world. It is this thought that motivates the prayer with which the hymn ends: 'Come, Prince of Peace, and reign!'

TUNES: *Rinkart* (melody and bass by J. S. Bach, 1685–1750), or *Darmstadt* (melody by A. Fritsch, 1679).

174 Christ is the world's Light, he and none other
F. Pratt Green*,
*b.*1903

Dr Erik Routley described this as 'perhaps the most immediately successful hymn of the recent wave of modern hymn-writing in Britain.' It is almost certainly Fred Pratt Green's best known hymn. It was written for the Methodist supplement *Hymns and Songs*, 1967, to be used with the tune *Christi Sanctorum*, a melody derived from the *Paris Antiphoner*, 1681, and harmonised by R. Vaughan Williams.

The theme of the hymn is the uniqueness of Christ. He is the world's Light, the world's Peace, the world's Life – *he and none other*.

He is the world's *Light* because he is the revelation of God to mankind. 'If we have seen him, we have seen the Father.'

He is the world's *Peace* because in reconciling us to God he also reconciles us to one another. 'Who else unites us, one in God the Father?'

He is the world's *Life* because by his death he vanquished death and by his rising again he restored to us eternal life. 'He, who redeems us, reigns with God the Father.'

These three stanzas are concerned with the three great gospel themes of revelation, reconciliation and redemption. Therein lies the uniqueness of Christ. And that being so, what remains for us but to say 'Glory to God on high'?

TUNE: See above.

175 We have a gospel to proclaim   *E. J. Burns, b.*1938

Edward Joseph Burns, a Lancashire clergyman, wrote this hymn in the spring of 1968 in connection with the Bishop of Blackburn's 'Call to Mission'. The purpose of the 'call' was to awaken the churches of the diocese to their responsibility for local evangelism. In each deanery meetings were organised to provide instruction on four of the basic elements of the gospel: the Incarnation, the Atonement, the Resurrection and the Ascension/Pentecost.

Mr Burns composed the hymn for his own deanery of Chorley. Its contents and construction clearly reflect its origin. The bold affirmation of the first stanza serves as an introduction. The four stanzas that follow relate in turn to the four great themes of the 'good news' of Christ which it is the Church's task to tell forth:

> 'Tell of his birth at Bethlehem . . .'
> 'Tell of his death at Calvary . . .'
> 'Tell of that glorious Easter morn . . .'
> 'Tell of his reign at God's right hand . . .'

The final stanza provides a fitting conclusion to a hymn which is being increasingly used by the churches in fulfilling their evangelistic mission.

TUNE: *Fulda*, from William Gardiner's *Sacred Melodies*, 1815.

THE CHURCH TRIUMPHANT

176 For all the saints who from   *W. Walsham How*★,
their labours rest   1823–97

Many church people instinctively associate All Saints' Day
with Bishop Walsham How's famous hymn, undoubtedly the
finest of the many he wrote. It was first published in 1864 and
soon became immensely popular, sung to Sir Joseph Barnby's
For all the Saints which he composed for it in 1869. That tune
has now been superseded almost entirely by Dr Vaughan
Williams's *Sine Nomine* ('without a name') which he wrote for
the *English Hymnal*, 1906.

There is real poetry in this hymn. It has the imaginative
touch, the inspirational quality, required by a hymn on the
Communion of Saints. It originally consisted of eleven
stanzas. By common consent three of these (which referred
in turn to the Apostles, Evangelists and Martyrs) are now
omitted.

The hymn begins on the note of thanksgiving: thanksgiving
for the saints who by faith confessed Christ before the world
and found in him 'their rock, their fortress, and their might'
(vv.1,2). This leads to a prayer that we as Christ's soldiers
today may like them be 'faithful true, and bold' (v.3). Then
comes what is surely the pivotal verse, the heart of the entire
hymn (v.4):

> O blest communion, fellowship divine!
> We feebly struggle, they in glory shine;
> Yet all are one in thee, for all are thine.

Here we acknowledge the essential unity of the whole Church
of God in heaven and on earth as being 'knit together in one
communion and fellowship in the mystical body of Christ our
Lord' (Collect of All Saints' Day, *BCP*).

The remaining four stanzas fall into two pairs. The first pair
(vv.5,6) present a picture of the Church on earth as it bravely

continues its warfare, sustained by the hope of glory. The last pair (vv.7,8) set before us a vision of the Church in heaven, complete, victorious and glorified in the presence of the King.

TUNE: See above.

177 Give me the wings of faith to rise   I. Watts*, 1674–1748

Watts published this in his *Hymns and Spiritual Songs*, 1709, and entitled it 'The Examples of Christ and the Saints'. It is one of his masterpieces, both in form and language. Modern hymnals make no attempt to 'improve' it, apart from altering one line. No Christian poet, observed Arthur Gregory, 'has touched the sorrows of our hearts more tenderly or comforted the bereaved more wisely' than Watts has done in this hymn.

In developing his theme he first reminds us of the example of the 'saints' and their testimony to the triumphs of Christ's grace in their lives; and then he points us to the supreme example of Christ himself in whose footsteps they trod. The saints are *our* example only insofar as they followed Christ's example. And that is what we are called upon to do:

> Our glorious Leader claims our praise
> For his own pattern given;
> While the long cloud of witnesses
> Show the same path to heaven.

Here we may note that 'How bright these glorious spirits shine' (a paraphrase of Rev.7:13–17) is based on a hymn by Watts but has little of his original work in it. Completely revised and rewritten, it appeared in the *Scottish Paraphrases*, 1781.

TUNE: *Song 67* (Orlando Gibbons, 1583–1625).

178 Let saints on earth in concert sing   C. Wesley*, 1707–88

> Come, let us join our friends above
> That have obtained the prize,

> And on the eagle wings of love
> To joy celestial rise.

That is how Wesley began his fine hymn on the Communion of Saints and how it still begins in many hymnals. The popular version. 'Let saints on earth', made for *A&M* 1861, is a considerably altered one. The original hymn is the first of Wesley's *Funeral Hymns*, second series, 1759. As would be expected, the Methodist hymn books keep closest to this. Other books compromise and combine authentic Wesley with some of *A&M*'s adaptation. Happily they all retain unchanged the central stanza in which the sense of the one-ness of all God's people in heaven and on earth finds superb expression:

> One family we dwell in him,
> One Church above, beneath,
> Though now divided by the stream,
> The narrow stream of death:
> One army of the living God,
> To his command we bow;
> Part of his host hath crossed the flood,
> And part is crossing now.

As Dr J. E. Rattenbury comments, 'Death, it is true, like love, "renders all distinctions void", but it cannot destroy the fellowship which love makes.'

TUNE: *Dundee* (*Scottish Psalter*, 1615).

179 O what their joy and their glory must be   *P. Abelard, 1079–1142*
   Tr. J. M. Neale*, 1818–66

Peter Abelard, a French priest, was a man of brilliant intellect and passionate feelings. By his early affair with his beloved Heloise he brought disgrace upon himself, and to hide his shame he became a monk, while Heloise entered a convent. Many years later she was appointed abbess of a newly-founded convent near Nogent-sur-Seine. She and her nuns found themselves in need of many things, including hymns for their worship. She wrote to Abelard, explained the situation and

sought his help. Within a very short time he replied by sending
her a complete hymnal which he had compiled for the purpose, covering the whole liturgical year. It was an astonishing
achievement and demonstrated Abelard's outstanding intellectual gifts. From this medieval hymn book comes our *O
quanta qualia*, translated by Dr Neale and published in his
Hymnal Noted, 1858.

The hymn is a joyful celebration of the life of heaven. It was
designed to be sung on Saturday evenings in preparation for
Sunday, the Christian Sabbath. Hence the reference in the first
stanza to 'those endless sabbaths the blessed ones see'. And
again:

> There dawns no sabbath, no sabbath is o'er,
> Those sabbath-keepers have one and no more;
> One and unending is that triumph-song
> Which to the angels and to us shall belong.

TUNE: *Regnator orbis* (melody from La Feillée's *Méthode*,
1808).

180 He wants not friends that   R. Baxter★,
hath thy love   1615–91

The six stanzas of this hymn – first published as such in the
English Hymnal, 1906 – are a selection of verses from a poem
entitled 'The Resolution' in Richard Baxter's *Poetical Fragments*, 1681. It is dated 3 December 1663 and headed by the
note, 'Written when I was silenced and cast out.' Evidently at
that time of apparent forsakenness he found consolation in the
knowledge that he was not alone or without friends. By his
faith he was bound in the glorious fellowship of God's saints
both on earth and in heaven.

Baxter was a Puritan, and his verses bear witness to the
fact that the doctrine of the Communion of Saints is not confined to the Catholic or High Church tradition. Nowhere
is the doctrine stated more clearly or beautifully than in the
lines:

Still we are centred all in thee,
    Members, though distant, of one Head;
In the same family we be,
    By the same faith and Spirit led.

Before thy throne we daily meet,
    As joint petitioners to thee;
In spirit we each other greet,
    And shall again each other see.

TUNES: *Angels' Song* (Orlando Gibbons, 1583–1625);
Uffingham (J. Clarke, c.1673–1707); and others.

181 Jerusalem the golden   *Bernard of Cluny, 12th century*
                                         Tr. J. M. Neale*, 1818–66

This celebrated hymn is a very small part of an extraordinary
poem of nearly 3,000 lines entitled *De Contemptu Mundi* ('On
Contempt of the World') written by Bernard of Cluny. His
exact dates are unknown. Early in the 12th century he became
a monk and entered the great Abbey of Cluny – the largest,
wealthiest and most powerful religious establishment in
France – and remained there till his death. His poem, written
about 1145, is a burning invective against the wickedness,
vices and follies of the world. And by the 'world' Bernard
meant not simply society at large but the religious world as he
encountered it within his monastery. From the distressing
spectacle of what he saw around him he turned his thoughts to
the heavenly realm where such evils are banished for ever and
God reigns supreme.

From this long poem Dr Neale made translations of selected
passages and published them in 1858. They now appear in our
hymn books as four separate hymns: 'The world is very evil',
'Brief life is here our portion', 'For thee, O dear, dear country',
and 'Jerusalem the golden' – this last by far the best known.

Concerning the poem as a whole, Dr Neale wrote: 'The
greater part is a bitter satire on the fearful corruptions of the
age. But as a contrast to the misery and pollution of the earth,
the poem opens with a description of the peace and glory of

heaven, of such rare beauty as not easily to be matched by any medieval composition on the same theme.' It is this aspect of the poem that is represented in our hymn. Its imagery, as will be recognised, is borrowed from the book of Revelation.

TUNE: *Ewing* (A. Ewing, 1830–95).

182 Ten thousand times ten thousand   *H. Alford*, 1810–71

Henry Alford, Dean of Canterbury from 1857 till his death, is best known for his harvest hymn 'Come, ye thankful people, come' (284). That was written in 1844. His hymn on the Church Triumphant was a good deal later. He completed the first three stanzas in 1867 and added the fourth in 1870. The hymn was sung at his funeral on 17 January 1871.

Dean Alford was one of the leading New Testament scholars of his day. Not surprisingly therefore he derives the imagery of his hymn from the Bible, chiefly from the book of Revelation. St John in his vision of heaven saw a mighty throng around the throne of God, 'and the number of them was ten thousand times ten thousand', offering praise to the Lamb that was slain (Rev. 5:11,12). This becomes the hymn's starting point with its picture of 'the armies of the ransomed saints' entering the golden gates, their fight with sin and death finished for ever.

In the second stanza the 'rush of Alleluias' and the 'ringing of a thousand harps' are also from the Apocalypse (19:1,3,4,6; 14:2). The third stanza portrays the reunion with loved ones 'on Canaan's happy shore' and is designed to afford consolation to the bereaved. The final verse is a prayer for the coming of Christ, the completion of the Church and the consummation of the heavenly kingdom.

TUNE: *Alford* (J. B. Dykes, 1823–76).

183 There is a land of pure delight   *I. Watts**, 1674–1748

Isaac Watts was born in Southampton and spent his early life in the town. He was therefore familiar with the view across the gulf-river, Southampton Water, to the green meadows near

Netley on the other side; and it is that vista which is said to have suggested this hymn and inspired the lines:

> Sweet fields beyond the swelling flood
> Stand dressed in living green.

This may well be true. But Watts's mind was richly stored with biblical imagery and in the hymn he takes us to the Old Testament story of the exodus and the Israelites' first glimpse of the promised land across the Jordan after their forty years of wandering:

> So to the Jews old Canaan stood,
> While Jordan rolled between.

Watts thus uses the Jordan as a symbol of death and Canaan as a picture of heaven, the land of pure delight.

The hymn, published in his *Hymns and Spiritual Songs*, 1707, is entitled 'A Prospect of Heaven makes Death easy'. For the Christian believer death is not something to be feared, no 'King of Terrors'. It is but 'the narrow sea' which separates this life from the heavenly one and we can face it without fear:

> Could we but stand where Moses stood,
>   And view the landscape o'er,
> Not Jordan's stream, nor death's cold flood,
>   Should fright us from the shore.

TUNE: *Beulah* (G. M. Garrett, 1834–97).

SECTION FOUR
CHRISTIAN DISCIPLESHIP

REPENTANCE AND FORGIVENESS

184 Rock of ages, cleft for me   *A. M. Toplady, 1740–78*

The legend still persists that Augustus Toplady wrote this hymn while he was sheltering from a thunderstorm in a cleft rock at Burrington Combe in the Mendip Hills, Somerset. It is an attractive story but it has no historical foundation. It is true that Toplady was curate of the nearby village of Blagdon from 1762 to 1764, but the hymn was not written till twelve years later (1776). Further, the legend about his sheltering in the rock only began to circulate seventy years after his death.

Almost certainly he found the theme of his hymn in some words from Dr Brevint's *Christian Sacrament and Sacrifice,* 1745:

O Rock of Israel, Rock of salvation, Rock struck and cleft for me, let these two streams of blood and water which once gushed out of thy side bring down pardon and holiness into my soul; and let me thirst after them now, as if I stood upon the mountain whence sprung this water, and near the cleft of that Rock, the wounds of my Lord.

Here are the ideas which Toplady wove into his hymn and which underlie its message. It is a hymn about sin and salvation; or to put it in personal terms, about the sinner in his helpless need and Jesus Christ in the all-sufficiency of his atoning sacrifice. He, the Rock of ages, is the sinner's sole refuge. Man can do nothing to save himself. All his efforts are in vain. He can only cry:

> Nothing in my hand I bring,
> Simply to thy cross I cling.

Note the figures of speech used in this third stanza to describe saving faith: it is *clinging* to Christ crucified, *coming* to him, *looking* to him, *fleeing* to him. Nothing else is required on man's side. The grace of God does the rest. The secret of the hymn's popular appeal lies just here, that it deals with the two basic realities of the gospel, sin and grace.

TUNE: *Petra* 76 (R. Redhead, 1820–1901); or in USA *Toplady* (T. Hastings, 1784–1872).

185 Jesu, Lover of my soul   *C. Wesley**, 1707–88

Written not long after Wesley's evangelical conversion (21 May 1738) this hymn reflects the startling change which the experience made to his faith. He tells in his *Journal* how a month or two before the event, when he was seriously ill, his Moravian friend Peter Bohler came to visit him. 'Do you hope to be saved?' asked Bohler as he stood by the sick man's bedside. 'Yes,' answered Wesley. 'For what reason do you hope it?' asked Bohler. 'Because I have used my best endeavours to serve God,' said Wesley. Bohler shook his head but said no more. And Wesley wrote: 'I thought him very uncharitable, saying in my heart, "What, are not my endeavours a sufficient ground of hope? Would he rob me of my endeavours? I have nothing else to hold to."'

It was a very different Wesley who later wrote:

> Other refuge have I none,
> Hangs my helpless soul on thee.

Instead of resting on his own endeavours, he was now trusting wholly in what another had done for him:

> Thou, O Christ, art all I want,
> More than all in thee I find.

And again:

> Plenteous grace with thee is found,
> Grace to cover all my sin.

Here is the classical expression of evangelical religion, the language of a man who has found full assurance of salvation in Christ.

The hymn was criticised by W. E. Gladstone as lacking cohesion and being just a jumble of ideas and metaphors haphazardly strung together. But he was mistaken. A hymn is not to be judged purely as poetry. A good hymn may not necessarily be a good poem. It may fail as a poem and succeed as a hymn. History is agreed that 'Jesu, Lover of my soul' is not a failure. It is full of memorable pictures and phrases and has a way of speaking to the heart that is equalled by few hymns.

TUNES: *Hollingside* (J. B. Dykes, 1823–76), or *Aberystwyth* (J. Parry, 1841–1903).

186 Just as I am, without one plea   *Charlotte Elliott,*
1789–1871

At the age of thirty-two Charlotte Elliott, the daughter of the Revd Charles Elliott, suffered a serious illness which left her a semi-invalid for the rest of her life. A year or so later she passed through a spiritual crisis which resulted eventually in the writing of this hymn.

At the time her father was vicar of Clapham, London. There came to stay at the house the Swiss evangelist Dr César Malan, who observing the young woman closely felt that something was amiss. He therefore asked her outright if she were a Christian. She much resented the question and told him so. But later she apologised and told him that she did not know how to come to Christ. 'Come to him just as you are,' was the answer. She did so and found peace of heart.

Not till twelve years later did she write the hymn. She was then living with her brother Henry, who was vicar of St Mary's, Brighton. A big bazaar was being held in the parish to raise money for a new school; but when the rest of the household set out for it, she herself was too unwell to leave her room. Left on her own she was overwhelmed by a sense of her own weakness and uselessness and lapsed into a mood of doubt and despondency. Seeking something on which to rest her faith, she recalled the earlier crisis when she was anxiously seeking Christ and what Dr Malan had told her: 'Come to him just as you are.' The words took hold of her afresh that afternoon and brought her peace and assurance again. Reaching for paper and pencil she wrote with no apparent effort the words of this hymn which has brought consolation and help to untold thousands down the years. One stanza at least reflects her state of mind when she wrote it:

> Just as I am, though tossed about
> With many a conflict, many a doubt,
> Fightings within, and fears without,
> O Lamb of God, I come.

TUNES: *Misericordia* (H. Smart, 1813–79); *Saffron Walden* (A. H. Brown, 1830–1926); in USA *Woodworth* (W. B. Bradbury, 1816–68); and others.

187 I heard the voice of Jesus say   *H. Bonar**, 1808–89

This was once, and not so very long ago, the best known of Dr Bonar's many hymns. It now appears to have lost something of its popular appeal. As Dr Routley observed, some hymns edify one generation and miss the target with another. In any case a deeply personal and subjective hymn like this would not be everyone's choice; and admittedly it is more suitable for use in mission services than in normal Christian worship. Its charm lies in what Bishop Bickersteth called its 'severe simplicity'. It is one of Bonar's earlier hymns and was probably written for the children of his Sunday school.

He published it in his first collection of hymns in 1846 and entitled it 'The Voice from Galilee'. Each of the three stanzas falls into two distinct parts. In the first we hear the voice of Jesus, in words borrowed from the Gospels, inviting us to accept what he has to offer: rest from our burdens (Matt. 11:28), living water to quench our thirst (John 4:10),

and light for life's journey (John 8:12). The second part is our
response of faith to his invitation.

The traditional tune *Vox dilecti*, which Dr Dykes wrote for
the hymn when it appeared in *A&M* 1868, effectively marks
this change from the first half of the verse to the second. A
popular alternative tune is *Kingsfold*, an English folk-song
which Vaughan Williams arranged for the hymn in *EH* 1906.

TUNE: See above.

188 Amazing grace (how sweet   *J. Newton**,
the sound!)   1725–1807

> Amazing grace (how sweet the sound!)
>   That saved a wretch like me!
> I once was lost, but now am found;
>   Was blind, but now I see.

When John Newton wrote those words he was recording a
piece of spiritual autobiography. Before his conversion he had
been, on his own confession, 'an infidel and libertine', and had
lived a godless and dissolute life. But now all that was
changed. He had become a new man in Christ; and it was
God's *grace* that had done it – his free, unmerited, unlimited
love to sinners. That was why the word sounded so sweetly
to him.

To the end of his long and eventful life Newton never got
over the wonder of what God had done for him. Like the
apostle Paul he could say, 'By the grace of God I am what I am'
(1 Cor. 15:10). When a very old man he was questioned by a
friend about his health. He admitted that his powers were
failing and that his memory had almost gone. 'But,' he said,
'there are two things I can never forget, that I am a great sinner
and that Jesus Christ is a great Saviour.'

> Through many a danger, toil, and snare,
>   I have already come;
> 'Tis grace that brought me safe thus far,
>   And grace will lead me home.

TUNE: *Amazing grace* (American folk hymn melody), and others.

189 Eternal Light! Eternal Light! *T. Binney*, 1798–1874

> Eternal Light! Eternal Light!
> How pure the soul must be,
> When, placed within thy searching sight,
> It shrinks not, but with calm delight
> Can live, and look on thee.

God, says the apostle Paul, 'dwells in unapproachable light' (1 Tim.6:16). It is of that light, God's eternal light, that Thomas Binney writes in this hymn. He composed it around 1826 at Newport, Isle of Wight, where he was Congregational minister at the time. Three years later he went to London to serve the Weigh House Chapel, Eastcheap, and rapidly won fame as a preacher.

The idea of the hymn came to him one evening when after watching the sunset he saw the stars beginning to shine; and it then occurred to him that the sky is never without light. It has eternal light; and that same evening, before retiring to bed, he wrote the hymn. It asks and answers the question, How can fallen man with his darkened mind approach the presence of God and bear on his naked spirit 'the uncreated beam' of his eternal light? With man it is impossible. But what is impossible with man is possible with God:

> There is a way for man to rise
> To that sublime abode:
> An offering and a sacrifice,
> A Holy Spirit's energies,
> An advocate with God.

This is the answer of divine grace to the seemingly insoluble problem of human sin; and thus:

> The sons of ignorance and night
> May dwell in the eternal light
> Through the eternal love!

TUNES: Traditional, *Newcastle* (H. K. Morley, 1875); or *Binney's* (Eric H. Thiman, 1900–75).

190 And can it be that I should gain *C. Wesley**, 1707–88

Of all Charles Wesley's hymns this has always been a great favourite among the Methodists. It was published in London in 1839, a year after Wesley's evangelical conversion. Entitled 'Free Grace', it was probably written very soon after that event and is doubtless his own description of the radical spiritual change he then underwent. The verse of scripture that struck home to his heart at the time was Galatians 2:20: 'The Son of God loved me, and gave himself for me' – with its stress on the personal pronoun. Christ died *for me*! Wesley never ceased to wonder at the fact. So now he writes:

> Died he for me, who caused his pain?
>   For me, who him to death pursued?
> Amazing love! how can it be
> That thou, my God, shouldst die for me?

He goes on to dwell on the mystery and the mercy of the atoning sacrifice, the self-giving of the Son of God who 'emptied himself of all but love' to redeem mankind. Then comes the glowing stanza in which he portrays his conversion in language borrowed from the story of Peter's release from prison (Acts 12:6–9):

> Long my imprisoned spirit lay
>   Fast bound in sin and nature's night;
> Thine eye diffused a quickening ray –
>   I woke, the dungeon flamed with light;
> My chains fell off, my heart was free,
> I rose, went forth, and followed thee.

TUNE: *Sagina* (Thomas Campbell, 1825–76).

191 Jesus, whose all-redeeming love   G. W. Briggs*, 1875–1959

From Canon Briggs's *Hymns of the Faith*, 1957, and surely one of his finest hymns. Erik Routley described it as 'a perfect example of the hymn-writer's art, with its skilful blending of the very simple with the occasional great colourful word.'

The hymn's theme, Jesus the friend of sinners, reflects in particular Luke's portrait of him as the one who came to seek and save the lost and welcomed all who came to him. The self-righteous Pharisees were scandalised by the disreputable company he kept and complained, 'This man receiveth sinners, and eateth with them' (Luke 15:2AV). The accusation was true, of course – gloriously true; and it is that truth which finds expression in the first two stanzas (note that they are linked together):

> Jesus, whose all-redeeming love
>   No penitent did scorn,
> Who didst the stain of guilt remove,
>   Till hope anew was born;
>
> To thee, physician of the soul,
>   The lost, the outcast came;
> Thou didst restore and make them whole,
>   Unburdened of their shame.

The verses that follow dwell upon the love of Jesus for the lost (v.3), love as wide as the Father's boundless mercy (v.4), and concludes with a personal prayer of repentance and faith (v.5).

TUNE: *Stracathro* (melody by C. Hutcheson, 1792–1860), and others.

192 O happy day that fixed my choice   P. Doddridge*, 1702–51

John Bunyan in his spiritual autobiography, *Grace Abounding to the Chief of Sinners*, says that it is 'profitable for Christians to be often calling to mind the very beginnings of grace with their souls'. This in effect is what Dr Doddridge is doing in his hymn. With wonder and gratitude he is looking back to his conversion, to the beginnings of grace with his soul.

But what is conversion? One of the values of Doddridge's hymn is that it answers this question. Conversion, he reminds us, involves a *choice*: a deeply personal choice when we say Yes to Jesus as our Saviour and our God. It involves, too, a spiritual *transaction* between ourselves and him, a covenant relationship in which we become his and he becomes ours. And so drawn by his love – for the initiative is always his – we *follow on* in his service, *confess* him before men and find our *rest* in him. Such then is conversion. But it is no more than a beginning. It involves commitment to Christ for life:

> High heaven, that heard the solemn vow,
>   That vow renewed shall daily hear;
> Till in life's latest hour I bow,
>   And bless in death a bond so dear.

Many Christians, probably most, cannot recall precisely the 'happy day' of their conversion. With them it was not a sudden or dramatic affair. But whenever or however it happened they can thank God for the beginnings of his grace with their souls, though known to him alone, and daily renew their vows of love and loyalty to Christ.

TUNES: The chorus often attached to the hymn (not by Doddridge) is best discarded. A wide choice of LM tunes is then available, including *Melcombe* (S. Webbe the elder, 1740 –1816), and *Festus* (adapted from a melody in Freylinghausen's *Gesangbuch*, 1704).

193 Souls of men, why will ye scatter   *F. W. Faber**, 1814–63

Frederick William Faber was brought up in a strict evangelical and Calvinistic tradition. In his earlier years he had been strongly attracted by the *Olney Hymns*, and when he entered the Church of Rome it became one of his aims to write hymns for RCs with the same popular appeal as those of Newton and Cowper. He comes nearer to doing something like this in the present hymn than in any of his others.

In its original form the hymn had thirteen stanzas. Hymnals reproduce no more than eight, often less. Faber entitled it 'Come to Jesus', but that is not its major theme. As a whole, and in its finest parts, it is a superb expression of the Love of God. The original third stanza was:

> It is God: his love looks mighty,
>   But is mightier than it seems!
> 'Tis our Father: and his fondness
>   Goes out far beyond our dreams.

The verses that follow enlarge upon this. God's mercy is as wide as the sea. His justice is tempered by his kindness. He feels for earth's sorrows and failings. He welcomes the penitent sinner. There is grace enough for all:

> For the love of God is broader
>   Than the measures of man's mind;
> And the heart of the Eternal
>   Is most wonderfully kind.

TUNE: *Animae Hominum* (A. Blanchet, 1868–1926), and others.

194 Forgive our sins as we forgive *R. E. Herklots, b.* 1905

The idea of writing this hymn came to Miss Rosamond Herklots in a curious way. As she was digging up dock weeds in the garden one day she realised that just as their deep and stubborn roots were a hindrance to the growth of the nearby flowers, so the bitter resentments we harbour in our lives hinder our spiritual growth and need to be rooted out.

The thought developed into the hymn, written in June 1966 and printed soon afterwards in the parish magazine of St Mary's Church, Bromley, Kent. It was included in the supplement *100 Hymns for Today*, 1969, and since then has gained

wide recognition. Its theme – echoing in its opening line the
familiar words of the Lord's Prayer – is the incompatibility of
our asking God to forgive us when we are unwilling to forgive
others.

> How can your pardon reach and bless
>   The unforgiving heart
> That broods on wrongs, and will not let
>   Old bitterness depart?

It has been rightly said that 'unforgiving, unforgiven' is a
law of the kingdom of God (cf. Matt. 18:23–35). So the hymn
goes on to show us, in the light of the Cross, how vast is our
indebtedness to God and how trivial the debts our fellow men
owe to us (v.3); and in the last stanza we pray the Lord to rid
our souls of all resentment and to enable us to live in peace both
with him and with one another.

TUNE: *St Bernard*, adapted from *Tochter Sion* (Cologne,
1741). Other CM alternatives are available.

195 Thou didst leave thy throne   *E. E. S. Elliott*, 1836–97

This has been described as the Christmas hymn which is sung
at all seasons. It was written in 1864 by Miss Emily Elliott – a
niece of Charlotte Elliott (see 186) – and published a few years
later in a children's magazine which she edited for the Church
Missionary Society.

As a hymn intended for children it is rightly pictorial in
character. It has as its text Luke 2:7: 'There was no room for
them in the inn.' So it begins with Bethlehem and the
Saviour's 'lowly birth' in the stable. From there it moves on
through his earthly life and his homeless state, with nowhere
to lay his head (Matt. 8:20). And then it comes to the cross:

> Thou camest, O Lord, with the living word
>   That should set thy people free;
> But with mocking scorn and with crown of thorn
>   They bore thee to Calvary.
>   O come to my heart, Lord Jesus,
>   There is room in my heart for thee.

But Calvary is not the end. Heaven's arches that rang to celebrate the birth of Jesus (v.2) will ring again at his 'coming to victory'. And we pray that as now *we* find room for him in our hearts, so then *he* will find room for us in his heavenly home.

The prayer expressed in the refrain makes this a suitable communion hymn.

TUNE: *Margaret* (T. R. Matthews, 1826–1910).

196 I will sing the wondrous story   *F. H. Rowley,*
1854–1952

Frances Rowley was an American Baptist minister. In 1886, when he was in charge of a church at North Adams, Massachusetts, he had the assistance of a young colleague called Peter Bilhorn, who was a gifted singer. It was the era of Moody and Sankey, a time of religious revival. After one of the Sunday services, Bilhorn said to Dr Rowley, 'Why don't you write a hymn for me to set to music?' He agreed to do so and composed this hymn the same evening. Sankey included it in his *Sacred Songs* and it soon became popular.

It is an example of the American gospel song at its best. The evangelistic note is strong and clear. The 'wondrous story' finds its centre in Christ and the cross – 'the Christ who died for me' – and is illustrated by the parable of the lost sheep:

> I was lost, but Jesus found me,
>   Found the sheep that went astray,
> Raised me up and gently led me
>   Back into the narrow way.

TUNE: *Hyfrydol* (R. H. Prichard, 1811–87).

197 A Man there lived in Galilee   *S. C. Lowry,* 1855–1932

The popularity of this hymn is largely due to what has been called 'the ravishing Tyrolean melody' to which it is now sung. The tune, which is that of a carol from the Tyrol, first became known in Britain by its inclusion in the *Oxford Book of Carols*, 1928, to an arrangement by Martin Shaw.

When the hymn first appeared (in *School Worship*, 1926) it was set to the traditional English melody *Forest Green* which we associate with 'O little town of Bethlehem'. It then included a refrain to be sung after each verse:

> O son of man, O more than man,
>   Canst thou our comrade be?
> Then help us all, who hear thy call,
>   To rise and follow thee.

This is now omitted because the Tyrolean melody does not lend itself to the necessary repetition of its second half. In one respect the omission is unfortunate, for the refrain expresses our personal response to the Son of Man whose life and death and exaltation we celebrate in the three stanzas. However, there is plenty of simple gospel teaching in these verses and they make abundantly clear the claims of Christ upon our lives.

For Lowry's 'Son of God, eternal Saviour', see 291.

TUNE: See above.

FAITH AND HOPE

198 All my hope on God is founded   *R. Bridges**, 1844–1930
Based on J. Neander, 1650–80

This hymn should be ascribed to Robert Bridges rather than to Joachim Neander (see 12). The latter's *Meine Hoffnung stehet feste* simply provided a starting point and a theme. The verses, which were intended to be sung as a grace after a meal, were based on 1 Timothy 6:17, a passage in which the wealthy are warned 'not to set their hopes on uncertain riches but on God, who furnishes us with everything richly to enjoy'.

This may be said to be the theme which Bridges adopted and

developed. The believer must repose his hope not in man or
the passing things of earth (v.2) but in *God*, whose great
goodness calls forth our praise (v.4):

> Daily doth th'Almighty Giver
>   Bounteous gifts on us bestow;
> His desire our soul delighteth,
>   Pleasure leads us where we go.
>   Love doth stand
>   At his hand;
>   Joy doth wait at his command.

And the greatest of all God's gifts, as the final stanza asserts, is
'the gift of Christ his Son.'

Bridges' hymn was first published in the *Yattendon Hymnal*,
1899, and soon found a place in many other books. However,
it did not achieve its present popularity until it began to be
sung to Herbert Howells' inspiring tune *Michael*. He composed
it in the early 1930s at the request of the director of music of
Charterhouse School. Dr Howells related that on receiving the
request he wrote the tune at the breakfast table where he was
opening his mail. It was named after his son who died in
childhood.

TUNE: *Michael* (Herbert Howells, 1892–1983).

199 Fight the good fight with all thy might

J. S. B. Monsell*,
1811–75

Monsell's popular hymn was published in 1863 under the title
'The Fight for Faith'. But it is not in fact a Christian battle-
song, as the opening line suggests. Its fighting strength, as Dr
Albert Bayly remarks, lies in its imperatives, ten in all. In its
entirety it is a hymn of faith in its varied aspects. *Faith* is
certainly the hymn's main emphasis, as *Christ* is its key (the
word occurs seven times). It is a thoroughly biblical hymn.
Each of its four stanzas enshrines words borrowed from the
New Testament epistles, as follows (quotations are from
AV):

Stanza 1. 'Fight the good fight of faith, lay hold on eternal life' (1 Tim.6:12).

Stanza 2. 'Let us run with patience the race that is set before us, looking unto Jesus' (Heb.12:1,2).

Stanza 3. 'Casting all your care upon him, for he careth for you' (1 Pet.5:7).

Stanza 4. 'Christ is all, and in all' (Col.3:11).

Of Dr Monsell's numerous hymns only this and 'O worship the Lord in the beauty of holiness' (68) are now well known. He sought to introduce into his hymns a 'more fervent and joyous' note than was common in Victorian hymnody. He died tragically as the result of an accident when he was vicar of Guildford. The church was under reconstruction and while inspecting work on the roof he fell and sustained fatal injuries.

TUNES: *Duke Street* (J. Hatton, *d.*1793) is probably first choice. But note also *Cannock* (Walter K. Stanton, 1891–1978) and *Rushford* (Henry G. Ley, 1887–1962). *Pentecost* is best avoided.

200 My faith looks up to thee   *R. Palmer★*, 1808–87

Dr Ray Palmer became one of America's most distinguished Congregationalist ministers, but this hymn was written in his earlier days, shortly after he graduated from Yale in 1830 at the age of twenty-two. No particular occasion called it forth. He wrote it, he recalled, with very little effort as a spontaneous expression of his faith and of what Christ meant to him. When he had completed it he slipped the manuscript into his pocket-book, and there it remained until a few days later when he met in Boston the musician Dr Lowell Mason (1792–1872), who was then compiling a new hymn book. Asked by Dr Mason if he had some hymn he might contribute to the book, the young man took out his pocket-book and handed over his hymn. On reaching home Dr Mason was immediately struck by the simplicity and sincerity of the verses and composed the tune *Olivet*, with which the hymn has always been associated.

Meeting Palmer in the street some days after this, Dr Mason said, 'Mr Palmer, you may live many years and do many good things, but I think you will be best known to posterity as the author of "My faith looks up to thee".' The words proved prophetic to some extent. Dr Palmer wrote many other hymns in the course of his ministry, including 'Jesus, thou joy of loving hearts' (151); but his first hymn is the one by which he is best remembered 150 years and more later.

TUNE: *Olivet* (see above).

201 My faith, it is an oaken staff   *T. T. Lynch*, 1818–71

Few if any church people today will have heard of *The Rivulet*, a small collection of hymns published in 1855 by a Congregational minister, Thomas Toke Lynch. But at the time it aroused a storm of controversy because its contents – so its critics asserted – were more like nature poems than hymns and lacked any specifically Christian theology. To us now it all appears to have been much-ado-about-nothing, and in any case the controversy soon subsided; but unhappily it affected Lynch's already feeble health and hastened his early death.

From his *Rivulet* come several familiar hymns, including 'Dismiss me not thy service, Lord' and 'Gracious Spirit, dwell with me'; but probably the finest of all is this hymn which was entitled 'Faith in Christ'. The first three stanzas are affirmations of faith, which is likened to the Christian pilgrim's staff and the Christian soldier's 'trusty blade'. Christ is accordingly portrayed as the pilgrim-soldier's Guide and Captain. This leads appropriately to the fourth stanza, which is a prayer:

> My faith, it is an oaken staff,
>   O let me on it lean!
> My faith, it is a trusty sword,
>   May falsehood find it keen!
> Thy Spirit, Lord, to me impart,
> O make me what thou ever art,
> Of patient and courageous heart,
>   As all true saints have been.

TUNE: *The staff of faith* (traditional Swiss melody).

202 I'm not ashamed to own my Lord   I. Watts*,
                                                 1674–1748

In his *Hymns and Spiritual Songs*, 1707, Watts headed this hymn
'Not ashamed of the Gospel', and added the reference 2
Timothy 1:12: 'I am not ashamed, for I know whom I have
believed, and am persuaded that he is able to keep that which I
have committed unto him against that day' (*AV*). The hymn is
not only a bold confession of Christ. It is also an expression of
complete trust in him and a readiness to defend his cause. The
third stanza in particular echoes the apostle's words:

> Firm as his throne his promise stands,
>   And he can well secure
> What I've committed to his hands
>   Till the decisive hour.

Certain alterations were made to the hymn in the *Scottish
Paraphrases*, 1781, and these are adhered to in the *Church
Hymnary*. It was in this form that Professor Henry
Drummond sang it to the Scots melody *Martyrdom* on his
death-bed. When he had finished he exclaimed to his friend
Dr Barbour, 'There's nothing to beat that, Hugh.' He died a
day or two later.

TUNES: *Martyrdom* (H. Wilson, 1766–1824); *Kilmarnock*
(N. Dougall, 1776–1862); and others.

203 My hope is built on nothing less E. Mote, 1797–1874

A cabinet maker by trade and quite irreligious, Edward Mote
was converted under the preaching of the Revd John Hyatt, of
Tottenham Court Road Chapel. 'I went astray from my
youth,' he confessed. 'My Sundays were spent on the streets in
play. So ignorant was I that I did not know there was a God.'
His life underwent a complete change. He ultimately became a
Baptist pastor and for the last twenty-six years of his life
ministered at Horsham, Sussex.

The hymn, entitled 'The immutable basis of a sinner's
hope', was written about 1834. Concerning its origin, he told

how one morning during his working life, as he was walking up Holborn Hill, the refrain came into his mind:

> On Christ the solid rock I stand,
> All other ground is sinking sand.

Later the same day he wrote four verses to accompany the chorus and sang them to a sick woman whom he had been asked to visit. They brought her great comfort and she asked for a copy. Two other stanzas were added later and the completed hymn was published in Mote's *Hymns of Praise*, 1836. Bishop Edward Bickersteth called it 'a grand hymn of faith'. There is no doubt as to its clear evangelical message from its opening stanza onwards:

> My hope is built on nothing less
> Than Jesus' blood and righteousness;
> I dare not trust the sweetest frame,
> But wholly lean on Jesus' name.

TUNES: *St Catherine* (H. F. Hemy, 1818–88), or *Bute* (J. Currie, *b*. 1934).

204 Be still, my soul: *Katharina von Schlegel*, 1697–?
 the Lord is on thy side   *Tr. Jane L. Borthwick*, 1813–97

Jane Borthwick made her translation of the German original, *Stille, mein Wille; dein Jesus hilft siegen*, as long ago as 1855. By now it might well have been forgotten were it not for its association in more recent times with the chorale-like melody from the symphonic poem *Finlandia* by Jean Sibelius (1865–1957). It is not known who was first responsible for linking the words and music together, but they are admirably matched. The hymn has thus taken on a new lease of life.

Miss Borthwick was a devoted member of the Free Church of Scotland, actively engaged in missionary and social work. With her sister Sarah (Mrs Findlater) she published a series of translations of German hymns under the general title of *Hymns from the Land of Luther*. The present hymn, from the second series, is headed 'Submission', accompanied by the words of Jesus: 'In your patience possess ye your souls' (Luke 21:19 *AV*). This is the key to the theme which runs all through the hymn: the Christian's attitude of complete trust and submission to the Lord in times of grief, pain or bereavement.

TUNE: *Finlandia* (see above).

205   God moves in a mysterious way   *W. Cowper**, 1731–1800

This is the greatest hymn on the subject of divine providence, and only a man of Cowper's poetical genius and spiritual perception could have written it. No doubt it was born of his own experience. He had passed through a period of utter despondency when everything was dark, and life, it seemed, had no meaning. Then in God's mercy the cloud lifted. Faith and hope were rekindled, and he wrote the hymn, entitling it 'Light Shining out of Darkness'.

God moves in a mysterious way. The opening words provide a clue to what follows. They recognise that God's ways often *are* mysterious to us, 'unfathomable', beyond our comprehension. That is something we must accept. But it does not mean that life is all mystery and that we have nothing to hold on to when things are dark. *God* is there, in the situation in which we find ourselves. And he *moves*: he is active, not passive. He 'works his sovereign will' in that very situation. The dreaded clouds are 'big with mercy'; so we can take courage and believe in his benevolent purposes.

> Judge not the Lord by feeble sense,
>   But trust him for his grace;
> Behind a frowning providence
>   He hides a smiling face.

The text of scripture Cowper attached to the hymn was John 13:7 *AV*, the words of Jesus to his disciples: 'What I do thou knowest not now, but thou shalt know hereafter.' Life's mysteries will one day be made clear. This is the shining truth Cowper emphasises throughout. We may have sublime confidence in God's unerring wisdom, and we can trust him as fully in the darkness as in the light.

TUNES: *London New* (Edinburgh, 1635); *Dundee* (from the *Scottish Psalter*, 1615).

206 Nearer, my God, to thee   *S. F. Adams,* 1805–48

Sarah Flower Adams (her married name) was a Unitarian. She possessed considerable poetical talent and was a friend of Browning. This hymn and a dozen others were written for *Hymns and Anthems*, published in 1841 for use in Unitarian congregations. Her other hymns are now forgotten. 'Nearer my God to thee' remains as her memorial. It has been translated into many languages and finds a place in almost all hymnals.

The hymn is based on the well known Bible story of Jacob's dream at Bethel (Gen. 28:11–19). At the time Jacob was in dire trouble. He had grievously wronged his brother and miserably failed his God. Now he was a fugitive from both. But in his dream that night he saw a ladder reaching from earth to heaven, with angels ascending and descending it; and he heard God say to him, 'I am with thee, and will keep thee in all places whither thou goest.' It was a revelation of divine mercy. He learnt that God had not forsaken him after all. Wherever he might wander heaven was always open to him. God was nearer to him than he realised.

This is the background to Sarah Adams's hymn and this is the thought she develops. The refrain 'Nearer to thee' occurs twelve times in the complete five stanzas. Our trials – our 'crosses', the metaphor used in the opening verse – may bring us closer to God. But so also may our joys. The writer did not forget this and in her final stanza (omitted from many hymnals) she wrote:

> Or if on joyful wing
>   Cleaving the sky,
> Sun, moon, and stars forgot,
>   Upwards I fly,
> Still all my song shall be,

Nearer my God to thee,
Nearer to thee.

TUNES: Traditional, *Horbury* (J. B. Dykes, 1823–76).
Others: *Liverpool* (John Roberts, 1822–77); *Proprior Deo* (A. S.
Sullivan, 1842–1900); and in USA *Bethany* (Lowell Mason,
1792–1872).

207   In heavenly love abiding   *Anna L. Waring, 1820–1910*

Anna Waring was a Welsh woman, born in Neath, Glamor-
ganshire. She grew up as a Quaker; but later, drawn by her
desire for the sacraments, she became an Anglican. She taught
herself Hebrew and daily read the Psalms in the original
tongue. In Bristol she visited the prison and worked for the
Discharged Prisoners' Aid Society. She wrote thirty-nine
hymns, including 'Father, I know that all my life'.

The present hymn was published in 1850. Entitled 'Safety in
God' it is based on Psalm 23, particularly verse 4: 'Yea, though
I walk through the valley of the shadow of death, I will fear no
evil, for thou art with me'. Hence the lines:

Wherever he may guide me,
    No want shall turn me back;
My Shepherd is beside me,
    And nothing can I lack.

All through the hymn runs this note of serene confidence in
the Lord's unchanging love, his constant nearness, his watch-
ful care; and this means that the future is bright with promise:

My hope I cannot measure,
    My path to life is free;
My Saviour has my treasure,
    And he will walk with me.

My 'treasure' here means my heart, my supreme love.
    TUNE: *Penlan* (David Jenkins, 1849–1915).

208 O Love that wilt not let me go

G. Matheson,
1842–1906

George Matheson suffered a cruel affliction in his youth. From childhood his sight had been impaired and by his eighteenth year he became practically blind. Yet despite this handicap he graduated with academic distinction from Glasgow University in 1862 and went on to become one of the outstanding ministers and preachers of the Scottish Church.

Legend connects the writing of this hymn with his blindness. The story goes that the girl he was hoping to marry broke off the engagement on learning of his loss of sight and that it was this that turned his thoughts to the Love that would not let him go. But the story is purely imaginary. The hymn was not written till much later, when he was forty years of age. He had sustained a sad bereavement and as he sat in his study brooding over his sorrow on a summer evening in 1882 the words came to him by a sudden inspiration. Its composition, he declared, occupied only a few minutes. 'I was suffering from extreme mental distress and the hymn was the fruit of suffering.'

Ida and Leslie Church offer this helpful reflection on the four verses:

The Love that won't let go – but offers rest.
The Light that gives to eyes, blinded by sorrow, sight to see God's fairer day.
The Joy that comes in the dark and sorrowful hour and points to daybreak without a cloud in the sky.
The Cross that raises us when we have abandoned our selfishness and let Love in.

Dr Matheson explained what he meant by the term 'blossoms red' in the last verse: 'I took red as the symbol of that sacrificial life which had bloomed by shedding its life.' White blossoms come from prosperity, red from sacrifice.

TUNE: *St Margaret*, written for this hymn by Dr A. L. Peace (1844–1912) for the *Scottish Hymnal*, 1885.

209 Loved with everlasting love

G. W. Robinson,
1838–77

The Revd Henry Martyn (1781–1812), remembered and honoured for his heroic missionary work in India and Persia, made reference to this hymn in his *Journal* and wrote: 'Since I have known God in a saving manner, painting, poetry and music have had charms unknown to me before; for religion has refined my mind and made it susceptible of impressions from the sublime and beautiful.'

He was clearly referring to the hymn's second stanza:

> Heaven above is softer blue,
>   Earth around is sweeter green;
> Something lives in every hue
>   Christless eyes have never seen;
> Birds with gladder songs o'erflow,
>   Flowers with deeper beauties shine,
> Since I know, as now I know,
>   I am his and he is mine.

The hymn is not as well known now as it used to be, but for this stanza alone it could claim a place in our hymnals.

George Wade Robinson, an Irishman and graduate of Trinity College, Dublin, entered the Congregational ministry. In his short life of thirty-nine years he served churches in London (St John's Wood), Dudley and Brighton and published two volumes of poetry.

TUNE: *Everlasting love* (J. Mountain, 1843–1933), and others.

210 I bind unto myself today

St Patrick, 372–466
Tr. C. F. Alexander*, 1818–95

This is a free paraphrase and expansion of the famous *Lorica* or 'Breastplate' ascribed to St Patrick. The legend is that it was sung by the saint when as a Christian missionary he landed in Ireland in 432. The purpose of the song was to seek God's protection for himself and his monks against the pagan Irish king, whose forces were lying in ambush for them. Whatever truth there may be in the story (the details of which must be sought elsewhere) the Gaelic words of the *Lorica* are certainly very ancient, comprising at once an incantation, a war-song and a creed.

It seems that Mrs Alexander wrote the hymn in 1889 for the new and enlarged edition of the *Irish Church Hymnal*, which was published two years later. Dean H. H. Dickinson of the Chapel Royal, Dublin Castle, explained how it came about: 'I wrote to her suggesting that she should fill a gap in our Irish Church Hymnal by giving us a metrical version of St Patrick's "Lorica", and I sent her a carefully collated copy of the best prose translations of it. Within a week she sent me that exquisitely beautiful as well as faithful version which appears in the appendix to our Church Hymnal.'

The hymn rapidly found its way into hymn books, set to the traditional Irish hymn melody *St Patrick*, familiar to us in the arrangement made by Sir Charles Stanford (1852–1924).

TUNE: See above.

211 Firmly I believe and truly   *J. H. Newman**, 1801–90

Like 'Praise to the Holiest' (83) this hymn comes from Newman's *Dream of Gerontius*. The words are spoken by the aged monk as he approaches death. They are of the nature of a *credo*, a confession of Christian faith, and as such they found their way into *EH* 1906. They have since come into wide use in church worship.

The first four stanzas affirm faith in God the Holy Trinity; in the incarnation of the Son and his crucified manhood; in the sufficiency of his grace as the Holy and the Strong; in the Church and in 'her teachings as his own'. The fifth stanza is a doxology to end the hymn on a note of adoration.

One question arises. Are all the Church's teachings Christ's own? As a Roman Catholic Newman of course had no doubt on that score; he believed in an infallible Church. Many would be happier if the line were to read, 'And *his* teachings as her own'. All must agree that it is Christ's teachings that validate the Church's, not the other way round.

TUNES: *Halton Holgate* (W. Boyce, 1710–79), or *Shipston* (traditional English melody).

212 I am trusting thee, Lord Jesus   *Frances R. Havergal**, 1836–79

> I am trusting thee, Lord Jesus,
>   Trusting only thee;
> Trusting thee for full salvation,
>   Great and free.

This was Miss Havergal's own favourite among her hymns. It was found in her pocket Bible after her death. She wrote it while on holiday in Switzerland in 1874. In a letter to a friend that same year she related how her hymns came to be written. She refuted the idea that they were the result of any particular talent. 'I can never set myself to write verse,' she said. 'I believe my King suggests a thought and whispers me a musical line or two, and then I look up and thank him delightedly, and go on with it. That is how the hymns and poems come.'

'Trusting Jesus' is the title given to this hymn. Ever since she first trusted Jesus as her Saviour when a schoolgirl of fifteen she had possessed a strong and assured faith. And, for her, *faith* meant full and unreserved commitment to Christ as her Master and Lord. Here she is trusting him for 'full salvation': not only for pardon but for power, and for more still:

> I am trusting thee for cleansing
>   In the crimson flood;
> Trusting thee to make me holy
>   By thy blood.

This stanza is normally omitted, and probably rightly so; but it indicates what for *her* full salvation meant. The crucified Saviour was at the heart of her faith and the ultimate secret of her deeply consecrated life.

TUNE: *Bullinger* (E. W. Bullinger, 1837–1913), and others.

213 The Lord's my shepherd, I'll not want

Scottish Psalter, 1650

First published in the *Scottish Psalter*, 1650, and of virtually unknown authorship, this metrical version of the 23rd Psalm has now established itself as the universal favourite, firmly attached to the 19th century tune *Crimond*. It has been described as 'probably the most perfect metrical psalm in Christendom'. Queen Elizabeth chose it for her marriage service in Westminster Abbey, in 1947, and that at once made both words and music widely known.

Dr Patrick Millar, the leading authority on Scottish psalmody, in his analysis of the psalm concludes that it is an amalgam, combining elements from seven different sources. The composer of the tune was for long a matter of dispute, but there is now little doubt that it was written by Miss Jessie S. Irvine (1836–87), whose father was for thirty years minister of the church at Crimond in Aberdeenshire.

Many metrical versions of this best-loved psalm have been made over the years. Some of the earlier ones are desperately poor. Even Tate and Brady made little of it in their *New Version* of the Psalms, 1696. On the other hand there are some delightful and worthy paraphrases such as George Herbert's 'The God of love my shepherd is' and Joseph Addison's 'The Lord my pasture shall prepare'. For Sir Henry Baker's hymn based on the psalm, see 150.

TUNE: See above.

214 Lift up your hearts! We lift them, Lord, to thee

H. M. Butler, 1833–1918

This challenging and exhilarating hymn was written by one of the outstanding scholars of his day. At the age of twenty-six Henry Montagu Butler became Headmaster of Harrow, his old school, and remained there till 1885. He exercised an enormous influence over the lives of the boys (who included some of the future leaders of the nation) and revolutionised the school's whole approach to education.

He wrote the hymn in 1881 for the *Harrow School Hymn*

Book. It draws its inspiration from the *Sursum corda* in the Communion service, 'Lift up your hearts', followed by the response of the congregation, 'We lift them to the Lord.' The words are of very early origin. They are quoted by Cyprian, the 3rd century Bishop of Carthage, who interprets them as summoning the worshippers in the eucharist to fix their thoughts wholly on *God*.

This is the meaning Dr Butler attaches to them. His hymn compels us to face the fact that our lives have been too earth-bound. Our spiritual level in the past ('the former years') has been too low. So now the call comes to us to lift our hearts to a higher plane: above the dark and shameful things of life to him who is the Lord of Light and Truth (stanzas 2 and 3). But more. In the fourth stanza we are also bidden to lift to him, in prayer and dedication, every good gift with which he has endowed us, for 'Low lies the best till lifted up to heaven'. The final verse, with its reference to life's 'after years', is a reminder that the words were originally written with schoolboys in mind – and for them the future was all-important.

TUNE: *Woodlands* (written for the hymn by W. Greatorex, 1877–1949, when director of music at Gresham's School, Holt, Norfolk).

215 Lord of all hopefulness,   *Jan Struther*,
Lord of all joy   1901–53

Jan Struther was the pen-name of Mrs Joyce Placzek, adapted from her maiden name of Anstruther. A Londoner by birth, she followed a literary career and frequently contributed poetry and prose to various periodicals. She became well known for her novel *Mrs Miniver*, 1939, later made into a film.

This hymn was written for *Songs of Praise*, 1932, to fit the Irish tune *Slane* (see 262) at the request of Percy Dearmer. He described it as 'a lovely example of the fitting together of thought, words and music.' In *SP* it has the heading 'All-Day Hymn' and this denotes its distinctive character. In their final lines the four stanzas refer respectively to morning, noon, evening and night. The prayer in each is addressed to God in appropriate terms; e.g. in the first to 'Lord of all hopefulness,

Lord of all joy'; in the second to 'Lord of all eagerness, Lord of all faith'; and so on.

The whole hymn is a fine piece of literary craftmanship. But more: it is also a work with a warm human touch, a healthy spiritual tone, and well merits its popularity.

TUNES: *Slane* (see above); or *Minniver* (written for it by Cyril Taylor, *b.*1907).

216 Thou art the Way: by thee alone
G. W. Doane,
1799–1859

When the first edition of *Hymns Ancient & Modern* appeared in 1861 it contained only one hymn by an American author. It was this one, published in 1824 by George Washington Doane, who was later, in 1832, consecrated Bishop of New Jersey. He achieved distinction as a scholar, church leader and man of letters.

The words of Jesus, 'I am the way, the truth, and the life' (John 14:6), have been an inspiration to many in a variety of ways. Thomas Aquinas reflected on them thus: 'Without the Way, there is no going; without the Truth, there is no knowing; without the Life, there is no living.' Later Erasmus took the words and made them into a prayer. The University of Glasgow adopted them as its motto: *Via, Veritas, Vita*.

Bishop Doane fashions them into a hymn. As we sing it we acknowledge that Christ is all that he claimed to be: the Way by whom alone we come to the Father; the Truth who as the self-revelation of God 'true wisdom can impart'; and the Life, whose resurrection proclaims him to be the conqueror of death. The final stanza sums it up in the form of a prayer:

> Thou art the Way, the Truth, the Life:
>   Grant us that Way to know,
> That Truth to keep, that Life to win,
>   Whose joys eternal flow.

TUNE: *St James* (Raphael Courtville, 1697), and others.

217 How firm a foundation, ye saints of the Lord

? R. Keen,
c.1787

This hymn first appeared in a collection published in 1787 by the Baptist minister, Dr John Rippon. It had no author's name attached to it, simply the initial 'K'. Who this 'K' was remains something of a mystery. Happily however it is not a matter of any great importance and without going into the question at further length we may accept the general verdict that the author was probably Richard Keen, the precentor of Dr Rippon's church in London.

Whatever its precise origin, the hymn is a noble one, better known in America than in Britain and more familiar to Free Churchmen than to Anglicans. The hymnals make a selection from its seven stanzas. It is based on Isaiah 43:1–5 *NIV*, part of which reads: 'Thus says the Lord, "Fear not, for I have redeemed you; I have called you by name, you are mine. When you pass through the waters I will be with you . . . When you walk through fire you will not be burned . . . Do not be afraid, for I am with you."' The hymn dwells on this promise of divine protection and applies it to believers as they face the 'deep waters' and 'fiery trials' of life. Then at the end it moves away from its Old Testament background to this triumphant conclusion:

> The soul that on Jesus has leaned for repose
> He will not, he will not, desert to its foes;
> That soul, though all hell should endeavour to shake,
> He'll never, no never, no never forsake.

TUNE: *Montgomery* (probably by S. Jarvis, 1762).

218 Blessed assurance, Jesus is mine

Frances J. van Alstyne,
1820–1915

The American Mrs van Alstyne is best known by her maiden name of Fanny Crosby. Blind almost from birth, she wrote an enormous number of hymns and gospel songs. This, and 'To God be the glory' (44), are among the better ones that have survived. They were much used in the Moody and Sankey missions during the last century and now, after a long interval, some have become popular again through the Billy Graham crusades.

The present hymn is typical of the kind of gospel hymns Fanny Crosby poured out by the hundred. It is all very simple and truly evangelical; but while it has an emotional appeal it lacks literary form and poetical distinction. It is doubtless the rousing tune *Blessed assurance*, published in 1873, that has carried it along through the years. This was the work of Mrs Phoebe Knapp (1839–1908), the wife of a wealthy business-man, who in her day was one of the best known American writers of hymn tunes and sacred songs.

TUNE: See above.

219 Great is thy faithfulness, O God my Father
T. O. Chisholm, 1866–1960

This fine gospel song came to Britain from America through Billy Graham's Harringay crusade of 1954. Its author Thomas Chisholm, born in Kentucky, served in turn as a school teacher and journalist before becoming a Methodist minister. The hymn was published in 1923, set to the familiar tune written for it by William M. Runyan (1870–1957). He too was a Methodist minister and became widely known in America as a composer of sacred music and gospel songs.

That 'God is faithful' is one of the fundamental truths of the Bible, both Old and New Testament. A popular hymn cele-brating it is much to be welcomed. The first stanza empha-sises God's unchanging and unchangeable character. With him there is 'no shadow of turning' (cf. Jas. 1:17). The constancy of the created order bears witness to this, as the second stanza affirms. Best of all, there is the assurance of God's pardon, peace and presence, of daily strength and future hope – 'Bless-ings all mine, with ten thousand beside' (v.3). Hence the refrain:

Great is thy faithfulness! Great is thy faithfulness!
Morning by morning new mercies I see;
All I have needed thy hand has provided,
Great is thy faithfulness, Lord, unto me!

TUNE: See above.

220 When we walk with the Lord

J. H. Sammis,
1846–1919

> Trust and obey,
> For there's no other way
> To be happy in Jesus,
> But to trust and obey.

Dr Daniel B. Towner (1850–1919), musical director of the Moody Bible Institute, Chicago, recalled that during Moody's mission at Brockton, Massachusetts, a young man stood up at one of the testimony meetings and said, 'I am not quite sure, but I am going to trust, and I am going to obey.' Towner made a note of the words and passed them on with their story to John Sammis, a Presbyterian minister. He at once wrote the above well known chorus, enshrining the young man's testimony, and later added the four verses, beginning:

> When we walk with the Lord
> In the light of his word
> What a glory he sheds on our way!
> While we do his good will,
> He abides with us still,
> And with all who will trust and obey.

Towner composed the tune *Trust and obey* for the hymn, which he published in his *Hymns Old and New*, 1887. Sankey included it in his collections and it has remained ever since one of the most popular gospel songs.

TUNE: See above.

221 O Master, let me walk with thee

W. Gladden,
1838–1918

Washington Gladden was one of America's best known Congregationalist ministers. He served a number of pastorates, his last, longest and most influential being in Columbus, Ohio, where he remained for thirty-two years. His liberal theological outlook found expression in the 'social gospel' of which he was a powerful and fearless advocate.

The hymn by which he is now remembered was written in 1879 as a poem entitled 'Walking with God'. The opening lines provide the key to its message:

> O Master, let me walk with thee,
>   In paths of service glad and free.

The hymn develops the theme that to walk with God involves the service of mankind: bearing 'the strain of toil, the fret of care', being patient with the 'slow of heart', guiding 'the wayward feet . . . in the homeward way', and in ever closer fellowship with the Master working with patience, trust and hope, and 'in peace that only thou canst give'.

The hymn soon became very popular in the USA; but as it was often set to unsuitable tunes Dr Gladden stipulated that permission to reproduce it would only be granted if it were sung to *Maryton*, composed by Canon H. P. Smith (1825–98) for the hymn 'Sun of my soul'.

TUNE: See above.

222 Will your anchor hold in the storms of life?

Priscilla J. Owens,
1829–99

A hymn beloved by fisherfolk, lifeboat crews and seamen in general. Its author, Miss Priscilla Jane Owens, an American of Scottish and Welsh descent, lived in Baltimore and for fifty years engaged in Sunday school work. Most of her hymns, which include 'We have heard a joyful sound', were written for children's services.

This hymn follows a simple and well ordered pattern. The four stanzas pose a series of questions, all based on the imagery of the perilous sea, challenging our Christian faith in the great crises of life – and the final crisis of death. The refrain supplies the answer to the questions and is an affirmation of trust in Jesus:

We have an anchor that keeps the soul,
Steadfast and sure while the billows roll;
Fastened to the Rock which cannot move,
Grounded firm and deep in the Saviour's love.

For the biblical image of the anchor, see Hebrews 6:19.

The tune *Will your anchor hold?* was written by William J. Kirkpatrick (1838–1921), who is best known as the composer of the familiar tune to 'Away in a manger' (61).

TUNE: See above.

223 Lord, it belongs not to my care *R. Baxter**, 1616–91

St Paul found himself 'in a strait betwix two' when he confronted the issues of life and death, as he told the Philippians. 'My desire is to depart and be with Christ, for that is far better. But to remain in the flesh is more necessary on your account' (see Phil. 1:21–26).

Richard Baxter felt much like the apostle:

> Lord, it belongs not to my care
>   Whether I die or live;
> To love and serve thee is my share,
>   And this thy grace must give.

> If life be long, I will be glad
>   That I may long obey;
> If short, yet why should I be sad
>   To soar to endless day?

The hymn was first published in his *Poetical Fragments*, 1681. In a later edition he entitled it 'The Covenant and Confidence of Faith', with the added note: 'This covenant my dear wife in her former sickness subscribed with a cheerful will.' This referred to the fact that his wife had sung the hymn on her deathbed. The work as we have it is a shortened version of the original poem, which comprised eight stanzas of eight lines.

Richard Baxter, one of the greatest of the Puritans, was also, as George Macdonald remarked, 'One of the purest and wisest and devoutest of men – and no mean poet either.' The hymn reveals something of his poetical gifts, though the text has been slightly altered.

TUNES: Various, including *St Hugh* (E. J. Hopkins, 1818–1901); *Cheshire* (Este, *Psalms*, 1592); and *Song 67* (Prys' *Psalter*, 1621).

224 Abide with me; fast falls the eventide

H. F. Lyte★, 1793–1847

When Henry Francis Lyte wrote 'Abide with me' he was a dying man, and he knew it. Not surprisingly therefore it is a hymn about death. It was not intended to be an evening hymn. The words 'fast falls the eventide' refer not to the ending of the natural day but to the eventide of life. When Lyte wrote:

> Swift to its close ebbs out life's little day,
> Earth's joys grow dim, its glories pass away . . .

he was simply expressing what was true for him. For twenty-five years he had been vicar of the Devonshire fishing village of Brixham. Now, at the age of fifty-four, broken in health and saddened by dissensions within his congregation, he was about to depart to the south of France. On Sunday 4 September 1847 he preached his farewell sermon in the morning and rested in the afternoon. After tea he retired to his study. When an hour or two later he rejoined his family he held in his hand the manuscript of his immortal hymn. The following day he left for Nice, where he died of consumption on 20 November.

The hymn is based on the prayer of the two disciples on the Emmaus road when, at the end of their journey, they sought to detain the stranger who had joined them. 'Abide with us,' they said, 'for it is towards evening, and the day is far spent.' Thus invited he entered their home – and there, as he broke bread before them, they recognised him as the risen and living Lord. (See Luke 24:13–35.)

If the hymn is about death, it is also about the faith that faces death fearlessly and triumphantly in the light of the cross and the empty tomb. The Christian knows that because Jesus died, sin has been dealt with and put away; and because he lives, death has been overcome and the gate of everlasting life been thrown open wide. In that confidence he sings:

> I fear no foe, with thee at hand to bless;
> Ills have no weight, and tears no bitterness.
> Where is death's sting? Where, grave, thy victory?
> I triumph still, if thou abide with me.

Nurse Edith Cavell repeated the hymn as she awaited execution on 12 October 1915 and faced the firing squad with the words, 'Heaven's morning breaks, and earth's vain shadows flee'.

TUNE: *Eventide* (written for the hymn by Dr W. H. Monk and published in the first edition of *A&M*, 1861).

225 Now is eternal life   *G. W. Briggs*★, 1875–1959

> Now is eternal life,
>   If ris'n with Christ we stand,
> In him to life reborn,
>   And holden in his hand;
> No more we fear death's ancient dread,
> In Christ arisen from the dead.

In saying that eternal life is ours *now*, a present possession and not something that awaits us in heaven, Canon Briggs is affirming a great New Testament truth. St John's Gospel is full of it. Whoever believes in Christ *has* eternal life (3:16; 6:47; etc.). The believer has already passed from death to life (5:24), so that he who lives and believes in him shall never die (11:26).

This eternal life is not mere endless existence as we now know it. It is life of a new, divine, spiritual quality; and it is ours because:

> By death destroying death,
>   Christ opened wide life's gate.
> He lives, who died; he reigns on high;
> Who lives in him shall never die.

This is our Easter faith and experience as those who are risen with Christ. Eternal life is ours today and every day. For the believer it is Easter all the year round.

TUNE: *Christchurch* (C. Steggall, 1826–1905).

226 For ever with the Lord!   *J. Montgomery**, 1771–1854

James Montgomery declared that he had received more expressions of thanks for this hymn than for any other he had written except 'Prayer is the soul's sincere desire'. It is not as often sung nowadays as it used to be, but that may be due to its theme. Hymns about death and the life beyond require discriminate use. But for the type of hymn it is, Montgomery's is almost unsurpassed – 'sincere, restrained, an expression of living faith, not dimmed or entangled by a clutter of elaborate imagery or points of theological dispute' (H. A. L. Jefferson).

Montgomery published it in his *Poet's Portfolio*, 1835, headed, 'At Home in Heaven. 1 Thessalonians 4:17.' The text refers to Christ's coming for his people and declares, 'So shall we ever be with the Lord.' The hymn is largely woven round those words. It views our present life as a pilgrimage to heaven, the 'Father's house on high', from which we are separated so long as we are 'here in the body pent' – that is, confined. Yet even now we are not without the Lord's presence and help, and therefore we can face the last enemy with serene faith:

> So when my latest breath
>   Shall rend the veil in twain,
> By death I shall escape from death,
>   And life eternal gain.

TUNE: *Nearer Home* (I. B. Woodbury, 1819–58), or *Old 25th* (*Anglo-Genevan Psalter*, 1558).

227 My soul, there is a country   *H. Vaughan*, 1621–95

It is a strange fact that the *Sacred Poems*, 1650, of Henry Vaughan, the Welsh country doctor and metaphysical poet, were more or less forgotten for two hundred years until H. F. Lyte republished them in 1847. Dr Vaughan had been deeply influenced by the poems of George Herbert. The reading of them entirely changed his spiritual outlook and revolutionised his poetry. He nicknamed his devotional verse *Silex Scintillans*, 'Sparks from a Flint', the sparks being flashes of truth and the flint his own stony heart.

His poem 'My soul, there is a country' is a vision of heaven. He entitled it 'Peace', for

> There above noise, and danger,
>   Sweet peace sits crowned with smiles . . .

while the fourth stanza declares:

> If thou canst get but thither,
>   There grows the flower of peace.

The final verse begins 'Leave then thy foolish ranges' – an expression which some must find puzzling. To range is to wander; and so, as G. R. Balleine explains, our 'foolish ranges' are our aimless wanderings through life which the poet urges us to exchange for the peace and security of heaven. Henry Vaughan had lived much of his adult life during the Civil War. He was weary of strife and his longing for peace at last is all the more understandable.

TUNE: *Christus der ist mein Leben* (Melchior Vulpius, *c*.1560–1616).

PILGRIMAGE AND CONFLICT

228 Guide me, O thou great Jehovah   *W. Williams, 1717–91*

This hymn, a product of the Evangelical Revival in Wales in the 18th century, has gained immense popularity through its association with the tune *Cwm Rhondda*. It was composed for a Welsh song festival in 1905 by John Hughes (1873–1932), an official of the old Great Western Railway and precentor of Salem Baptist Church, Pontypridd.

William Williams, the author, is the foremost figure in the story of Welsh hymnody. Converted as a young man through the preaching of the revivalist Howel Harris, he took holy orders in 1740; but three years later he left the Established Church and spent the rest of his life as an itinerant evangelist. By all accounts he was a great preacher; but he was an even greater poet and has deservedly been called the poet laureate of the Welsh revival.

'Guide me, O thou great Jehovah' was published in Welsh in 1745. The English translation by Peter Williams (no relation) appeared in 1771. The imagery of the whole hymn is drawn from the story of the Exodus and the Israelites' journey through the wilderness to the promised land. Thus the 'Bread of heaven' (v.1) refers to the manna (Exod. 16:4–18; John 6:30–36); 'the crystal fountain' to the water from the smitten rock (Exod. 17:4–6). For 'the fiery, cloudy pillar' see Exodus 13:21; and for 'the verge of Jordan' see Joshua 3:14–17. Probably few people who sing the hymn realise that in the words 'Death of death and hell's Destruction' Christ is being addressed. He himself is the destroyer of death, the vanquisher of hell (2 Tim:1.10; Rev.1:17,18).

TUNE: *Cwm Rhondda* (see above).

229 Who would true valour see   *J. Bunyan, 1628–88*

Although John Bunyan's celebrated Pilgrim Song was written nearly 300 years ago, it did not find its way into our hymn books till 1906. It then appeared in the *English Hymnal* in Percy Dearmer's edited version as 'He who would valiant be'. At the same time it was set to the tune *Monk's Gate* which Dr R. Vaughan Williams (the musical editor of *EH*) composed for it, based on an old Sussex folksong.

Ever since then the tune has continued to be used for whatever version of the words is sung. On the other hand, Dr Dearmer's adaptation has tended to drop out of use and recent hymnals have reverted to the song as Bunyan originally wrote it.

It comes from the second part of *Pilgrim's Progress*, 1686, and is connected with Mr Valiant-for-Truth. This brave man tells Greatheart about his pilgrim life, of the trials he has met with, of the battles he has fought and won. At this point in the story Bunyan inserts the song. It is important to note that the words are not put into the mouth of Valiant, as though he were boasting of his valour and pointing to himself as an example. The words are not his but Bunyan's. Before proceeding with the story the author directs the reader to 'come hither' and take a good look at Valiant so as to see in him a picture of a courageous and victorious pilgrim.

This is the purpose of the song. The first stanza stresses the need for constancy in the face of discouragements; the second describes the fearless spirit with which the pilgrim must meet and conquer his foes; and the third points to the goal of the journey, the life eternal which is the pilgrim's heavenly inheritance.

TUNE: *Monk's Gate* (see above).

230 Children of the heavenly King   *J. Cennick*, 1718–55

Life is a journey. That is the theme of John Cennick's hymn; and its message is summed up in the line 'We are travelling home to God' (v.2) – words which indicate the direction and destination of the journey. We come *from* God; we are going *to* God; and to be *with* God is home.

How do we travel? Cheerfully, says the hymn, singing our Saviour's worthy praise and gladly leaving all below. And expectantly, too, with our eyes fixed on the celestial city where we shall see the Lord and be reunited with those who have gone before. It is all very simple, simple enough to be a children's hymn; but Cennick was a master of simplicity, and this in a hymn-writer is a virtue, not a fault.

Early in his career Cennick had close associations with Whitefield and the Wesleys. He himself was a Methodist convert and became the first Methodist lay preacher. Later he joined the Moravians and travelled far and wide as an evangelist in their service. He wrote a great many hymns. For his share in 'Lo! he comes' see 46. Apart from the present hymn the only other verse for which he is now remembered is the grace, 'Be present at our table, Lord'.

TUNE: *Innocents* (from the *Parish Choir*, 1850; probably by W. H. Monk, 1823–89).

231 O happy band of pilgrims   *J. M. Neale*, 1816–88*

> O happy band of pilgrims
> If onward ye will tread,
> With Jesus as your fellow,
> To Jesus as your Head!

Happy band? Is that the right word? According to the hymn the pilgrims have a lot to put up with on their journey: labour, hunger, trials, troubles, sorrows, temptations. What is Dr Neale thinking of?

When he published the hymn in his *Hymns of the Eastern Church*, 1862, he indicated that it was based on some verses of Joseph the Hymnographer (840–83), a Sicilian who in the service of Christ suffered persecution, became an exile and refugee, and later, captured by pirates, was taken as a slave to Crete. But his faith never faltered and he met all his hardships and deprivations in a joyful and triumphant spirit.

Neale acknowledged in due time that his hymn owed little if anything to Joseph. It was entirely his own composition, the outcome of his reflections on the man's heroic life. Evidently he saw in Joseph the pattern of a Christian pilgrim who cheerfully suffered pain, peril and persecution for his Lord.

There are two words in the hymn which show how we may find happiness in our pilgrimage. The first is at the beginning – *onward*. That indicates progress; but it is progress 'with Jesus' as our companion and leader. The other word is in the last stanza – *upward*: looking upward as we journey to 'where such a light affliction' will win us 'such a prize'. Sufferings borne for Jesus' sake are jewels of eternal value, rungs in the ladder that leads to heaven.

TUNE: *Kocher*, sometimes called *Barton* (J. H. Knecht, 1752–1817). Other choices are available.

232 Through the night   B. S. Ingemann, 1789–1862
   of doubt and   Tr. S. Baring-Gould*, 1834–1924
   sorrow

A hymn from Denmark – and the only well known Scandin-
avian hymn to find a place in our hymnals. The Danish original
was written by Professor Bernhard Ingemann, who won
national fame as the author of many historical romances as
well as poems and hymns. The English version by Sabine
Baring-Gould, published in his *People's Hymnal*, 1867, was
later considerably improved when it appeared in *A&M* 1875.

The hymn's imagery comes from the OT story of the
Israelites' journey to the promised land. This is given a
Christian interpretation and applied to the pilgrim Church on
earth. In the central verses the emphasis is on the Church's
unity. The word *one* is constantly repeated: one object of the
journey, one faith, one hope, one song, one conflict, one
march.

But unity is not the main theme of the hymn. 'The overall
impression it creates,' writes Erik Routley, 'is one of movement and pilgrimage, and in doing that it does good service . . . No church member can be anything but profited by
being reminded that he is a traveller, and that his journey is not
a fruitless one.' This then is essentially a song of *hope*. We are
pilgrims with a purpose. Far from drifting along in an aimless
manner we are on the march, with the promised land (heaven)
ever in view and with 'songs of expectation' on our lips. And
at last that expectation will be realised:

> One the gladness of rejoicing
> On the far eternal shore,
> Where the one almighty Father
> Reigns in love for evermore.

TUNE: *Marching* (written for this hymn in 1915 by Martin
Shaw, 1875–1958).

233 O God of Bethel,   *P. Doddridge*★, 1702–51,
    by whose hand   *and others*

This was David Livingstone's favourite hymn. He often sang it as he pursued his perilous journeys through darkest Africa; and it was sung by the great congregation that gathered for his funeral in Westminster Abbey in April, 1874.

The hymn as Doddridge wrote it, in five stanzas, differs a good deal from its present form. The original manuscript still exists, dated 16 January 1739, and headed 'Jacob's Vow; from Genesis 28:20–22'. The hymn is virtually a paraphrase of these verses:

> Jacob vowed a vow, saying, If God will be with me, and will keep me in this way that I go, and will give me bread to eat, and raiment to put on, so that I come again to my father's house in peace; then shall the Lord be my God.

The compilers of the Scottish paraphrases carried out a careful revision of Doddridge's work in 1745 and 1781; and in the process they made good use of a version of the hymn by John Logan (1748–88), minister of South Leith. The final result was the hymn as we have it today: a strangely composite production, as it has been said, yet of great excellence. The Scottish revisers replaced Doddridge's fifth stanza with one of their own, beginning 'Such blessings from thy gracious hand our humble prayers implore'; but surely the fourth verse makes a very satisfying finish:

> O spread thy covering wings around,
>   Till all our wanderings cease,
> And at our Father's loved abode
>   Our souls arrive in peace.

TUNES: *Salzburg* (J. M. Haydn, 1737–1806); *Martyrdom* (H. Wilson, 1766–1824); or *Stracathro* (C. Hutcheson, 1792–1860).

234 Lead us, heavenly Father, lead us   *J. Edmeston,*
                                                    1791–1867

James Edmeston was an eminent architect who spent most of
his life at Homerton in the East End of London. He came from
a Nonconformist background, but at an early age he joined the
Church of England and for many years served as church-
warden of his local church. Among his pupils was Sir Gilbert
Scott, whose grandson designed Liverpool Cathedral.

Edmeston had what Percy Dearmer describes as the 'regrettable practice' of writing a hymn every Sunday evening, to
be read at family worship. This explains why he wrote nearly
2,000 hymns in all. Of these, only 'Lead us, heavenly Father'
has gained widespread popularity. It was written in 1821
for the children of the London Orphan Asylum, to which
Edmeston was a regular visitor.

The hymn is a prayer, an invocation of the Holy Trinity, the
three stanzas being addressed in turn to the Father, Son and
Holy Spirit. It is the final stanza which has made it something
of a wedding hymn, with its references to 'heavenly joy' and
'love with every passion blending'. The second stanza is open
to criticism because it describes Jesus in the wilderness as 'lone
and dreary'. Alone, yes; but surely not *dreary*. To avoid this
difficulty the *Baptist Hymn Book* has altered the last two lines of
the stanza:

> Son of Mary, lone and weary,
>   Victor through this world didst go.

TUNE: *Mannheim* (F. Filitz, 1804–76).

235 Be thou my guardian and my guide   *Isaac Williams,*
                                                    1802–65

The Revd Isaac Williams was an Oxford scholar, a close friend
of Keble and Newman, and the author of one of the famous
'Tracts for the Times'. Among his poetical works he published
Hymns on the Catechism, 1842, from which the present hymn is
taken. It was designed to illustrate the petition in the Lord's

Prayer, 'Lead us not into temptation'. Its theme makes it specially suitable for Lent.

As the work of a man who had entertained hopes of succeeding Keble as Professor of Poetry at Oxford it is not a particularly distinguished piece of writing; but it has the merit of being short and simple and down to earth. It recognises the reality of temptation in human life; it reminds us of our own inherent weakness in the battle with sin; and it reveals the possibility of achieving victory through reliance on the saving power of God.

TUNE: *Abridge* (I. Smith, c.1735–1800).

236 Father, hear the prayer we offer   L. M. Willis, 1824–1908

Another hymn we owe to America. The original version by Mrs Maria Willis appeared in a monthly magazine in 1859 and began, 'Father, hear the prayer I offer.' Five years later, rephrased in the plural form and altered in several ways, it was included in *Hymns of the Spirit*, a Unitarian hymn book. It is noteworthy that the hymn has no specifically Christian content.

Mrs Willis was the wife of a doctor of medicine and spent most of her life at Rochester, New York. The idea behind her hymn is that there is an active as well as a passive side to the religious life. It is not simply a matter of resting in green pastures and beside still waters, as portrayed in the twenty-third Psalm. There is another side to the picture. Life is a 'steep and rugged pathway', and the hymn is a prayer that we may be given the courage and strength to tread it 'rejoicingly' with the Lord at our side.

TUNE: *Marching* (M. Shaw, 1875–1958), or *Sussex* (English traditional melody arranged by R. Vaughan Williams).

237 Lead, kindly Light, amid the   J. H. Newman★, encircling gloom   1801–90

Newman wrote this hymn in the summer of 1833 while a passenger on an Italian cargo boat heading for Corsica. He was returning to England after a holiday in Sicily, but the home-ward journey was irritatingly slow. 'We were becalmed for a whole week in the Straits of Bonifacio,' he wrote in his *Apologia*, 'and it was there that I wrote the lines "Lead, kindly Light" which have since become so well known.'

At the time, then aged thirty-two and vicar of St Mary's, Oxford, he was in an unsettled state of mind. He was already grappling with those deep religious questions which some twelve years later led him to enter the Church of Rome. Hence the lines he wrote that day were a prayer for divine guidance. When in due course he published the poem he entitled it 'The Pillar of Cloud', likening himself to the Israelites on their journey through the wilderness, led step by step by the light of God's presence. 'Lead thou me on': the phrase is repeated five times and is the essence of the prayer.

The three stanzas are concerned respectively with the present, the past and the future. In the first he acknowledges 'The night is dark, and I am far from home,' and in simple trust he asks to be shown the next step. In the second he looks back to his youth and recalls with shame how proud and self-willed he had been, choosing his own way, not God's. Then in the final stanza he faces the future and does so with serene confidence. There may be difficulties and dangers to be overcome, but he knows that the pillar of cloud will continue to illuminate his way until the darkness gives place to morning light.

TUNES: *Lux benigna* (J. B. Dykes, 1823–76); *Sandon* (C. H. Purday, 1799–1885); *Alberta* (W. H. Harris, 1883–1973).

238 A safe stronghold our God is still
M. Luther*, 1483–1546
Tr. T. Carlyle, 1795–1881

Of Martin Luther's thirty-seven hymns *Ein' feste Burg* is by far the best known. First printed in 1529, it is now sung in over fifty languages all round the world. English translations alone are said to number about sixty. Thomas Carlyle's translation is the most widely used in Britain; in the USA a version by Dr Frederick Hedge (1805–90) beginning 'A mighty fortress is our God' is the most popular. Both renderings powerfully express the fighting spirit of this 'Marseillaise of the Reformation', as Heine called it.

The first stanza is based on Psalm 46, 'God is our refuge and strength, a very present help in trouble.' Here in his battle for truth Luther sees himself in conflict with the devil, 'the ancient prince of hell', with all his supernatural power and cunning. Against such a foe 'force of arms' (i.e. human weapons) cannot prevail, and well he knows it (v.2):

> But for us fights the proper Man,
> Whom God himself hath bidden.
> Ask ye, Who is this same?
> Christ Jesus is his name –

and he, who is none other than the Lord of hosts, is unconquerable in the battle.

The opening lines of the third stanza –

> And were the world all devils o'er,
> And watching to devour us –

recall Luther's defiant words on his way to the Diet of Worms: 'Though there were as many devils in Worms as there are tiles on the roofs, I will go on nevertheless.' The final stanza makes special reference to God's word, 'written with his finger', viz. the holy scriptures, Luther's most trusted weapon.

TUNE: *Ein' feste Burg*, Luther's own tune to this hymn. He was a musician as well as a poet.

239 Oft in danger, oft in woe

H. Kirke White, 1785–1806, *and others*

A hymn with a strange and sad history. Henry Kirke White, the son of a Nottingham butcher, early developed a flair for poetry and attracted the attention of Southey. He won a scholarship to Cambridge and entered St John's College with a view to taking holy orders. He showed brilliant promise; but his health broke down through overwork and he died of consumption at the age of twenty-one. A few months earlier

he had sat an examination and having quickly completed the
task he occupied the remaining time in writing a hymn on the
back of the examination paper, beginning:

> Much in sorrow, oft in woe,
> Onwards, Christians, onwards go;
> Fight the fight, and, worn with strife,
> Steep with tears the bread of life.

Six further lines followed, all of them like 'worn with strife'
and 'steep with tears' reflecting his wretched state of health.

The hymn was left uncompleted; but in 1812 the fragment
was published by Dr William Collyer in his collected hymns,
with some added lines of his own, long forgotten. Next
involved was Mrs Fuller Maitland, who in 1827 published a
new version of the hymn in her *Hymns for Private Devotion*. She
had showed her eighteen-year-old daughter, Frances Sara,
White's unfinished lines and suggested she might like to
complete them. The girl went to her room and soon after
returned with the hymn in the form in which her mother later
published it – much the same as we now have it. A few minor
alterations were later made by Bishop Bickersteth when he
included it in his *Christian Psalmody*, 1833; and so in this
roundabout way the hymn has come into our books, with its
challenging call to arms in the service of Christ.

TUNE: *University College* (H. J. Gauntlett, 1805–76).

240 Onward! Christian soldiers   S. Baring-Gould*, 1834–1924

When in 1864 Sabine Baring-Gould became curate-in-charge
of the mission church at Horbury Bridge, near Wakefield,
Yorkshire, he found that one of the big occasions in the year
was the Whit-Monday procession when the Sunday school
children marched to a neighbouring village for a united festival. 'I wanted the children to sing when marching,' he wrote,
'but couldn't think of anything quite suitable, so I sat up at
night, resolved to write something myself.' The result was
'Onward! Christian soldiers'. Its subsequent popularity, he

declared, greatly surprised him; but undoubtedly Sir Arthur Sullivan's fine tune *St Gertrude* was an important factor.

It is very obviously a processional hymn. The Church is *marching*, and marching into battle. The 'cross of Jesus going on before' is of course the processional cross. The often-disputed words 'We are not divided, All one body we' had a purely local reference when Baring-Gould wrote them. He was thinking of the children of the two villages united in their common faith. We can understand that; but it must be admitted that to modern ears the hymn as a whole has a too martial, triumphal, even bombastic air to make it readily acceptable. Present-day hymns about the Church adopt a different tone. However, the lines which state that the Church will never be vanquished by 'the gates of hell' remain true, for:

> We have Christ's own promise,
> And that cannot fail.

The promise is in Matthew 16:18.

TUNE: See above.

241 Soldiers of Christ, arise   *C. Wesley**, 1707–88

Most of us are accustomed to singing this as a hymn of five or six short-metre verses. In the form that Wesley published it in 1749 there were no less than thirty-two such verses – an impossible length for a hymn. John Wesley recognised this and broke it up into three parts in his *Collection*, 1780.

The hymn is based on the well known passage in Ephesians 6:10–18 *AV* in which the apostle describes the Christian life as a spiritual conflict with the powers of evil and writes: 'Put on the whole armour of God, that ye may be able to stand against the wiles of the devil.' The Greek for 'whole armour' is *panoplia*, hence the reference to 'the panoply of God'. The armour is not of our own making. It is provided by God. All we have to do is to *take* it and use it – *all* of it. Hence:

> Leave no unguarded place,
> No weakness of the soul;

> Take every virtue, every grace,
> And fortify the whole.

And again:

> To keep your armour bright,
> Attend with constant care,
> Still walking in your Captain's sight,
> And watching unto prayer.

The imagery of the hymn, as commentators rightly point out, has a somewhat remote and unrealistic sound to us today. Armour has no place in modern warfare. But Wesley is merely using the biblical imagery, not his own, and whatever language is employed, the battle still goes on. There is nothing unreal about that. The Church on earth is always the Church militant.

TUNES: In SM version, *Ethelwald* (W. H. Monk, 1823–89); in DSM, *From strength to strength* (E. W. Naylor, 1867–1934).

242 Stand up, stand up for Jesus   G. *Duffield*, 1818–88

Dr George Duffield, a Presbyterian minister, stated that he caught the inspiration for this hymn from the dying message of a young clergyman of the Episcopal Church of the USA to the members of the YMCA in Philadelphia – 'Tell them to stand up for Jesus.' It was the year of the great American revival, 1858. Under the auspices of the YMCA the Revd Dudley Tyng had been conducting a mission for young men in the largest hall in the city. On the previous Sunday evening he had preached to a crowd of 5,000 from the text, 'Come now, ye that are men, and serve the Lord' (Exod. 10:11 *AV*). Hundreds responded to his call and enlisted in the service of Christ. On the following Wednesday he met with a terrible accident and died a few hours later. His friend George Duffield, visiting him on his deathbed, heard his last message and preached at his funeral, concluding his sermon with the lines of this hymn which he had written for the occasion.

Printed later in leaflet form, the hymn found its way into a church newspaper and thence into a new American hymn book. It was soon being sung all over the States and later made a big impact in Britain.

The story behind the hymn explains its distinctive character and challenging message. It is a summons to all 'soldiers of the Cross' to engage in the holy war (Eph.6:10–20) and to take a firm stand for Christ. In one stanza there is a reference to the text of Dudley Tyng's last sermon:

> Ye that are men now serve him
>   Against unnumbered foes;
> Let courage rise with danger,
>   And strength to strength oppose.

TUNE: *Morning Light* (G. W. Webb, 1803–87).

243 Jesus, good above all other   *P. Dearmer**, 1867–1936

Canon Percy Dearmer was one of the leading figures in the story of English hymnody in the first part of this century. His outstanding achievement was the editorship of *Songs of Praise*, 1925, and the enlarged edition of 1931. A considerable number of his hymns and translations are included in that book, under his own name or various initials.

Among his hymns in present use none is better known than the present one, which was intended for use by children. It is not entirely original, being based on a hymn by Dr J. M. Neale which begins:

> Jesus, kind above all other,
> Gentle Child of gentle mother,
> In the stable born our Brother,
>   Whom the angelic hosts adore.

With this verse, slightly adapted, as its starting point the hymn unfolds in a simple way the story of Jesus' earthly life, his death, resurrection and exaltation, and his sympathy with

212 CHRISTIAN DISCIPLESHIP

human need; and it concludes, as it begins, with a prayer for grace to persevere.

The hymn was originally written for the *English Hymnal* to carry the German 14th century carol tune *Quem Pastores*.

TUNE: See above.

LOVE, JOY, PEACE

244 Of all the Spirit's gifts to me   *F. Pratt Green*★,
*b.*1903

'The fruit of the Spirit is love, joy, peace . . .' writes St Paul in Galatians 5:22. They are not the only fruit: six others are listed. Nevertheless, as the hymn says, we 'take and treasure most these three'. *Love* naturally heads the list, for God is love and love is the summing up of all true spiritual life. This is the Spirit's primary grace:

> He shows me love is at the root
> Of every gift sent from above,
> Of every flower, of every fruit,
> That God is love.

Joy – Christian joy, not mere *joie de vivre* – springs from love; it is love singing and making melody in the heart, 'however great is my distress' (v.3). And *peace* is that serenity of mind which enables us to face each day and all the unknown future without fear (v.4). So love, joy and peace are ours in the Spirit – not simply to be possessed but above all to be shared in our needy world (v.5).

Dr Pratt Green wrote the hymn for a United Women's rally in Croydon in 1979, to be sung to the tune *Ripponden* by Norman Cocker (1889–1953).

TUNE: See above.

245 Hark, my soul, it is the Lord   *W. Cowper**, 1731–1800

This is surely the loveliest of all Cowper's hymns. It is also
one of the earliest he wrote. In many respects it is typical
of his work: deeply personal and introspective in character,
beautifully and poetically expressed, and rich in scriptural
allusions.

The hymn is based on the searching question Jesus put to
Simon Peter after the resurrection, 'Lovest thou me?' (John
21:15). Love certainly is the theme; but the stanzas are not
primarily concerned with *our* love for the Lord. They are
occupied far more with *his* love for us: the love that reveals
itself in what he has done for our souls (v.2), the love that far
surpasses human love at its best (v.3: 'Can a woman's tender
care . . . ?' – a beautiful paraphrase of Isaiah 49:15). And the
expression of this love reaches its peak in the magnificent
fourth stanza:

> Mine is an unchanging love,
> Higher than the heights above,
> Deeper than the depths beneath,
> Free and faithful, strong as death.

That verse, as Erik Routley rightly says, sets the scale of the
whole hymn and gives relevance to everything else in it. In the
end we can only say, in response to the initial question, 'We
love him because he first loved us.'

TUNE: *St Bees* (J. B. Dykes, 1823–76) remains the
favourite, but the hymnals offer alternatives.

246 Immortal love for ever full   *J. G. Whittier*, 1807–92

John Greenleaf Whittier, the American Quaker poet, is most
widely known as the author of 'Dear Lord and Father of
mankind' (256). He was the son of a New England farmer, but
as a young man – and much against his father's wishes – he
forsook the land and turned to literature, especially poetry. As
a Quaker he was not accustomed to singing hymns in worship;

but some of his verse quickly found its way into the hymn books and there it has remained.

His Christian faith was of a simple, mystical character. He had no interest in institutional religion and cared little for dogmas. For him, what mattered was not the Christ of the creeds but the Christ of experience. This is reflected in the present hymn, which is part of a long poem entitled 'Our Master'. The supreme emphasis throughout is on the *inwardness* of true religion. The 'immortal love' of God which 'our outward lips confess' can only be comprehended by the love of the heart. Christ is not past history, nor have we to seek his presence in the heights or depths:

> But warm, sweet, tender, even yet
>   A present help is he;
> And faith has still its Olivet,
>   And love its Galilee.

The hymn beginning 'O Lord and Master of us all' is a further selection of stanzas from the same poem and pursues much the same theme.

TUNE: *Bishopthorpe* (J. Clarke, *c.*1659–1707) is the favourite in Britain; in USA *Serenity* (W. V. Wallace, 1812–65).

247 Gracious Spirit, Holy Ghost   *C. Wordsworth**, 1807–85

St Paul's great panegyric of Love in 1 Corinthians 13 is one of the classics of literature as well as of scripture. That being so, it is surprising that so few attempts have apparently been made to produce a metrical paraphrase of it as a hymn. We must therefore be grateful to Bishop Wordsworth for his version, published in his *Holy Year*, 1862, for Quinquagesima Sunday. It has been subject to a certain amount of criticism for various reasons and it is certainly not free from fault; but a hymn about love deserves to be treated with charity.

The bishop wrote eight stanzas, covering the whole of the Pauline passage. Most hymnals print five or six of these. Some omit the verse:

Faith will vanish into sight;
Hope be emptied in delight;
Love in heaven will shine more bright;
    Therefore give us love.

The reason given for the omission is that Paul wrote, 'Now *abide* faith, hope, love, these three,' implying that they continue for ever and that therefore the hymn is wrong. But the apostle inserts before the verb the emphatic 'now' (*nuni*), which seems to mean 'now as things are', and this should not be overlooked.

The final stanza ('From the overshadowing . . .') refers to the Holy Spirit under the symbol of the dove, as at our Lord's baptism (Mark 1:10).

TUNE: *Charity* (J. Stainer, 1840–1901).

248 Sometimes a light surprises   *W. Cowper**, 1731–1800

How good it is to find Cowper in a serene mood. This is certainly the happiest of all his hymns. For a time, at least, the darkness that so often clouded his mind has lifted and he is surprised by joy. Cowper himself entitled the hymn 'Joy and Peace in Believing'. It is notable not only for its biblical language but also for its metaphors, all drawn from the world of nature.

The first stanza alludes to Malachi 4:2: 'The sun of righteousness shall arise with healing in its wings,' and to 2 Samuel 23:4: 'Like rain that makes grass to sprout from the earth'; the second to Matthew 6:34: 'Do not be anxious about tomorrow, for tomorrow will be anxious for itself.' The third stanza is based broadly on the words of Jesus in the same passage about how God clothes the lilies of the field and feeds the birds of the air (Matt. 6:28,26). The final verse is a magnificent paraphrase of Habakkuk 3:17,18:

    Though vine nor fig-tree neither
       Their wonted fruit should bear,
    Though all the field should wither,
       Nor flocks nor herds be there,

> Yet God, the same abiding,
>   His praise shall tune my voice,
> For while in him confiding,
>   I cannot but rejoice.

TUNES: Various, including *Offertorium* (adapted from M. Haydn, 1737–1806) and *Bentley* (J. Hullah, 1812–84).

249 Jesu, the very thought of thee   *Latin, 12th century*
*Tr. E. Caswall**, 1814–78

The Latin original of this hymn, *Jesu dulcis memoria*, used to be attributed to St Bernard of Clairvaux (1090–1153), the greatest of medieval saints. More recent research has established that this is almost certainly a mistake. In a study of the hymn published in Rome in 1944 Dom André Wilmart stated that the oldest manuscripts go back to about the year 1200; and he further affirmed that since the earliest and best texts were copied in England, and passed from England to France and Germany, 'It is difficult to resist the conclusion that the poem is the work of an Englishman, and written at the end of the twelfth century.'

This imparts a particular interest to the hymn from the English point of view. It contains many echoes of the genuine prose works of St Bernard and clearly owes not a little to him. The note of personal and passionate devotion to Christ, so characteristic of the saint, comes over in the translations. The best known of these is Edward Caswall's 'Jesu, the very thought of thee', a rendering of the whole poem in his *Lyra Catholica*, 1849. Dr J. M. Neale also produced a version of part of the poem beginning, 'Jesu! the very thought is sweet,' published in 1851. His translation is the more literal, Caswall's the more lyrical. In either case no more than a selection of verses is required for hymn-singing. Most hymnals break up their selection into two or three parts.

For 'Jesus, thou joy of loving hearts', derived from the same source, see 151.

TUNES: Various, including *St Agnes* (written for the hymn by J. B. Dykes, 1823–76); *Mendip* (traditional English melody); and *Metzler's Redhead* (R. Redhead, 1820–1901).

250 How sweet the name of Jesus sounds J. Newton*, 1725–1807

In his *Olney Hymns* John Newton gave as a scripture reference to this hymn Song of Solomon 1:3: 'Thy name is as ointment poured forth.' Ointment not only emits a sweet and fragrant odour; it also possesses healing properties. So does the name of Jesus for the believer:

> It soothes his sorrows, heals his wounds,
>   And drives away his fears.
>
> It makes the wounded spirit whole,
>   And calms the troubled breast.

But that is not what the hymn as a whole is about. It is a joyful celebration of the Saviour's name by a man to whom that name, which he had once blasphemed, had come to mean everything:

> Dear name! the rock on which I build,
>   My shield and hiding-place;
> My never-failing treasury, filled
>   With boundless stores of grace.

Note the titles applied to Jesus: rock, shield, hiding-place, treasury. But Newton cannot stop there. He is now in full cry and out of his rich experience he writes:

> Jesus! my Shepherd, Saviour, Friend,
>   My Prophet, Priest, and King;
> My Lord, my life, my Way, my End,
>   Accept the praise I bring.

The last two stanzas take up the theme of praise and develop it. Here on earth we cannot praise Christ as he deserves; but meanwhile we must use what remains of life and proclaim his love to the end of our days – as indeed Newton himself did.

TUNE: *St Peter* (A. R. Reinagle, 1799–1877), and others.

251 Happy are they, they that love God
R. Bridges*, 1844–1930
Based on C. Coffin, 1676–1749

The Latin hymn *O quam jovat fratres* by the French priest Charles Coffin (see 49) was rendered into English by John Chandler in the hymn beginning:

> O Lord, how joyful 'tis to see
> The brethren join in love to thee!

Dr Bridges's version, published in his *Yattendon Hymnal*, 1899, is quite independent of this. In fact it is not so much a translation as a free paraphrase of the first three stanzas, with two additional ones of his own.

The general theme of the original hymn is the unity of those who are brothers in Christ, as is clear from Chandler's translation. This theme underlies Bridges's hymn and it ends with an appropriate reference to the 'happy brotherhood' of Christ's people. In his second stanza he portrays them joining together in praise and prayer to God. In the third stanza, however, what in Chandler is 'the house of God' (the church) becomes the Christian home, blessed with the peace of Christ. The last two stanzas reflect on the thought that earth's sorrows are a path which leads us nearer to Christ and its pain is something God uses for the good of those who love him.

TUNE: *Binchester* (Wm. Croft, 1678–1727).

252 Come, thou fount of every blessing
R. Robinson, 1735–90

Born at Swaffham in Norfolk, the son of poor parents, apprenticed as a boy to a London hairdresser, and a somewhat dissolute youth – such was the unpromising beginning to the life of Robert Robinson, the author of this hymn. But then the grace of God intervened. At the age of seventeen he came under the influence of George Whitefield, was converted, and dedicated himself to Christ's service. Six years later (1758) when in charge of a Methodist chapel in Mildenhall, Suffolk, he wrote this hymn, a hymn of providence and grace, as it has well been called.

Clearly it reflects something of the author's own spiritual history and is an outpouring of praise for what God had done for him:

> Jesus sought me when a stranger,
>   Wandering from the fold of God . . .

And so he cries:

> Oh, to grace how great a debtor
>   Daily I'm constrained to be!
> Let thy grace, Lord, like a fetter,
>   Bind my wandering heart to thee.

The reference to his 'wandering heart' is not without significance. Robinson was a passionate and rather unstable character, and sad to say in his later life he lost the assured faith of his youth and drifted towards Unitarianism.

TUNES: *Ebenezer* (T. J. Williams, 1869–1944); *Corinth* (S. Webbe, 1740–1816); and others.

253 I'll praise my Maker while I've breath   *I. Watts*★, 1674–1748

This is one of Isaac Watts's versions of Psalm 146 in *The Psalms of David Imitated*, 1719, headed 'Praise to God for his goodness and truth.' The psalm begins with the words: 'Praise the Lord, O my soul! While I live I will praise the Lord; I will sing praises to my God while I have any being.' Watts treats the psalm with his customary freedom, but in the process he produces a magnificent hymn.

> I'll praise my Maker while I've breath;
> And when my voice is lost in death,
>   Praise shall employ my nobler powers;
> My days of praise shall ne'er be past,
> While life, and thought, and being last,
>   Or immortality endures.

The hymn was a particular favourite with John Wesley, who included it in his first collection of psalms and hymns published in Georgia in 1737. It was very much in his mind at the end of his life. He gave it out before the last sermon he preached at the City Road Chapel, London, on 22 February 1791. A week later, two days before he died, while in a state of great weakness, he astonished his friends by breaking out and singing with vigour the first and second verses. The following night, as his life ebbed peacefully away, he was heard often trying to repeat the hymn, but he could only get out, 'I'll praise, I'll praise'; and so praising his Maker with his last breath he ended his marvellous life of nearly eighty-eight years.

TUNES: *Monmouth* (G. Davis, c.1768–1824), or *Dresden* (J. Schmidlin, 1796).

254 Fill thou my life, O Lord my God   H. Bonar*, 1808–89

The whole of the Christian's life should be a doxology, giving glory to God. So the great Scottish hymn-writer teaches us in this hymn. He published it in the third series of his *Hymns of Faith and Hope*, 1866, and entitled it 'Life's Praise'. There were six stanzas of eight lines. Not surprisingly it has been shortened to about half that length in our hymnals and has benefited as a result. Bonar was inclined to be too prolific with his verse.

His theme is excellently expressed and illustrated in his hymn. He insists that the praise of the lips is not enough, nor even the praise of the heart. It is the *life* that matters – 'a life made up of praise in every part'.

> Praise in the common things of life,
>   Its goings out and in,
> Praise in each duty and each deed,
>   However small and mean.

Again, to praise God in church is insufficient, good though that be. In a stanza now omitted Bonar wrote:

Not in the temple-crowd alone,
Where holy voices chime,
But in the silent paths of earth,
The quiet rooms of time.

Thus the whole of life is sanctified and becomes a hymn of
praise to the Lord.

TUNE: *Arden* by Sir George Thalben-Ball (*b*.1896) is a
welcome alternative to the over-worked *Richmond* (T.
Haweis, 1734–1820).

255 Peace, perfect peace, in this   *E. H. Bickersteth,*
dark world of sin?   *1825–1906*

In August 1875 Edward Henry Bickersteth, then incumbent of
a church in Hampstead, was on holiday in Harrogate. On a
Sunday morning he heard a sermon in the parish church by the
vicar, Canon Gibbon, on the text, 'Thou wilt keep him in
perfect peace, whose mind is stayed on thee' (Isa.26:3 *AV*).
With the text and sermon much in mind he sat down after
lunch and within a few minutes composed the hymn. Later
that afternoon he read it to an aged relative, then on his
deathbed, whom he visited, and it brought comfort to the
dying man. It was published in the author's *Songs in the House
of Pilgrimage*, 1875.

The hymn takes the form of question and answer. The first
line of each verse (except the last) asks a question; the second
line supplies the answer. The questions are real enough. For
example, how can we find peace when there is so much evil in
the world? When we are overburdened with work? When
sorrows surge around us? When the future is uncertain and
unknown? The questions are many; but significantly the
answer is one and the same in every case. Each of the second
lines mentions the name *Jesus*. He is the ultimate answer to
every question.

Edward Bickersteth later became Dean of Gloucester, and
finally Bishop of Exeter. In addition to writing many hymns
and poems he was editor of the *Hymnal Companion to the Book*

of Common Prayer, 1870, which for the next sixty years super-seded all other Evangelical hymn books in the C of E.

TUNES: Either the traditional tune *Pax Tecum* (G. T. Caldbeck, 1852–1918), or the now-preferred *Song 46* (Orlando Gibbons, 1583–1625).

256 Dear Lord and Father of mankind   *J. G. Whittier,*
1807–92

This very popular hymn is derived from the poem *The Brewing of Soma*, 1872, by John Greenleaf Whittier, the Amer-ican Quaker poet (see 246). Soma was a drink brewed by the Indians to produce a state of religious frenzy in their endeavour to have communion with the deity. In the poem he draws a parallel between this and the stirring of the emotions in Christian worship through music, ceremonial, and the like, and writes:

> In sensuous transports, wild as vain,
> We brew in many a Christian fane
> The heathen Soma still!

From these 'foolish ways' (as he regards them) Whittier turns away in the stanzas that follow – the stanzas that make up our hymn – and describes what is for him the authentic spirit of Christ's religion: the Quaker ideal of simplicity, stillness, silence. Real worship, he insists, is something in-ward, not outward, concerned with the heart and life rather than with churchly activities. He illustrates his theme from scripture: the silent response of the first disciples to the Lord's call by the lakeside; the prayer life of Jesus in quiet communion with the Father; the manna noiselessly falling from heaven in the wilderness; the 'still small voice' with which God spoke to Elijah on Mount Carmel.

It is all beautifully done, with poetic artistry, and what is said is true as far as it goes. But it is only a half-truth. There is another side to the picture. The worship of the apostolic church was not silent but vocal and musical with 'psalms and hymns and spiritual songs'. Nor did it lack outward forms; the

Lord's Supper was faithfully observed in obedience to his command. Nevertheless we gratefully accept what the poet has to teach us about the place of silence in worship and the need to cultivate a calm and restful spirit in our daily lives:

> Drop thy still dews of quietness,
>   Till all our strivings cease;
> Take from our souls the strain and stress,
> And let our ordered lives confess
>   The beauty of thy peace.

TUNE: *Repton* (from the oratorio *Judith* by Sir Hubert Parry, 1848–1918), or *Rest* (F. C. Maker, 1844–1927).

CONSECRATION AND SERVICE

257 Take my life, and let it be
Frances R. Havergal*,
1836–79

Miss Havergal put on record when and how her consecration hymn (as she called it) came to be written. The date was 4 February 1874; the occasion was the end of a five-day visit to friends at Arley House, Worcestershire. She had prayed that God would so use her witness in the home that all ten members of the family might become genuine and rejoicing Christians. And he answered her prayer.

'Before I left the house everyone had got a blessing,' she wrote. 'The last night of my visit . . . I was too happy to sleep and spent most of the night in praise and renewal of my own consecration; and these little couplets formed themselves, and chimed in my heart one after another, till they finished with *Ever*, ONLY, ALL for thee!'

From this it is clear that she wrote the hymn in couplets, twelve in all, and in this form they were printed in her *Loyal Responses*, 1878. The first of them is general and introduces the theme:

> Take my life, and let it be
> Consecrated, Lord to thee.

The ten that follow are specific and show that true consecration involves the whole of life, the entire personality: mind and body, words and deeds, intellect and will – not forgetting money and possessions. The final couplet integrates these into one, namely the consecrated self.

In our hymn books the couplets are paired, to form six four-line verses. The author's father, the Revd Williams H. Havergal (1793–1870), a leading church musician of his day, wrote the tune *Consecration* for the hymn. It is often sung to the familiar *St Bees* by J. B. Dykes, or to *Nottingham*, a tune in former times erroneously ascribed to Mozart.

TUNES: See above.

258 O thou who camest from above   *Charles Wesley**,
1707–88

From Wesley's collection entitled *Short Hymns on Selected Passages of Scripture*, 1762. The scripture passage indicated is Leviticus 6:13 *AV*: 'The fire shall ever be burning upon the altar; it shall never go out.' The reference is to the Jewish burnt offering in which the entire sacrifice was consumed by fire and the fire was kept burning continually until the offering was completely consumed.

Wesley interprets this as a symbol of the Christian believer's entire and unceasing devotion to God. *Fire* is the key word of the hymn, as it was of the Wesleys' faith. Theirs was the religion of the burning heart. Charles once remarked that his spiritual experience at almost any time might be found in the first two verses of the hymn. The 'flame of sacred love' burned constantly within him and was expressed in 'humble prayer and fervent praise'. Objection has sometimes been taken to the word 'inextinguishable' in the second stanza as being too difficult to sing; but suggested amendments have not found favour. In the last line of the hymn the original reading was '*my* sacrifice' (as in *EH*). John Wesley changed the 'my' to *the*; but this destroys the antithesis between '*thy* endless mercies' and '*my* sacrifice'. Death is the Christian's final oblation and completes all that he has to offer to God in this life.

TUNE: *Hereford* (S. S. Wesley, 1810–76, sometime organist of Hereford Cathedral).

259 O for a closer walk with God   *W. Cowper*★, 1731–1800

As it happens we know the precise date of this hymn's composition: 9 December 1769. In a letter written to a friend the following day Cowper refers to the serious illness of his faithful friend and housekeeper, Mrs Unwin – 'the chief of blessings I have met with in my journey.' The poet was deeply anxious about what might befall her and of what would happen to him in the event of her death. It was a moment of spiritual crisis in his life; and he composed the hymn, he explains, in an endeavour 'to surrender up to the Lord' his 'dearest comforts'. The hymn is headed 'Walking with God' and the Bible reference is Genesis 5:24 *AV*: 'Enoch walked with God, and he was not, for God took him.'

After praying in the first verse for 'a calm and heavenly frame' and for light upon his way, in view of his troubled and uncertain state, in the next two stanzas Cowper looks back to his evangelical conversion: to the 'blessedness' he had known 'when first (he) saw the Lord' (v.2) and cries (v.3):

> What peaceful hours I once enjoyed!
>   How sweet their memory still!
> But they have left an aching void
>   The world can never fill.

Several hymnals omit one or both of these verses as being unsuitable for use in public worship. This is understandable. Yet the words strike a realistic note and answer to something that many Christians know to be only too true in their own spiritual history.

The fourth stanza is a penitential prayer to the Holy Spirit for the renewal of peace; the fifth a firm resolve to dethrone every idol that would usurp the place of God; while the final verse echoes the words of the first – not now in the form of yearning and longing but in the language of faith and certainty.

TUNE: *Caithness* (from the *Scottish Psalter*, 1635).

260 Teach me, my God and King   *G. Herbert**, 1593–1633

George Herbert is numbered among the metaphysical poets of the 17th century and this poem-cum-hymn is an excellent example of that aspect of his work. He entitled it *The Elixir*. The term refers to the search of the medieval chemists for a magical formula or touchstone which could turn base metal into gold. Herbert takes up this idea and asserts that there is indeed an elixir that can transform and ennoble the whole of life. It is found in the phrase 'For thy sake'. God measures the value of our service not simply by *what* we do but by *why* we do it. Our humblest deeds are turned to gold when our motive is solely the seeking of his glory.

This is the theme of the hymn, as the first stanza states:

> Teach me, my God and King,
> In all things thee to see,
> And what I do in anything
> To do it as for thee.

The poet provides a simple and homely illustration of how this heavenly elixir works:

> A servant with this clause
> Makes drudgery divine;
> Who sweeps a room, as for thy laws,
> Makes that and the action fine.

In his *Priest to the Temple* George Herbert wrote: 'Nothing is little in God's service. If it once have the honour of that Name, it grows great instantly.' Little is much when God is in it.

TUNE: *Sandys* (from Sandys' *Christmas Carols*, 1833).

261 Jesus calls us! O'er the tumult   *C. F. Alexander★,*
1818–95

Saints' days hymns are normally little used and therefore little
known. Mrs Alexander's hymn for St Andrew's Day is the
great exception. She wrote it for the SPCK's *Hymns for Public
Worship*, 1852, basing it on the Gospel of the day: the story of
Jesus' call, 'Follow me', addressed to the fishermen brothers
Simon Peter and Andrew by the Sea of Galilee (Matt. 4:18–20).

The hymn's theme throughout is the *call* of Christ. And it is
about priorities. Christ's call comes to us today just as clearly
as it came to Andrew long ago (stanzas 1 and 2). For him
it involved sacrifice: he 'turned from home, and toil, and
kindred' and left all for Jesus' sake. So must we (v. 3):

> Jesus calls us from the worship
>   Of the vain world's golden store,
> From each idol that would keep us,
>   Saying, 'Christian, love me more.'

This central stanza is also the heart of the hymn. It expresses
what is involved in Christ's call – both negatively and posi-
tively. We are called *from* love of the world, with its wealth and
idols, *to* a wholehearted love for him. He must be our first
love. Anything else is an idol. The fourth stanza illustrates this
further. Things like joys and pleasures as well as work and
cares may hinder our devotion to the Lord.

TUNE: *St Andrew* (E. H. Thorne, 1834–1916), or *Wrays-
bury* (E. J. Hopkins, 1818–1901).

262 Be thou my vision,   *Ancient Irish,*
**   O Lord of my heart**   *Tr. Mary E. Byrne, 1880–1931*
and Eleanor H. Hull, 1860–1935

We owe our version of this popular hymn, derived from an 8th
century Irish poem, to two scholarly Irish women. The words
were translated into English prose in 1905 by Miss Byrne, a
graduate of the University of Ireland and an expert in the
ancient language of her native land. Dr Hull, the author of

several books on Irish literature, then turned the prose into verse and published it in her *Poem Book of the Gael*, 1912.

The hymn is a prayer – a prayer for a vision of God, that he may be our all-in-all throughout life's journey. Take note of the personal pronouns. They provide the clue to the hymn and to what we are asking when we sing it.

TUNE: *Slane*, a traditional Irish air from Joyce's *Old Irish Folk Music and Songs*, 1920.

263 O Jesus, I have promised   *J. E. Bode*, 1816–74

John Ernest Bode may be classified among the 'one-hymn' writers. Like most such, he wrote a great many other hymns (he published two volumes of verse), but this is the only one that has survived. It was written about 1866 for the confirmation of his daughter and two sons when he was vicar of Castle Camps, Cambridge. It consisted of six stanzas. Most hymnals reduce it to four or five.

The hymn makes no particular mention of confirmation, though the opening line refers to the promises made by the candidates. But the hymn clearly has a wider use than as a confirmation hymn. It is a prayer for the realisation of Christ's presence at all times: in the battle with sin; amid the temptations of the world outside; when struggling with 'the storms of passion' within. It is a reassuring hymn, for in so far as it has to do with promises, the promises are mutual:

> O Jesus, thou hast promised,
>   To all who follow thee,
> That where thou art in glory
>   There shall thy servant be;
> And, Jesus, I have promised
>   To serve thee to the end;
> O give me grace to follow,
>   My Master and my Friend.

TUNES: *Wolvercote* (W. H. Ferguson, 1874–1950), or *Thornbury* (Basil Harwood, 1859–1949).

264 Thine for ever! God of love

Mary F. Maude,
1819–1913

Mrs Maude wrote this hymn in 1847 for the older girls in the Sunday school of St Thomas's, Newport, Isle of Wight, of which her husband was the vicar. She was helping in the preparation of the girls for confirmation when she was taken seriously ill. On her recovery she went away for convalescence and during her absence sent a series of letters to the girls. 'In one of these letters,' she said, 'I wrote, quite spontaneously, the hymn "Thine for ever! God of love". It was no effort to me whatever, the words came unsought.' The following year the letters were published in booklet form, including the hymn, which eventually found its way into *A&M* and other books as a confirmation hymn.

Understandably modern hymnals tend to omit the fourth stanza, beginning:

> Thine for ever! Shepherd keep
> These thy frail and trembling sheep.

Nowadays confirmation candidates – or anyone else, for that matter – would hardly relish being described in these unflattering terms. The Victorians, it seems, didn't mind so much.

The phrase on which the hymn is built, *Thine for ever,* comes from the Order of Confirmation in the *BCP*. At the laying on of hands the bishop prays, 'Defend, O Lord, this thy child with thy heavenly grace, that *he* may continue thine for ever . . .'

TUNE: *Newington* (Archbishop W. D. Maclagan, 1826–1910).

265 Breathe on me, Breath of God

Edwin Hatch,
1835–89

Edwin Hatch was an Oxford scholar who achieved international fame as a theologian. After ordination he served a curacy in an East End of London parish and in 1859 accepted an appointment as Professor of Classics at Trinity College, Quebec. Eight years later he returned to Oxford where he held various distinguished posts. Like many great scholars he was a humble, self-effacing man and his hymns were not published till after his death.

It was said of Edwin Hatch that his religion was 'as simple and unaffected as a child's'. This hymn bears witness to that fact. Yet there is profundity as well as simplicity in its prayer to the Holy Spirit. In both Hebrew and Greek the word for *spirit* is the same as that for 'wind' or 'air'; hence the Spirit of God may rightly be called the Breath of God. To breathe is to live. The Holy Spirit is the 'life-giver', as the creed states. 'Life anew', the life of the Spirit, is therefore the theme of this hymn. It reaches its climax in the final stanza with its reference to 'the perfect life of (God's) eternity', the life which is untouched by death.

TUNE: Choices include *Carlisle* (C. Lockhart, 1745–1815); *Veni Spiritus* (J. Stainer, 1840–1901); *Hampton* (Williams' *Psalmody, c.*1770).

266 Blest are the pure in heart   *J. Keble★, 1792–1866 and W. J. Hall, 1793–1861*

The authorship of this beautiful hymn has a curious history. John Keble's name is always and rightly attached to it, for it originated with him. But he was not the only person who had a hand in it. The other person was a less distinguished and little-known clergyman, but one who deserves to be named, for he had equal honours in creating the hymn.

It happened like this. In 1827 Keble published his famous *Christian Year*. In it was a long poem for the feast of the Purification (Candlemas), beginning, 'Blest are the pure in heart' – the *first* stanza of the hymn. The next fifteen verses are quite unfamiliar until we come to the final one:

> Still to the lowly soul
> He doth himself impart . . .

And thus we discover the hymn's *third* stanza. What then of the two remaining ones, the *second* and *fourth*?

It is here that William John Hall comes into the story. He was a minor canon of St Paul's and later vicar of Tottenham. In 1836 he published what became known as the *Mitre Hymn Book* and in it he included our hymn. He had taken the two stanzas of Keble's poem and (with his permission) welded them with two others of his own composition. The result is a hymn which despite its dual authorship possesses a marked unity and is a devotional gem.

TUNE: *Franconia* (W. H. Havergal, 1793–1870).

267 O for a heart to praise my God   *C. Wesley*★, 1707–88

Its opening line might give the impression that this is a hymn of praise. A closer look however shows that it is made up of prayer rather than praise; and the prayer is for true holiness of heart – 'a heart from sin set free'. Wesley headed the hymn with the words, 'Make me a clean heart, O God,' from Psalm 51:10 *BCP*.

What is the secret of a clean heart? The second stanza supplies the answer:

> A heart resigned, submissive, meek,
>   My great Redeemer's throne,
> Where only Christ is heard to speak,
>   Where Jesus reigns alone.

Perhaps that line, 'My great Redeemer's throne', is the key to the hymn. If we are to be holy Christ must not only reside in our hearts: he must rule them. Only so shall we have 'a heart in every thought renewed and *full of love divine*'. The Wesleys thought of Christian holiness in terms of perfect love. To be holy is to be full of love, like Christ himself. Hence the hymn ends fittingly with the prayer:

> Thy nature, gracious Lord, impart;
>   Come quickly from above,
> Write thy new name upon my heart,
>   Thy new, best name of love.

TUNE: *Stockton* (T. Wright, 1763–1829), or *Abridge* (I. Smith, *c.*1725–1800).

268 Love divine, all loves excelling
C. Wesley*,
1707–88

Wesley got the idea of this hymn from a popular song of the day, some verses from Dryden's play *King Arthur* set to music by Purcell, beginning:

> Fairest isle, all isles excelling,
>   Seat of pleasure and of loves,
> Venus here will choose her dwelling,
>   And forsake her Cyprian groves.

The words and music between them set the poet's imagination to work. The theme that suggested itself to him was that of divine love, and the hymn that resulted is a prayer for that love to enter into our lives. The prayer is addressed to Christ, and its essence is that he may come to us personally and 'fix in us (his) humble dwelling'. Hence the couplet:

> Visit us with thy salvation,
>   Enter every trembling heart.

This prayer for Christ's indwelling presence is also a prayer for sanctification. The one follows from the other:

> Finish then thy new creation,
>   Pure and spotless let us be.

It is known that Wesley originally wrote *sinless* for 'spotless'. Probably his brother John made the change. But both brothers firmly believed that God's 'great salvation' was sufficient to deliver the Christian from the power as well as from the guilt of sin, so that those who are his 'new creation' in Christ (2 Cor.5:17) are enabled consistently to lead pure, strong and holy lives. This is true sanctification; and even now we are being 'changed from glory into glory' (2 Cor.

3:18), till at last we take our place in heaven. And that will be glorification.

TUNES: The choice probably lies between *Love Divine* (J. Stainer, 1840–1901), *Hyfrydol* (R. H. Prichard, 1811–87), and *Blaenwern* (W. P. Rowlands, 1860–1937).

269 Who is on the Lord's side? *Frances R. Havergal*, 1836–79*

This is not, as might appear at first sight, an evangelistic hymn, a call to the unconverted. It is a summons to professing Christians to give themselves wholeheartedly to the service of Christ. Miss Havergal wrote it in 1877 and published it the following year in her *Loyal Responses*, heading it with the text, 'Thine are we, David, and on thy side, thou son of Jesse' (1 Chr. 12:18). The men who spoke those words were pledging their loyalty to the king; and this is the key to the understanding of the hymn:

> Who is on the Lord's side?
> Who will serve the King?
> Who will be his helpers,
> Other lives to bring?

The hymn is about serving the King. And clearly by such service Miss Havergal does not mean doing odds and ends of church work, but winning others for Christ – the greatest service we can render. She also makes it plain that this is costly service. She describes it in military terms. The servant is the soldier, entering the King's army, fighting under his banner, facing a strong foe. Such is Christ's call to us. Our response to the call is expressed in the varied refrains which follow the stanzas.

The author's own tune for the hymn, *Hermas*, has been superseded by either *Armageddon* (a German melody adapted by J. Goss, 1800–80) or the more recent Welsh tune *Rachie* (Caradog Roberts, 1879–1935).

TUNE: See above.

270 May the mind of Christ my Saviour

Katie B. Wilkinson,
1859–1928

Written it is believed about 1912, this hymn was first published in the Children's Special Service Mission hymnal,
Golden Bells, 1925. It has long been a favourite in Evangelical
circles and now appears to have an even wider appeal. It is
essentially a hymn of dedication, expressed in a prayer for a life
in conformity to the mind of Christ (Phil. 2:5), enriched by the
Word of God, ruled by the peace of God (cf. Col. 3:15) and
filled with the love of Jesus. The final stanza is omitted in some
books:

> May his beauty rest upon me
>   As I seek the lost to win,
> And may they forget the channel,
>   Seeing only him.

Little is known of the author, Mrs Katie Barclay Wilkinson.
She was a member of the Church of England and is chiefly
remembered for her Christian work among girls in West
London. The familiar tune *St Leonards* was written for the
hymn by Arthur Cyril Barham-Gould (1891–1953), sometime vicar of St Paul's, Onslow Square, London. He was
living at St Leonards-on-Sea when he composed it.

TUNE: *St Leonards* (see above).

271 Faithful vigil ended

T. Dudley-Smith*, b. 1926

Bishop Dudley-Smith wrote this hymn at Eastbourne in the
summer of 1967 in order to provide a metrical version of the
Nunc Dimittis (Luke 2:29–32) as a companion to his well
known *Magnificat*: 'Tell out, my soul' (written in 1961; see 39).
As in the case of the latter, he based his hymn on the text of the
New English Bible which reads:

> This day, Master, thou givest thy servant his discharge in
>   peace; now thy promise is fulfilled.
> For I have seen with my own eyes the deliverance which

thou hast made ready in full view of all the nations:
a light that will bc a rcvclation to thc hcathcn, and glory to
   thy people Israel.

The hymn adheres closely to the *NEB* and therefore retains
the 'thee' and 'thou' forms, but it can readily be adapted to a
'you' version if preferred.
   In his song Simeon asks for 'his discharge in peace' (v. 1), for
God has fulfilled his promise to him that he would not die
before he had seen the Messiah. Now that moment has come
(v. 2):

> All thy Spirit promised,
>   All the Father willed,
> Now these eyes behold it
>   Perfectly fulfilled.

The song also foresees in the coming of Christ the accomplishment of God's saving purpose for all mankind; for the
messianic deliverance is to bring light to the dark pagan world
(cf. Isa. 49:6) as well as glory to Israel (v. 3).
   TUNES: *Faithful vigil* (D. G. Wilson, *b.* 1940); *Pastor Pas-*
torum (F. Silcher, 1789–1860); and others.

272 O Jesus Christ, grow   J. C. Lavater, 1741–1801
thou in me   Tr. Elizabeth L. Smith, 1817–98

The Lutheran pastor, Johann Caspar Lavater, exercised an
influential ministry in Zurich and was one of the most revered
German hymn-writers of his day. But his hymns – 'simple,
fresh, and popular in style,' as *Julian* describes them – were
more suited for private or family use than public worship. He
wrote 700 in all. The present one, *O Jesus Christ, wachs in mir*, is
considered to be his best. It was published in his *Christliche*
Lieder, 1780, headed 'Christ must increase, but I must de-
crease' (John 3:30). The translation by Mrs Elizabeth Lee
Smith, the wife of Dr Boyton Smith, of Union Seminary,
New York, first appeared in Britain in 1860.
   Lavater, though no scholar or theologian, was greatly loved

as a warm-hearted pastor and evangelical preacher. His deep devotional life is reflected in this hymn, which is a prayer for daily and continuous progress in the way of holiness through Christ's indwelling presence. Two stanzas will illustrate.

> Make this poor self grow less and less,
>   Be thou my life and aim;
> O make me daily, through thy grace,
>   More worthy of thy name.

> Let faith in thee and in thy might
>   My every motive move;
> Be thou alone my soul's delight,
>   My passion and my love.

TUNE: *Waverley* (R. Redhead, 1820–1901), and others.

SECTION FIVE
TIMES, SEASONS, OCCASIONS

MORNING

273 Christ, whose glory fills the skies   *C. Wesley**,
1707–88

Charles Wesley's lyrical 'Morning Hymn', published in 1740,
is characteristically different from the traditional type. It
makes no reference to the night's rest, the gift of sleep, the
tasks and perils of the day ahead. The poet's mind is on
Christ – and the hymn's opening word is the key to what
follows. We begin the day with Christ, whose glory fills the
skies (Ps. 19:1). He is 'the true light' of this dark world (1 John
2:8), the 'sun of righteousness' who shines on us with healing rays (Mal. 3:20 *AV*), the 'dayspring' or dawn chasing
the shades of night (Luke 1:78 *AV*), the 'day star' rising in our
hearts (2 Peter 1:19 *AV*).

In using all these biblical images Wesley's intention is to
infuse the new day with a spiritual lustre. It is to be a day
shared with Christ, for:

> Dark and cheerless is the morn
> Unaccompanied by thee.

To enjoy Christ's presence is our deepest need each day. It is to
have an 'inward light' which all the darkness in the world
cannot extinguish. Hence our prayer:

> Visit then this soul of mine,
> Pierce the gloom of sin and grief;

Fill me, radiancy divine,
   Scatter all my unbelief;
More and more thyself display,
Shining to the perfect day.

TUNE: *Ratisbon* (from J. G. Werner's *Choralbuch*, 1815),
and others.

274 Awake, my soul, and with the sun   *T. Ken**,
1637–1711

In 1674 Thomas Ken published his *Manual of Prayers* for the
boys of Winchester College. It was the school where he
himself had been educated and to which he later returned as
chaplain. To the manual he later added this famous morning
hymn, together with its equally famous companion, 'Glory to
thee, my God, this night' (278). Both were lengthy hymns,
consisting of a dozen or so stanzas; and oddly enough they
were accompanied by an equally long hymn to be sung at
midnight! Did the saintly Thomas Ken lack a sense of
humour? Or was it merely a lack of understanding of schoolboys' needs?

   The morning hymn is printed in some hymnals in two parts
(e.g. *A&M* and *EH*), the second part beginning with the
stanza 'Glory to thee, who safe hast kept'. Other books make a
selection of stanzas and present it as a single hymn. Happily
editors have not attempted to revise the original words, which
belie their age and are as suitable for today as for the 17th
century.

   The hymn as a whole is a summons to awake and tackle
the duties of the new day in a diligent and conscientious manner, as under the eye of 'all-seeing God'. Only at the end
does it take the form of prayer, concluding with the familiar
verse:

         Direct, control, suggest, this day
         All I design, or do, or say;
         That all my powers, with all their might,
         To thy sole glory may unite.

TUNE: *Morning Hymn* (F. H. Barthélémon, 1741–1808).

275 New every morning is the love

J. Keble★,
1792–1866

John Keble, like Thomas Ken a century and more earlier (see 274, 278), wrote a pair of well known hymns for morning and evening: this for the morning and 'Sun of my soul' (279) for the evening. First published in his *Christian Year*, 1827, they were originally of considerable length; but it must be remembered that Keble's famous book was not a hymnal but a collection of devotional poetry. This also explains the romantic spirit and pious character of the two hymns – so different in this respect from those of Bishop Ken.

'New every morning' is part of the first poem in the book. Its sixteen verses are entitled 'Morning', with the text, 'His compassions fail not; they are new every morning' (Lam. 3:22,23 *AV*). It is dated 20 September 1822. The poem begins with the words 'Hues of the rich unfolding morn', and the first five stanzas are a poetical description of the break of day. Then comes the verse, 'New every morning is the love,' followed by ten further stanzas. Some four or five of these are generally selected to make up the remainder of the hymn as we have it.

The familiar verse beginning 'The trivial round, the common task' becomes much more meaningful if it is preceded, as Keble intended, by the words:

> We need not bid, for cloistered cell,
> Our neighbour and our work farewell,
> Nor strive to wind ourselves too high
> For sinful man beneath the sky.

Two thoughts in particular are enshrined in this hymn. First, each new day takes on new meanings if we face it with God and allow him to hallow our thoughts. And second, God's service finds its fulfilment not only in religious works but in the commonplace things of life.

TUNE: *Melcombe* (S. Webbe, 1740–1816).

276 Forth in thy name, O Lord, I go   C. Wesley*, 1707–88

Published in Wesley's *Hymns and Sacred Poems*, 1749, and entitled 'For believers before work'. Wesley wrote hymns for every imaginable – and one might even say unimaginable – occasion, but in this case the occasion is entirely proper and of great importance. How are we to face our daily work? And what difference does it make that we do so as 'believers'?

In answering the question Wesley invests the subject of work, however mundane it may be, with a divine splendour. It is not just an irksome job to be done; it is part of our Christian service. It is the task God has assigned to us and in the doing of it we are to find his presence. We are therefore to do it as in his sight, to offer it to him for his approval, and to delight in using to the full every skill and faculty he has bestowed upon us.

These are indeed counsels of perfection. Yet Wesley was not unaware of the frailty of human nature, nor of the fact that every kind of work has its peculiar temptations; so his original hymn included a stanza which his brother John omitted and which is missing from nearly all hymnals:

> Preserve me from my calling's snare,
>   And hide my simple heart above,
> Above the thorns of choking care,
>   The gilded baits of worldly love.

TUNE: *Angels' Song* (Orlando Gibbons, 1583–1625).

EVENING

277 Hail, gladdening Light,   *Greek, 3rd century*
of his pure glory poured   *Tr. J. Keble* (1792–1866)

This ancient 'Candlelight Hymn' (*Phos Hilaron*) is probably the oldest surviving Christian hymn. It dates at least from the

3rd century, some scholars think the second. It had its origin in the Greek Church and was sung at the lighting of lamps in the evening service. Probably the hymn was also sung in the family circle at candle-lighting time. St Basil (*d*.379) quotes it as of unknown authorship and date. It is still sung in the Greek Church at Vespers.

John Keble's well known translation was published in 1834. It is rivalled by the later and freer version made by Robert Bridges beginning 'O gladsome light, O grace' which he wrote for the congregation at Yattendon where he lived. It became known through its inclusion in *EH* 1906. It now has a place in the office of Evening Prayer in the *Alternative Service Book*, 1980.

It should be noted that the hymn is addressed to Christ. He is the gladdening and holy Light, the glory of God and the giver of life to whom, with the Father and the Holy Spirit, we offer our praise as the evening lights shine around us.

TUNES: For Keble's version, *Sabaste*, composed for these words by Sir John Stainer (1840–1901); for Bridges's, *Nunc Dimittis*, written or adapted by L. Bourgeois for the *Genevan Psalter*, 1549.

278 Glory to thee, my God, this night   *T. Ken*★,
1637–1711

This lovely evening hymn, which has been described as the oldest and most popular of the traditional English evening hymns, is the companion to Bishop Ken's 'Awake my soul' (274). Both of them, written originally for the boys of Winchester College, have been in constant use for the past 300 years. They are not the sort of hymns that date, nor, despite their origin, are they restricted to people of any particular class or age.

All the elements that are required for an evening hymn are here: gratitude for the day that is past, penitence for what has been done amiss, prayer for protection, for 'sweet sleep' to renew our vigour, and for freedom from the fear of death. Hymnals make a selection from the original eleven stanzas for congregational use. Some (e.g. *CH*) begin the hymn with its original wording, 'All praise to thee, my God, this night'.

The final doxology which Ken added to both his hymns is one of the best known verses in English literature. It is often sung alone, as a grace before meals:

> Praise God, from whom all blessings flow,
> Praise him all creatures here below;
> Praise him above, ye heavenly host,
> Praise Father, Son, and Holy Ghost.

TUNE: The famous *Canon* by Thomas Tallis (1505–85), first published *c.*1561.

279 Sun of my soul, thou Saviour dear   *J. Keble*★, 1792–1866

For the background to Keble's famous evening hymn, see 'New every morning' (275). It is part of the second poem in his *Christian Year*, entitled 'Evening', with the text, 'Abide with us, for it is toward evening, and the day is far spent' (Luke 24:29 *AV*). It was written on 25 November 1820.

With the words ''Tis gone, that bright and orbèd blaze' the poem itself begins by describing a weary traveller as he pursues his journey after the sun has set and night draws on. Against this picture the opening stanza of the hymn as we have it takes on a new significance:

> Sun of my soul, thou Saviour dear,
> It is not night if thou be near;
> Oh, may no earth-born cloud arise
> To hide thee from thy servant's eyes.

The usual five stanzas that follow in our hymn books are a selection from the eleven which make up the rest of the poem. They are a prayer: a prayer for the Lord's presence, that he may 'abide' with us (a reference to the hymn's text) both in life and in death, by night as well as by day. But it is also, quite properly, a prayer for others: for the sinful who have wandered from God, for the sick, the poor and the mourners; and finally a prayer for God's blessing on the morrow, as we continue our journey through the world.

TUNES: *Abends* (H. S. Oakley, 1830–1903); or *Hursley* (from *Katholisches Gesangbuch, c.*1775).

280 The day thou gavest, Lord, is ended   *J. Ellerton**, 1826–93

Should this be regarded as an evening hymn or a missionary hymn? Both, is the simple answer. Inevitably it is classified as an evening hymn since its opening lines render it suitable only for use at evening worship. But it was in fact written by Canon Ellerton in 1870 as part of a *Liturgy for Missionary Meetings* and its missionary character is undeniable.

The hymn's dominant theme is the growing worldwide fellowship of the Church of Christ and its unbroken, unceasing offering of praise and prayer to God. The imagery of morning and evening, day and night, is no more than the background and is used simply by way of illustration.

> We thank thee that thy Church unsleeping,
>   While earth rolls onward into light,
> Through all the world her watch is keeping,
>   And rests not now by day or night.
>
> As o'er each continent and island
>   The dawn leads on another day,
> The voice of prayer is never silent,
>   Nor dies the strain of praise away.

Queen Victoria chose the hymn for her Diamond Jubilee in 1897 and it was sung at thousands of churches throughout Britain on Sunday, 20 June. The Queen may well have regarded her vast dominions – 'the empire on which the sun never sets' – as a symbol of the expanding Church in the world; but the hymn's final stanza wisely reminds us that while 'earth's proud empires pass away', God's kingdom 'stands and grows for ever' and will outlive all human institutions.

TUNE: *St Clement* (C. C. Scholefield, 1839–1904).

281 God, that madest earth and heaven

R. Heber*, 1783–1826
R. Whately, 1787–1896

Two authors for a hymn of only two verses is unusual, but for all that the result is entirely satisfactory. The hymn first appeared in this form in *Sacred Poetry*, 1838, issued for use in the schools of Dublin.

The first stanza comes from a hymn in the posthumous collection of Reginald Heber's works published by his widow in 1827. Tradition has it that he wrote it after hearing the familiar Welsh air *Ar Hyd y Nos* ('All through the night') in a house in which he was staying in Wales and that the hymn was first sung to that melody – as it has been ever since. The words of this stanza are a simple prayer for protection, sound sleep, holy dreams and fresh hopes for the coming day.

The second stanza was added by the scholarly Richard Whately, Archbishop of Dublin, for the book mentioned above. It is a free paraphrase of the antiphon in the office of Compline, which in the *BCP* (1928) runs: 'Preserve us, O Lord, while waking, and guard us while sleeping, that awake we may watch with Christ, and asleep we may rest in peace.' Whately's rendering of this in the verse, 'Guard us waking; guard us sleeping,' matches up well with Heber's words. It recalls the stanza in Bishop Ken's evening hymn: 'Teach me to live, that I may dread/The grave as little as my bed'.

TUNE: See above.

282 At even, when the sun was set   *H. Twells*, 1823–1900

When Canon Henry Twells composed this hymn in 1868 he was Headmaster of the Godolphin School, Hammersmith (1856–70). He has told how it came to be written. Sir Henry Baker had asked him to provide a new evening hymn for the Supplement to *A&M*:

Being at that time headmaster of a large grammar school, I wrote it one afternoon while the boys were taking examinations and I was supposed to be seeing 'all fair'. I am afraid I could not have been very energetic or lynx-eyed in my duties that day, but I little anticipated the popularity the hymn would attain.

Clearly he had in mind that afternoon the scene in Jesus' ministry depicted in Luke 4:40 at the end of a memorable sabbath at Capernaum: 'Now when the sun was setting, all those who had any that were sick with various diseases brought them to him; and he laid his hands on every one of them and healed them.' Twells wrote that this happened '*ere* the sun was set'; but most hymnals change this to *when*, as being closer to scripture and more in accordance with the Jewish observance of the sabbath.

The hymn mentions different classes of people in need of Christ's healing touch: the sick, the sad, the worldly, the restless, the conscience-stricken. A stanza usually omitted mentions yet other needs:

> And some are pressed with worldly care,
> And some are tried with sinful doubt;
> And some such grievous passions tear
> That only thou canst cast them out.

TUNE: *Angelus* (founded on a melody by G. Joseph, 1657).

283 Day is dying in the west   *Mary A. Lathbury,*
                                         1841–1918

This evening hymn by Miss Lathbury, the American Methodist writer (see 163), has a strong emotional appeal. 'The hymn,' writes Dr Albert Bayly, 'is close to the heart of nature and expresses the feelings engendered by the sunset and the twilight hours.' She wrote it in 1877 at the request of Dr John Vincent for use at the evening services of the Chautauque Centre.

The world of nature enters into each of the four stanzas: the

setting sun, the evening's deepening shadows, the night sky,
the starlight; but this element is blended with the spirit of
adoring worship as expressed in the refrain:

> Holy, holy, holy, Lord God of hosts;
> Heaven and earth are full of thee,
> Heaven and earth are praising thee,
> O Lord, most high.

The haunting tune *Sennen* (called *Evening Praise* in America), with its lullaby rhythm, has had a lot to do with the
hymn's popularity. It was composed for the words by William
F. Sherwin (1826–88), the musical director of the Chautauque
Centre.

TUNE: See above.

HARVEST THANKSGIVING

284 Come, ye thankful people, come   *H. Alford,*
                                                 1810–71

This, the most popular of all harvest hymns, appears in
somewhat different forms in our hymnals. Part of the explanation for this is that Henry Alford published two texts of the
hymn, the first in 1844 and the final one in his *Poetical Works*,
1865. But further alterations were carried out when the hymn
was included in *A&M* 1861. The author firmly repudiated this
version, and not without good reason. The tinkerings with the
text by the compilers of the hymn book were both clumsy and
unnecessary. For example, in the second stanza the lines:

> First the blade and then the ear,
> Then the full corn shall appear . . .

were changed to the insipid 'Ripening with a wondrous power/
Till the final harvest hour'; while in the fourth stanza the
words:

There for ever purified
In God's garner to abide . . .

became, for some obscure reason, 'All upon the golden floor/
Praising thee for evermore.' Happily most modern hymn
books adhere to the author's own text in one form or another.

The hymn is based largely on two of our Lord's parables: the
wheat and the tares (Matt. 13:24–30) and the seed growing
secretly (Mark 4:26–29). This fact accounts for the note of
judgment which is so prominent in the hymn.

Henry Alford, who became Dean of Canterbury in 1857,
was a distinguished scholar, a powerful preacher and the
author of numerous works. Generally speaking his poetry was
not of a very high order. For his hymn 'Ten thousand times ten
thousand', see 182. He also wrote the processional hymn
'Forward be our watchword' and the baptismal hymn 'In
token that thou shalt not fear'.

TUNE: *St George* (Sir G. J. Elvey, 1816–93).

285 We plough the fields,   *M. Claudius*, 1740–1815
     and scatter   *Tr. Jane M. Campbell*, 1817–78

Mathias Claudius, the author of this harvest hymn, was,
appropriately, a commissioner of agriculture in Germany
during part of his mixed career. He afterwards turned to
journalism and later still became auditor of a bank. The hymn
comes from his poem *Paul Eardmann's Festival*, 1782. It depicts
the celebration of harvest in a German farmhouse, in the
course of which the peasants join in a song of thanksgiving.
This song was published in a school worship-book in Hanover
some years later and rapidly became popular. Our English
version was made by Miss Jane Montgomery Campbell, the
daughter of a London clergyman who taught music in schools.
She contributed several translations to C. S. Bere's *A Garland
of Song*, 1862, this one among them.

The first stanza illustrates man's co-operation with God in
producing the harvest. *We* plough the land and sow the seed;
God provides the wind, sunshine and rain which make the
earth bring forth its fruits. The two remaining stanzas list a

number of other blessings which the heavenly Father lavishes upon his children; and so finally we acknowledge all these good gifts around us with humble, thankful hearts.

TUNE: *Wir pflügen* (attributed to J. A. P. Schulz, 1747–1800).

286 For the fruits of his creation   *F. Pratt Green**, *b*.1903

Fred Pratt Green's Harvest Song first appeared in the *Methodist Recorder* in August 1970. He had written it by request for the tune *East Acklam*, composed in 1957 by Francis Jackson for the hymn 'God that madest earth and heaven'. The new words were designed to meet the need for a new hymn on the theme of harvest. From the outset the author was besieged with requests from far and wide for permission to reproduce the hymn and it has now found its way across the world. Clearly, in providing a good contemporary harvest hymn it fills a gap.

As is proper, thanksgiving is the hymn's dominant note. In the first stanza it is thanksgiving for the natural harvest: for the fruits of God's creation which man enjoys through his 'ploughing, sowing, reaping'. In the third it is thanksgiving for the spiritual harvest – 'the harvests of the Spirit' – for God's goodness, truth and love. The middle stanza with its refrain 'God's will is done' challenges us to remember the needy peoples of our world, especially 'the hungry and despairing', and to share with them the plenty and bounty we enjoy.

TUNE: *East Acklam* (see above).

287 Praise and thanksgiving   *A. F. Bayly**, 1901–84

Our traditional harvest hymns are generally concerned with thanking God for his gifts to *us* with little or no recognition of the needs of the world at large. It is good that this fault is being rectified by contemporary hymn-writers like Fred Pratt Green (286) and Fred Kaan ('Now join we, to praise the creator'), as also here by Albert Bayly.

He wrote the hymn in June 1961. It was included in his

collection *Again I Say Rejoice*, 1967, with the recommen-
dation that it should be sung to the well known Old Gaelic
melody *Bunessan*. It begins by offering praise to God for all his
good gifts, including the harvest of the fields and the fruits of
the orchard. Then from praise it turns to prayer – and prayer
first for those whose labours make the harvest possible (v.2).
In the third stanza the scope of the prayer widens:

> Father, providing
> Food for thy children,
> Thy wisdom guiding
> Teaches us share
> One with another
> So that rejoicing
> With us, our brother
> May know thy care.

This is the heart of the prayer: *sharing* 'one with another'. By
such sharing our fellow men and women learn of the Father's
care for them; and as they partake of his blessings they will
acknowledge his gracious hand. This is his sovereign purpose
for his world (v.4).

TUNE: *Bunessan* (see above).

NATION AND SOCIETY

288 O God, our help in ages past

Isaac Watts*,
1674–1748

One of the finest hymns in the English language, this has
almost become a second national anthem. It is particularly
associated with State occasions and Remembrancetide. As
most people know, the hymn originally began, 'Our God, our
help'; but probably they are not aware that it was John Wesley
who changed the 'Our' to 'O'. For good or ill, the majority of
hymnals accept the alteration.

The hymn is based on the first seven verses of Psalm 90 which begins, 'Lord, thou hast been our dwelling place in all generations' (*AV*). Watts entitled his lines 'Man frail and God eternal'. This is the dominant note of the psalm, as it is also of the hymn as Watts wrote it; but we no longer use the hymn in its complete form. The three stanzas which dwell on human frailty have been dropped – which though it makes the hymn less complete also reduces it to a more convenient length.

The hymn calls for little comment or explanation; but there is one stanza which troubles a lot of people, specially on Remembrance Sunday:

> Time, like an ever-rolling stream,
>   Bears all its sons away;
> They fly, forgotten as a dream
>   Dies at the opening day.

Is it true that our sons are so soon forgotten and fade from our memory as swiftly as a dream? Surely not. But that is not the meaning of Watts's lines. The sons referred to are not *our* sons but the sons of *Time*: a figure of speech denoting the days and weeks and years that quickly pass away and are soon forgotten. But while time flies and memories fade, our God is for ever the same – 'our help in ages past', as he is also 'our hope for years to come'.

TUNE: *St Anne* (W. Croft, 1678–1727).

289 Eternal Ruler of the ceaseless round
J. W. Chadwick, 1840–1904

The background to this hymn is the American Civil War. This gives particular significance to its plea for peace and goodwill. John White Chadwick wrote it in 1864 for the graduating class of Harvard Divinity School, just prior to his becoming minister of the Second Unitarian Church, Brooklyn, New York. He remained there for forty years and became widely known for his sermons, books and poetry.

At the time the hymn was written the war had reached a turning-point. Following the bloody Battle of the Wilderness the nation was torn by a spirit of fear, bitterness and grief. Hence the reference in the first stanza to 'the night profound' which enshrouded the American people, and the prayer for God's guidance and strength. The tragedy was that men on both sides of the conflict claimed to be God's children, so that 'brothers' were fighting one another instead of being 'as one' with Christ. Verse three voices the longing for national unity:

> We would be one in hatred of all wrong,
>   One in our love of all things sweet and fair,
> One with the joy that breaketh into song,
>   One with the grief that trembleth into prayer,
> One in the power that makes the children free
> To follow truth, and thus to follow thee.

TUNE: *Song 1* (Orlando Gibbons, 1583–1625).

290 Rejoice, O land, in God thy might   *R. Bridges*★, 1844–1930

Who better to write a hymn for the nation than a future Poet Laureate? Dr Robert Bridges had that honour conferred upon him in 1913. The hymn was written a good deal earlier, in the year of Queen Victoria's Diamond Jubilee (1897), and was published in the *Yattendon Hymnal*, 1899.

Dr Bridges found his inspiration in some words of the prophet Joel: 'Fear not, O land; be glad and rejoice, for the Lord will do great things' (2:21). He was writing in the days when Britain had reached the peak of its greatness; but in his hymn he reminds us that a nation's true 'might' lies not in its wealth, conquests or armaments but in its obedience to the claims of God. Only then will it be 'with blessing crowned'. That blessing can never be presumed upon. There is no room for complacency – but room enough and to spare for repentance, recollection and reformation:

> He shall forgive thy sins untold:
> Remember thou his love of old;
> Walk in his way, his word adore,
> And keep his truth for evermore.

Dr Routley described Robert Bridges as a man in whom poetry and hymnody met. This hymn illustrates that fact.

TUNE: *Wareham* (W. Knapp, 1698–1768).

291 Son of God, eternal Saviour *S. C. Lowry*, 1855–1932

Lowry's hymn on the social implications of the gospel, first published in 1894, has stood well the test of time and still finds a place in modern hymnals.

It begins by recognising mankind's common brotherhood in Christ, the Son of Man, 'whose birth incarnate hallows all our human race'. Next it reminds us that his life of service must be the pattern of our own as we exercise our stewardship:

> As thou, Lord, hast lived for others,
>   So may we for others live;
> Freely have thy gifts been granted,
>   Freely may thy servants give.
> Thine the gold and thine the silver,
>   Thine the wealth of land and sea,
> We but stewards of thy bounty,
>   Held in solemn trust for thee.

In the stanza that follows (v.3) we pray that Christ's rule of peace may be established among us, to end our strife, quench our love of pleasure and shame our selfish greed, so that a brighter future may be ours in which all classes, high and low, are 'linked in bonds of common service for the common Lord of all' (v.4). This is our hope; so we ask:

> Grant, O grant, our hope's fruition:
>   Here on earth thy will be done.

Somerset Corry Lowry, born in Dublin, was educated in England and took holy orders in 1879. He served a number of parishes, published several devotional books, and wrote about sixty hymns. See also 197.

TUNES: *Bethany* or *Everton* (both by H. Smart, 1813–79).

292 God of grace and God of glory
H. E. Fosdick,
1878–1969

The great Riverside Church in New York was built specially for the ministry of Dr Harry Emerson Fosdick, probably the foremost American preacher of his day. On account of his ecumenical outlook he had stated his wish to serve a church free from denominational ties, membership of which would be open to all Christians. His wish was thus fulfilled and the church was opened on 5 October 1930. He wrote the hymn the previous summer, in anticipation of the event. It was sung then and also at the dedication of the building the following February.

In his autobiography he stated: 'That was more than a hymn to me when we sang it that day; it was a very urgent personal prayer. For with all my hopeful enthusiasm about the new venture, there was inevitably much humble and sometimes fearful apprehension.' Happily his fears proved to be un-founded. He drew large congregations to the magnificent new building and through his preaching, writing and broadcasting exercised a nationwide ministry.

The hymn, consisting in full of five stanzas (some books omit the final one), is little coloured by the occasion that called it forth. The sentiments it expresses are still a call to active Christian discipleship and its repeated prayer for wisdom and courage is as needful now as ever.

TUNE: *Rhuddlan* (Welsh traditional melody), or *Westminster Abbey* (adapted from H. Purcell, 1659–95).

293 O day of God, draw nigh
R. B. Y. Scott, b. 1899

A hymn by a Canadian scholar, and a distinguished one too. Robert Balgarie Young Scott was born in Toronto and educated at the university of that city. He was Professor of Old Testament in United Theological College, Montreal, from 1931 until his appointment as Professor of Religion at Princeton in 1956.

Apart from his many biblical works he is the author of some two dozen hymns. The present one was written for the

American Fellowship for a Christian Social Order and published in *Hymns for Worship*, 1939. It came into the *BBC Hymn Book* in 1951 and is now being widely used.

The 'day of God' which is its theme is that spoken of by the prophet Isaiah (chs. 24–27). It is at once a day of judgment and a day of salvation. The prayer expressed in the hymn is therefore a prayer for God's kingdom of justice and peace:

> Bring justice to our land,
> That all may dwell secure . . .
>
> Bring to our world of strife
> Thy sovereign word of peace . . .

Justice first, peace next: this is the biblical order. Peace is the fruit of righteousness (Isa. 32:17).

TUNES: *Hillsborough* (J. Gardiner, *b.* 1917), or *Bellswood* (by the Canadian composer J. Hopkirk, *b.* 1908).

294 I vow to thee, my country,   *C. Spring-Rice,*
all earthly things above   1859–1918

The Christian is a citizen of two countries: his own native land and the heavenly kingdom (Phil. 3:20). This hymn by Sir Cecil Spring-Rice, British Ambassador to the United States, 1912–18, takes cognisance of this fact. He wrote it on the eve of his final departure from Washington on 12 January 1918. Some six or seven years earlier, when Minister to Sweden, he had composed a poem entitled *Urbs Dei* (City of God), in two stanzas. The second of these, with its vision of that 'other country', a vision of gentleness and peace, is included (with minor alterations) in his new poem. The first stanza he entirely rewrote. In its previous form it had expressed a belligerent type of patriotism, glorifying and glamorising war. Since 1914 Spring-Rice had come to see that the only patriotism worth celebrating was the spirit of self-sacrificing love, as expressed in the cross of Christ. In a speech at Ottawa, a week after writing this poem, he said:

The Cross is a sign of patience under suffering, but not patience under wrong. The Cross is the banner under which we fight . . . We are all subjects of the Prince of Peace, who fought the greatest fight ever fought upon this earth, who won the greatest victory, and won it by his blood.

These words reveal what Sir Cecil meant by the lines:

The love that asks no question, the love that stands the test,
That lays upon the altar the dearest and the best;
The love that never falters, the love that pays the price,
The love that makes undaunted the final sacrifice.

He died suddenly on 14 February 1918.

TUNE: *Thaxted*, an adaptation by Gustav Holst (1874–1934) from the movement 'Jupiter' in his orchestral suite *The Planets*, written at Thaxted, Essex, in 1917.

295 We turn to you, O God of every nation   *F. Kaan, b.*1929

First published in Fred Kaan's *Pilgrim Praise*, 1967 (see 160), this hymn was written for a United Nations Sunday. But, as the author says, 'it has a wider application in that we bear a heavy responsibility for the family of nations Sunday after Sunday. Christ is crucified in our contemporary scene, and modern events cause him to suffer again . . . I believe that Babel and Pentecost are good words to describe what is and what is intended to be.'

This is a concise summary of the hymn's main message and comments on two of its phrases. The first is in the second stanza:

We turn to you, that we may be forgiven
For crucifying Christ on earth again.

The other is in the final stanza, which also includes a phrase from the well known prayer of St Ignatius Loyola:

Teach us, good Lord, to serve the needs of others,
    Help us to give and not to count the cost.
Unite us all, for we are born as brothers;
    Defeat our Babel with your Pentecost.

Babel is the symbol of division (Gen. 11:9), Pentecost of unity
in the Spirit (Acts 2). So we turn to God in penitence and pray
that he will free us from our pride and self-reliance and break
down the barriers that divide us.

TUNE: *Intercessor* (C. H. H. Parry, 1848–1918) is the
author's own choice for this hymn.

296 What does the Lord require   *A. F. Bayly**, 1901–84

This is one of a series of hymns which Albert Bayly wrote in
1950 on themes derived from the OT prophets. It is based on
the words of Micah 6:6–8 *AV*. The prophet asks, 'Wherewith
shall I come before the Lord, and bow myself before the high
God?' Not, he answers, with animal sacrifices or any such
offerings:

He hath shewed thee, O man, what is good; and what doth
the Lord require of thee, but to do justly, and to love mercy,
and to walk humbly with thy God?

This is the essence of true religion, and the hymn applies the
message to the world of our own day. For example, to the
world of finance and industry ('Masters of wealth and trade')
and the world of politics and government ('Rulers of men').
But the words speak to us all and are as applicable now as when
they were first written:

Still down the ages ring
    The prophet's stern commands:
To merchant, worker, king,
    He brings God's high demands:
        Do justly;
        Love mercy;
Walk humbly with your God.

How are we to fulfil these high demands? The final stanza supplies the answer: only by allowing Christ to fortify our wills with his grace. And this ending to the hymn adds a Christian dimension to the words of the ancient Hebrew prophet.

TUNE: *Sharpthorne* (written for the hymn by Erik Routley, 1917–82).

VARIOUS OCCASIONS

297 Father, let me dedicate   *L. Tuttiet*, 1825–97

> Father, let me dedicate
> All this year to thee,
> In whatever earthly state
> Thou wilt have me be;
> Not from sorrow, pain, or care,
> Freedom dare I claim;
> This alone shall be my prayer,
> 'Glorify thy name.'

This is probably the best known hymn written specifically for the new year. Canon Lawrence Tuttiet composed it, he said, because of the scarcity of hymns designed for this purpose. At the time he was vicar of Lea Marston, Warwickshire. It was published in 1864 and soon became popular in America as well as in Britain.

The burden of the hymn is the prayer repeated in the final line of each verse and which echoes our Lord's petition as he approached the cross: 'Father, glorify thy name' (John 12:28 *AV*). The prayer is applied to the various circumstances of life in the light of the unknown future and represents the spirit of true dedication and commitment.

TUNE: *Father, let me dedicate* (composed by Sir George Macfarren, 1813–87, for the 1875 edition of *A&M*)

298 Eternal Father, strong to save   *W. Whiting*, 1825–78

The sailors' hymn – the only hymn of the sea which has
achieved worldwide popularity – has been considerably
altered from its original form. It has also been considerably
improved in the process. As written in 1860 it began:

> O thou who bidd'st the ocean deep
> It own appointed limits keep;
> Thou who dost bind the restless wave,
> Eternal Father, strong to save.

When it appeared the next year in the first edition of *A&M* the
words of this opening stanza were changed to their now
familiar form. The remainder of the hymn also underwent a
certain amount of revision, with the author's consent.

The hymn follows the familiar Trinitarian pattern. The first
stanza, addressed to the Father, is based on the words of Job
38:10, 11, which tell how God prescribed the bounds of the sea
and said, 'Thus far you shall go, and no farther.' The second
recalls the stories of Jesus stilling the storm and walking on the
sea (Matt. 8:23–27 and 14:22–32). The third goes back to the
story of creation when the Spirit of God brooded over the face
of the deep and brought order out of chaos (Gen. 1:2). The final
stanza is a prayer to the Trinity for seafarers in danger's hour.

William Whiting has no claim to fame apart from this
hymn. He was for twenty years a master of Winchester
College Choristers' School and wrote the hymn for a pupil
who was about to sail for America.

TUNE: *Melita* (J. B. Dykes, 1823–76, composed for the
hymn in *A&M*, 1861. Its name, denoting Malta, is taken from
Acts 28:1 *AV*).

299 O God, by whose almighty plan   *H. C. A. Gaunt*,
                                                      1902–83

A modern hymn on the subject of healing is welcome. The
older hymns that have served for so long – e.g. Dean Plum-
tre's 'Thine arm, O Lord, in days of old' and Prebendary

Thring's 'Thou to whom the sick and dying' – are now somewhat dated and need in any case to be supplemented. Canon Howard Gaunt, who after being a schoolmaster for thirty-five years became Precentor of Winchester, wrote the hymn for a healing service in the cathedral.

It is a prayer, and follows the Trinitarian pattern. To God the Father, the creator from whom we derive our life, we pray for spiritual illumination, that we may have a deeper understanding of his truth. To Christ, who in his earthly ministry gave sight to the blind, made broken lives whole and healed the sick in mind, we pray:

> Grant us your faith, your love, your care,
> To bring to sufferers everywhere.

Our prayer to the Holy Spirit is for growing wisdom in the work of healing that we may be shown 'new paths to probe, new thoughts to trace':

> Grant us your wisest way to go
> In all we think, or speak, or do.

TUNE: *St Petersburg* (D. S. Bortnianski, 1752–1825).

300 God be with you till we meet again   *J. E. Rankin,*
                                                    1828–1904

Dr Jeremiah Eames Rankin was minister of the First Congregational Church, Washington, when he wrote this hymn in 1882. Sensing that there might be a 'story' behind it, someone asked him in what circumstances he had composed it. His answer was disappointing. He had written the hymn, he said, not with any special occasion or people in mind, but simply to make clear the original and true meaning of the word *goodbye*, which is 'God be with you'.

This perhaps is the hymn's chief value. It is quite frankly of a sentimental character, but of course farewells are often sentimental occasions. Unfortunately the poetical expression is poor in the extreme. Nevertheless the hymn retains a measure of popularity, due in part to the fact that for many people it has deeply personal associations, in part to the lack of suitable valedictory hymns, and in part to its traditional tune *God be with you*. As regards the latter, Dr Rankin said that at his invitation two men submitted tunes to him. One of these was an acknowledged musician; but the tune he selected as most suitable was by the other, an unknown schoolteacher, William G. Tomer (1832–96). It has been called 'a tedious, maudlin tune' and most modern hymnals replace it with Vaughan Williams' *Randolph*.

TUNE: See above.

BIOGRAPHICAL NOTES

ALEXANDER, CECIL FRANCES (1818–95). The second daughter of Major J. Humphreys, she was born at Redcross, Co. Wicklow, Ireland. At the age of twenty-five she published her *Hymns for Little Children*, with an introductory note by John Keble. Dedicated to her 'little godsons' the book was designed to illustrate and explain the Church Catechism. Two years later she married the Revd William Alexander and enjoyed an idyllic wedded life. Her husband later became Bishop of Derry and finally Archbishop of Armagh. Her poetical works reached a high level and were admired by Tennyson. She has rightly been called the greatest of British women hymn-writers. Her children's hymns are the best known of them all, but she also wrote many hymns for the saints' days and holy days of the Christian year.

ALFORD, HENRY (1810–71). The son of a clergyman and a Fellow of Trinity College, Cambridge, he was appointed Dean of Canterbury in 1857 and remained there till his death. In his own day, and for long afterwards, he was chiefly renowned as the author of his critical commentary on the Greek Testament, a work which marked a great advance in New Testament scholarship in the 19th century. He had an extraordinary capacity for literary work and his pen was never idle. A man of broad sympathies and strong Evangelical faith, he once wrote, in making inquiries about a curate he was seeking, 'I want him to teach and preach Jesus Christ and not the Church, and to be fully prepared to recognise the pious dissenter as a brother in Christ, and as much a member of the Church as ourselves.' He was deeply interested in hymnody and compiled several hymn books, for which he wrote and translated many hymns.

BAKER, SIR HENRY WILLIAMS (1821–77). Eldest son of Vice-Admiral Sir Henry Loraine Baker, Bart. He was educated at Trinity College, Cambridge, and ordained in 1844. Five years later he became vicar of Monkland, near Leominster, where he remained for the rest of his life. The light duties of a small country parish enabled him to devote most of his time to hymnody and in particular to promoting *Hymns*

Ancient and Modern, which was his brainchild. He was chairman of the committee responsible for the book and exercised a firm editorial control over its production. In addition to contributing many hymns and translations of his own, he encouraged others to write hymns for him (often freely editing their efforts) and enlisted the aid of gifted musicians to compose suitable tunes. The first edition was published in 1861 and its immediate success was a tribute to his genius and skill as a hymnist.

BARING-GOULD, SABINE (1834–1924). A man of remarkable versatility and industry who in the course of a long life was a prodigious author. He published nearly fifty volumes of fiction and a hundred or so more on religion, history, travel and other subjects, including his *Lives of the Saints* in fifteen volumes. On being ordained in 1864 he served for two years as curate at Horbury, Yorkshire, where he wrote his well known hymns for children, 'Onward, Christian soldiers' and 'Now the day is over'. On the death of his father in 1872 he inherited the family estate of Lew Trenchard, Devon, and when the living fell vacant he appointed himself rector of the small parish (1881). There he remained to the end of his life, devoting himself chiefly to literary work.

BAXTER, RICHARD (1615–91). One of the ablest and most devoted of the Puritan clergy, he was ordained to the ministry of the C of E in 1640. During the Civil War he attached himself to the Parliamentary Army, but after the Restoration he became chaplain for a short time to King Charles, who offered him the bishopric of Hereford. He declined the offer, and after the Act of Uniformity, 1662, he withdrew from the Established Church and lived in retirement till 1670. He then became a Nonconformist minister and though subject to much persecution (he was imprisoned by Judge Jeffries for two years) he patiently continued his ministry of preaching and writing. He was one of the pioneers of hymn-making in England and anticipated the work of Isaac Watts, insisting that in public worship singing should not be restricted to the metrical psalms but should include 'hymns more suitable to gospel times'.

BAYLY, ALBERT FREDERICK (1901–84). After training as a shipwright at the Royal Dockyard School, Portsmouth, he studied for the ministry of the Congregational Church at Mansfield College, Oxford, and was ordained in 1929. He served churches at Whitley Bay, Morpeth, Burnley, and Swanland (E. Yorkshire). His first collection of hymns, *Rejoice, O People*, was published in 1951 and others have followed since. His hymns reflect something of Isaac Watts's cosmic outlook and keen interest in the world of nature, being 'characterized by an awareness of the contemporary world in which we live, a faithfulness to the words and themes of scripture, and an intense feeling for the proper dignity of worship' (Eric Sharpe).

BONAR, HORATIUS (1808–89). The son of a Solicitor for Excise for Scotland, he was born in Edinburgh and educated at the High School and University of that city. In 1838 he was ordained and inducted at Kelso, where he remained for twenty-seven years. At the Disruption in 1843 he entered the Free Church of Scotland. He received the degree of Doctor of Divinity from the University of Aberdeen in 1853. On leaving Kelso he was appointed minister of the Chalmers Memorial Church, Edinburgh, and made Moderator of the General Assembly in 1883. A man of immense gifts and tireless energy, he distinguished himself as preacher, pastor, scholar and author. He is now remembered as the prince of Scottish hymn-writers. He wrote numerous hymns, which apparently he threw off with the greatest ease, many of them far too long. Hence Dr Louis Benson's description of them as 'spontaneous, careless, and sometimes ringing the changes fatiguingly', yet 'warmly evangelical, often poetical, and always sympathetic'.

BRIDGES, ROBERT SEYMOUR (1844–1930). Educated at Eton and Corpus Christi College, Oxford, he studied medicine at St Bartholomew's Hospital, London, and duly qualified; but he retired from medical practice in 1882 to devote himself to literature, having already made his name as a highly gifted poet. He settled at Yattendon, Berkshire, where he took over the training of the choir at the parish church. He gradually built up a collection of a hundred hymns of a high literary standard, of which forty-four were his own workmanship, and published it in 1899 as the *Yattendon Hymnal*. In 1913 he was appointed Poet Laureate. His many hymns and translations made a valuable contribution to the hymnody of the present century. Dr Erik Routley said of him that 'he did more than any other person to raise English hymnody to the level of respectable literature, redeeming it from both the crudity of the eighteenth century and the conventionality of the nineteenth.'

BRIGGS, GEORGE WALLACE (1875–1959). A classical scholar of Emmanuel College, Cambridge, he served as a chaplain in the Royal Navy, 1902–9. He then became vicar of St Andrew's, Norwich, in

1918, afterwards being appointed rector of Loughborough. He was a canon of Leicester Cathedral, 1927–34, and of Worcester, 1934–56. As adviser to various education authorities in connection with school worship he published several books of prayers and hymns for school use. He was also associated with the production of a number of hymn books, including *Songs of Praise*. His own hymns, published under the title *Songs of Faith*, 1945, maintain a high poetical standard, range over a wide variety of subjects, and are essentially biblical in character. He is now recognised as the leading English hymn-writer in the first half of the century.

CASWALL, EDWARD (1814–78). The son of a clergyman, he was educated at Marlborough and Oxford and took holy orders in 1840. Seven years later, under the influence of Newman, he was received into the Roman Catholic Church. On the death of his wife in 1850 he was re-ordained priest and joined Newman at his oratory in Edgbaston, Birmingham. There he spent the rest of his life, ministering to the sick and poor (by whom he was greatly loved) and devoting himself to the translation of early Latin hymns from the Roman breviaries. Some 200 of these were published in four volumes between 1849 and 1873. His only original hymn in common use is the Christmas carol, 'See amid the winter snow'.

COWPER, WILLIAM (1731–1800). One of the leading English poets of the 18th century and a man of tender, gracious personality whose life from his earliest years was marked by tragedy. After an unhappy boyhood he trained for the law; but though called to the Bar in 1754 he never practised, the legal profession proving too heavy a burden. Throughout his life he suffered from fits of deep depression, even periods of insanity. In 1767, at the invitation of John Newton, he came to live at Olney, Buckinghamshire, where he was cared for by Mrs Unwin, a clergyman's widow, who had become his faithful friend and housekeeper. As far as health permitted he shared with Newton in the work of the parish and joined with him in writing hymns to be sung at the weekly prayer meeting. These *Olney Hymns*, published in 1779, contained sixty-seven of Cowper's contributions. Only a handful of them now survive, but among them are some of the gems of English hymnody.

DEARMER, PERCY (1867–1936). Educated at Westminster School and Christ Church, Oxford, he was ordained in 1891 and served a number of London parishes. His chief ministry was as vicar of St Mary's, Primrose Hill, 1901–15. Oxford conferred on him the degree of DD in 1911. From 1919 till his death he was Professor of Ecclesiastical Art at King's College, London. In 1931 he was made a canon of Westminster. He had a deep interest in and an extensive knowledge of hymnody which he put to good account. He served as secretary of the committee that prepared the *English Hymnal*, 1906, and also acted as its editor. In collaboration with Ralph Vaughan Williams and Martin Shaw he published *Songs of Praise*, 1925, the *Oxford Book of Carols*, 1928, and the enlarged edition of *SP*, 1931. The latter contains a large number of his hymns and translations.

DIX, WILLIAM CHATTERTON (1837–98). One of the few laymen of the CofE in the 19th century to have achieved distinction as a hymn-writer. The son of a Bristol surgeon, he entered the world of commerce and spent most of his life as manager of a marine insurance company in Glasgow. On retirement he lived with a married daughter at Clifton, Bristol. He early developed an interest in literature, and writing became a favourite pastime. He published several volumes of verse. In addition to his many original hymns he versified translations of early Greek hymns by Dr R. F. Littledale, the eminent liturgical scholar.

DODDRIDGE, PHILIP (1702–51). A contemporary of Isaac Watts and like him a notable Nonconformist minister and scholar. At the age of twenty-seven he became pastor of Castle Hill chapel, Northampton, where he established a theological academy which trained over 200 men for the Dissenting ministry. He remained there till his untimely death through consumption at the age of forty-nine. His great scholarship was recognised by the degree of DD conferred on him by the University of Aberdeen. His hymns, 370 in all, were published posthumously by his friend Job Orton, who explained that they were composed to be sung after Doddridge had preached from the texts prefixed to them. They are therefore biblically based, didactic in tone and devotional in character; and while they lack Watts's literary grace and poetic inspiration, they possess a strong spiritual appeal and reflect the author's deep devotion to Christ.

DUDLEY-SMITH, TIMOTHY (b.1926). Educated at Tonbridge School and Cambridge University, and ordained in 1950, he began his ministry with a curacy in the Rochester diocese and then became head of the Cambridge University Mission in Bermondsey, 1953–5. After serving as editorial secretary of the Evangelical Alliance he was in turn assistant secretary and secretary of the Church Pastoral Aid Society from 1959 to 1973, when he was appointed Archdeacon of

Norwich. In 1981 he was consecrated Bishop of Thetford. He is recognised as one of the foremost English hymn-writers of today. His collected hymns have been published in the USA and Britain entitled *Lift Every Heart*.

ELLERTON, JOHN (1826–93). A faithful, earnest and much loved parish priest who is remembered chiefly for his notable work in the realm of hymnody. His hymns and translations, which numbered nearly a hundred, were at one time immensely popular and several of them are still in use, especially his evening hymns. But it is as a hymnologist that he achieved his highest distinction. He was in fact the Church's leading authority on hymns in the latter part of the century and influenced for good the development of hymn-singing in all the churches. With Walsham How he was joint editor of the SPCK's *Church Hymns*, 1871. He also served on the editorial committee for the 1889 edition of *A&M*, which contained twenty-six of his hymns. Throughout his life hymns were his joy and delight, and it is said that when he was lying semi-conscious on his deathbed hymns flowed from his lips in a never-ending stream.

FABER, FREDERICK (1814–63). A graduate of Balliol College, Oxford, he was ordained in 1837, but in 1846 seceded to the Church of Rome. He established in London an order of the 'Priests of the Congregation of St Philip, Neri' which later developed into the Brompton Oratory. He set himself the task of writing hymns which would do for English RCs what the *Olney Hymns* had done for Protestants. His total output was exactly 150 hymns, designed to correspond to the 150 biblical Psalms. The weakness of his verse is its tendency to an excessive sentimentality; but his best hymns, as *Julian* remarks, 'excel in directness, simplicity, and pathos'. That he possessed a measure of poetic genius cannot be doubted. When he told Wordsworth that he intended to enter the Church of Rome, Wordsworth replied, 'I do not say you are wrong, but England loses a poet.'

GREEN, FREDERICK PRATT (*b.*1903). Born in Liverpool and educated at the (Methodist) Rydal School, Colwyn Bay, he trained for the Methodist ministry at Didsbury College, Manchester, 1925–8. He served in various circuits in Yorkshire, London and the south of England. He was superintendent of the Dome Mission, Brighton, 1948–53, and chairman of the York and Hull District, 1957–64. His retirement to Norwich in 1969 gave him freedom and leisure to develop his poetical gift and as a member of the committee which prepared *Hymns and Songs*, 1969, he was encouraged to write words for selected tunes and provide hymns on particular themes. His hymns are now known throughout the world. In 1982 the degree of Doctor of Humane Letters was conferred upon him by Emory University, Atlanta, Georgia, in recognition of his services to hymnody. He contributed twenty-seven hymns to the Methodist *Hymns and Psalms*, 1984.

HAVERGAL, FRANCES RIDLEY (1836–79). Daughter of the Revd W. H. Havergal, one of the leading church musicians and composers of the century. At the age of fourteen, when at a boarding school, she came to a personal faith in Jesus Christ, committed her life to him and grew up to be a deeply consecrated Christian. She was a highly intelligent woman and mastered Hebrew and Greek as well as several modern languages. Her health was not robust, but as far as her strength allowed she devoted herself to writing books and poems and serving as a spiritual counsellor to the hundreds of people who sought her help. As a hymn-writer she is recognised as being, in a special sense, the singer of consecration. She was not a great poet; her hymns were the spontaneous expression of her own joyous faith and devotion to Christ. As *Julian* remarks, 'She lives and speaks in every line of her poetry.'

HEBER, REGINALD (1783–1826). An important name in the story of English hymnody. At Oxford he won the Newdigate Prize for poetry (1803) and later used his gift to write hymns for use in church worship. He was dissatisfied with the evangelical hymns of the previous century as lacking literary grace and being too subjective and pietistic. He therefore set about providing hymns of a more objective kind, dignified in tone and suitable for use with the *BCP*. With the assistance of other poets he began a collection of such hymns; but the task was never completed owing to his early death in India, where he had gone on his appointment as Bishop of Calcutta in 1822. His unfinished collection, published a year after his death, had a marked influence on the development of Anglican hymnody. 'His book offered a new standard of hymnody: that of a pure but carefully restrained devotion accommodated to the church year, and expressed in flowing rhythms with poetic grace and ornament' (Louis F. Benson).

HERBERT, GEORGE (1593–1632). Born at Montgomery Castle and the member of an old English family, he was educated at Westminster School and Cambridge University, where he was for some time Public Orator. He later served at the court of James I; but disillusioned with that sort of life he took holy orders in 1626. During his last three years he was rector of the Wiltshire village of Bemerton, where he showed himself a conscientious and devoted parish priest. He was also a gifted poet and musician. His religious verse was published a year after his death in *The Temple*. His main theme, as it has been said, is Christian love: the love that is in God and the charity that marks the true believer.

HOW, WILLIAM WALSHAM (1823–97). One of the best loved bishops of the CofE in the 19th century and also one of the finest hymn-writers of his time. In 1879, after thirty-three years spent in parochial work, he became suffragan bishop of East London, where his warm-hearted humanity and pastoral devotion won him the love of the East-Enders, especially the children. Ten years later, after declining several important bishoprics, he was persuaded to become the first bishop of the new diocese of Wakefield, where he spent the rest of his life. He was a good scholar and wrote a large number of biblical works; but it is by his hymns he is now remembered. Of the fifty-four he wrote, nearly a score are still in use. When he was asked his view on what constitutes a good hymn, he replied, 'A good hymn is something like a good prayer – simple, real, earnest, and reverent.' His own hymns fulfil these requirements.

KEBLE, JOHN (1792–1866). Entering Corpus Christi College, Oxford, at the age of fourteen, he distinguished himself by winning double first class honours four years later. He was ordained in 1816, published his celebrated *Christian Year* in 1827, and was Professor of Poetry at Oxford, 1831–41. His assize sermon on national apostasy, preached in the University Church in 1833, is regarded as the start of the Oxford Movement; but it was a profound grief to him when several of his friends, Newman chief among them, seceded to Rome some years later. He himself remained loyal to the CofE. He found deep fulfilment in his pastoral work as vicar of the Hampshire village of Hursley, where he remained for thirty years till his death. All who knew him bore witness to his humble, gracious and Christ-like character.

KELLY, THOMAS (1769–1854). The son of an Irish judge and educated at Trinity College, Dublin, he was ordained in the Church of Ireland in 1792, following a deep conversion experience. His fervent Evangelicalism proved too much for the Archbishop of Dublin and shortly afterwards he parted company with the Irish Church and became an Independent minister. His preaching attracted large congregations; and being a man of ample means he built several chapels and gave generously to the poor. His *Hymns on Various Passages of Scripture*, 1804, was followed by further and enlarged editions, until his hymns numbered 765 in all. Most of them are commonplace and of no value today, but at his best he rises to sublime heights. This can be seen in his two classic hymns, 'We sing the praise of him who died' and 'The head that once was crowned with thorns', which ensure him an honoured place among Irish hymn-writers.

KEN, THOMAS (1637–1711). Educated at Winchester and New College, Oxford, he later returned to Winchester as a prebendary of the cathedral and a Fellow of the school. It was during this period (1669–79) that he wrote his well known morning and evening hymns for which he is now remembered. The closing stanza of the hymns, 'Praise God from whom all blessings flow', has been called the Protestant Doxology and has probably been sung more frequently than any other verse of sacred song. In 1685 Ken became Bishop of Bath and Wells but did not long retain his see. He was one of the seven bishops imprisoned in the Tower of London for refusing to subscribe to the Declaration of Indulgence of James II. He spent his last years in retirement at Longleat House, Wiltshire, the home of Lord Weymouth. He was a man of true sanctity, great courage, and invincible fidelity to conscience.

LUTHER, MARTIN (1483–1546). The great German reformer exercised a powerful influence on the development of hymnody from the 16th century onwards. In fact, as *Julian* remarks, 'The church hymn, in the strict sense of the term, *as a popular lyric in praise of God to be sung by the congregation in public worship*, was born with the German Reformation.' When Luther finally broke with Rome he set about the positive task of rebuilding the Church and devoted several years to translating the Bible into German. Being a man of poetical and musical gifts he took a keen interest in hymnody, convinced of the value of hymns as a vehicle for propagating the reformed faith as well as a means of encouraging congregational worship. He himself wrote thirty-seven hymns and urged others to follow his example. 'It is my intention,' he said, 'to make German hymns for the people – that is, spiritual songs whereby the word of God may be kept alive among them by singing. We therefore seek everywhere for poets.'

LYTE, HENRY FRANCIS (1793–1847). The author of two such universal favourites as 'Abide with me' and 'Praise, my soul, the King of
heaven' is assured of a place in the story of English hymnody; yet
apart from these hymns Lyte's name is not widely known. Born in
Ireland of English parents, he graduated from Trinity College,
Dublin, and three times won the University's prize for an English
poem. Two years after his ordination in 1815 he left Ireland and went
as curate to Marazion, Cornwall, and while there underwent a
conversion experience which changed his whole outlook on life.
After serving other curacies he was appointed as the first incumbent
of the Devonshire fishing village of Lower Brixham, where he spent
his last twenty-five years. Towards the end of that time his health,
never robust, began to fail and he died of consumption at Nice, aged
fifty-four. He published several works of prose and verse, including
The Spirit of the Psalms, 1834.

MONSELL, JOHN SAMUEL BEWLEY (1811–75). The author of 'Fight
the good fight' deserves a note, not only on account of the hymns he
wrote but because of his admirable view that hymns should be 'more
fervent and joyous'. He was doubtless thinking of the morbid and
introspective character of so many Victorian hymns. 'We are too
distant and reserved in our praises,' he wrote; 'we sing not as we
should sing of him who is Chief among ten thousand, the altogether
Lovely.' He wrote nearly 300 hymns, most of which are bright and
joyful in tone. He was an Irishman, educated at Trinity College,
Dublin. On ordination in 1834 he was for some time chaplain to
Bishop Mant, author of 'Bright the vision'. On coming to England
in 1853 he was first vicar of Egham, Surrey, and then in 1870 rector
of St Nicholas, Guildford, where his life ended in a tragic accident
(see 199).

MONTGOMERY, JAMES (1771–1854). Dr Erik Routley described
him as the typical English hymn-writer and declared that he was,
without question, the greatest of Christian *lay* hymnists. He is
commonly ranked next to Watts and Wesley among the leading
hymn-writers. He was born in Scotland of devout Moravian parents
who in 1783 went as missionaries to the West Indies, where they
died. They left their son to be educated at a Moravian school in
Yorkshire, with a view to his becoming a minister; but the ministry
made no appeal to him and he felt the urge to write poetry.
Eventually he turned to journalism and in 1794 became the owner
and editor of the *Sheffield Iris*, a newspaper which he conducted for
thirty years. Many of his hymns (he wrote over 400) were first

published in this paper. As a whole they maintain a consistently high level. Some of his finest ones were written for missionary occasions. *Julian* spoke of his hymns as 'richly poetic without exuberance, dogmatic without uncharitableness, tender without sentimentality, elaborate without diffuseness, richly musical without apparent effort.'

NEALE, JOHN MASON (1818–66). A brilliant classical scholar of Trinity College, Cambridge, he was acquainted with twenty languages and used his gift for the translation of ancient Latin and Greek hymns. Archbishop Trench called him 'the most profoundly learned hymnologist of our Church'. His knowledge of liturgy in general was unsurpassed; yet on account of his advanced Tractarian views the Church practically ignored him and offered him no preferment. Even his DD degree came from America. His last twenty years were spent as warden of an almshouse for old men at East Grinstead on a salary of twenty-seven pounds a year! Nevertheless, here in almost complete obscurity he was extremely happy with his wife and four children, and the leisure he enjoyed gave him ample time to pursue his studies, make his translations and write his learned books. His contribution to the riches of the Church's hymnody is greater than that of any other of his century, but he claimed no copyrights for his works. 'A hymn,' he wrote, 'whether original or translated, ought, the moment it is published, to become the common property of Christendom, the author retaining no private right in it whatever.'

NEWMAN, JOHN HENRY (1801–90). After a distinguished career at Trinity College, Oxford, he was ordained in 1824. At that time he was an Evangelical, but he slowly gravitated to the High Church party and became the acknowledged leader of the Tractarian Movement. From 1828 to 1843 he was vicar of St Mary's, Oxford, where by his preaching he exerted a profound influence over the life of the University. In an agony of doubt and indecision he resigned the appointment and some two years later was received into the Roman Communion. Strangely enough, he was given no position commensurate with his great powers and for nearly forty years he lived a secluded and unfulfilled life at the Edgbaston Oratory of St Philip, Neri. Some consolation came to him in 1879 when the Pope elevated him to be a Cardinal; but his enormous gifts as a preacher, poet and master of English prose were largely misdirected or wasted.

NEWTON, JOHN (1725–1807). His epitaph, written by himself – to be seen in the Church of St Mary Woolnoth, London – tells in brief the story of this man's remarkable life:

JOHN NEWTON, Clerk, once an infidel and libertine, a servant of slaves in Africa, was by the rich mercy of our Lord and Saviour Jesus Christ preserved, restored, pardoned, and appointed to preach the Faith he had long laboured to destroy. Near sixteen years at Olney in Bucks, and twenty-seven years in this Church.

His early life, spent from the age of eleven at sea, was godless and dissolute. After serving in turn with the Merchant and Royal Navy he got deeply involved in the iniquitous slave-trade and was for some years captain of a slave ship. His conversion began with the reading of Thomas à Kempis and came to a climax when, faced with imminent death in a violent storm, he cried to God for mercy. He later left the sea, and under the influence of Wesley and Whitefield he spent nine years preparing for holy orders. Eventually in 1764 he was ordained as curate of Olney, where with the help of William Cowper he produced the famous *Olney Hymns*, 1779. The following year he moved to London as rector of St Mary Woolnoth and remained there till his death.

PALMER, RAY (1808–87). The son of an American judge, he graduated from Yale in 1830 and became minister of the Central Congregational Church, Bath, Maine, where the best of his hymns were written. In 1850 he was appointed minister of the First Congregational Church, Albany, New York, and in 1865 Corresponding Secretary of the American Congregational Union. A man of scholarly gifts and deep religious faith, he is said to have written more hymns than any other American. *Julian* remarks that 'the best of them, by their combination of thought, poetry, and devotion, are superior to almost all others of American origin.'

POTT, FRANCIS (1832–1909). One of the lesser names in the story of English hymnody but nevertheless a name associated with several well known hymns as author or translator. Educated at Brasenose College, Oxford, he was ordained in 1856 and spent his life in the parochial ministry. He was vicar of Ticehurst, Sussex, 1861–66, and then rector of Norhill, Bedfordshire, till his retirement to Speldhurst, Kent, in 1891. A competent scholar, he served on the committee that produced the first edition of *A&M* in 1861, and in the same year published his own collection of *Hymns fitted to the Order of Common Prayer*.

TATE, NAHUM (1652–1715). The son of an Irish clergyman and educated at Trinity College, Dublin, he later came to England and published a volume of verse in 1677. His appointment as Poet Laureate in 1690 was due to influence at Court rather than to his poetical talent, which was little more than mediocre. He joined forces with Nicholas Brady (1659–1726) – another Irishman, who became chaplain to William III and later rector of Stratford-on-Avon – to produce the *New Version* of the metrical psalms, published in 1696. For all its imperfections it gradually ousted the 'old' version by Sternhold and Hopkins (1562) and was often bound up with the *BCP*. Of its contents the best known are 'Through all the changing scenes of life' (Psalm 34; see 23) and 'As pants the hart for cooling streams' (Psalm 42).

WATTS, ISAAC (1674–1748). The son of a leading Dissenter in Southampton, he was educated at the local grammar school, where his brilliant intellectual gifts gained him honours. He early felt the call to the ministry, but being like his parents a staunch Nonconformist he was unable to accept the offer of a place at Oxford or Cambridge and did his training at one of the Dissenting academies. In 1702 he was appointed minister of Mark Lane Chapel, London; but in 1712 his health broke down and from then till his death he lived a quiet life as the guest of Sir Thomas and Lady Abney, devoting his time to writing. In 1728 the University of Edinburgh recognised his great learning by conferring on him the degree of DD. His tolerant spirit, his liberal views, and his deservedly popular hymns, did much to create better relations between Anglicans and Dissenters. He is rightly known as the father of English hymnody, as it was he who pioneered the practice of hymn-singing proper and effectively broke the Calvinistic tradition of using only metrical psalms in Christian worship. He wrote about 600 hymns, many of which are still in use, especially in the Free Churches.

WESLEY, CHARLES (1707–88). The prince of English hymn-writers, he was born at Epworth rectory, the youngest son of Samuel and Susannah Wesley. His brother John, the founder of Methodism, was four years his senior. He was educated at Westminster School and Christ Church, Oxford, where he graduated in 1729 and became a college tutor. After ordination in 1735 he joined forces with his brother, first as a missionary in the British colony of Georgia, and later, after his evangelical conversion in 1738, as an itinerant preacher in England. His outpouring of hymns began with his conversion and continued unbroken till his death. He was the poet of the Evangelical Revival and the Methodist movement owed much to his hymns. He wrote some 6,500 in all. Needless to say, not all are noteworthy, but among them are many of the glories of English hymnody. More of them are sung today than those of any other hymn-writer. They have enriched the life of the Christian Church throughout the world for the past two centuries and more.

WINKWORTH, CATHERINE (1829–78). A highly cultured woman, an expert linguist and a devout Christian, she earned for herself the title of the queen of translators by her valuable work in translating nearly 400 German hymns into English. She was born in London but lived most of her life in Manchester. Her later years were spent at Clifton, Bristol, where she took a prominent part in promoting the higher education of women and helped in the founding of the University. She died suddenly of heart disease at the age of forty-eight. Her memorial in Bristol Cathedral states that her translations 'opened a new source of light, consolation and strength in many thousand homes'. Several of them are to be found in all the standard hymnals, the best known being 'Now thank we all our God'.

WORDSWORTH, CHRISTOPHER (1807–85). A nephew of the poet, he was first and foremost a man of immense scholarship. After an exceptionally brilliant career at Cambridge he was ordained and while still under thirty was appointed headmaster of Harrow. In 1844 he became a canon of Westminster; but six years later he withdrew to a quiet country benefice in Berkshire where he proved a model parish priest until his elevation as Bishop of Lincoln in 1869. Among his many publications was a commentary on the whole Bible, a life's work in itself. While at Westminster he began work on his collection of hymns entitled *The Holy Year*, published in 1862. As a hymn-writer he was more concerned with doctrine than poetry, holding that it was the first duty of a hymn to teach the Faith in close adherence to scripture. His contemporary, Canon John Ellerton, described him as 'a most holy, humble, loving, self-denying man', and added: 'The man is reflected in his verse.'

INDEX OF AUTHORS AND TRANSLATORS

INDEX OF FIRST LINES

Hymns to be found under other first lines are bracketed